JOURNEYMAN

JOURNEYMAN

ONE MAN'S ODYSSEY THROUGH THE
LOWER LEAGUES OF ENGLISH FOOTBALL

BEN SMITH

Biteback Publishing

First published in Great Britain in 2015 by
Biteback Publishing Ltd
Westminster Tower
3 Albert Embankment
London SE1 7SP
Copyright © Ben Smith 2015

ISBN 978–1-84954-854-0

10 9 8 7 6 5 4 3 2 1

A CIP catalogue record for this book is available from the British Library.

Set in Adobe Garamond Pro

Printed and bound in Great Britain by
CPI Group (UK) Ltd, Croydon CR0 4YY

I would like to dedicate this book to all the family and friends who supported me throughout my career, but particularly my mum and dad, who both sacrificed time and money to help me turn my young footballing dream into a reality.

I also reserve a special mention for my long-suffering girlfriend Emma, who patiently followed me around England for ten years. I have promised her that any profits made from this book will go towards a wedding. I think that is called a win–win situation!

Thanks also to James Barrett, who has been a great support to me throughout the writing and editing process, helping make my thoughts and emotions structured and coherent.

Lastly, thanks to all the people who said I was not good enough; some of you were right but you all gave me the inspiration to try to shove those words back down your throats.

I did not have the football career I dreamt of but, on reflection, seventeen years of making a living from something you enjoy is not bad…

CONTENTS

INTRODUCTION

I HAVE ALWAYS been an avid reader and have read many footballers' autobiographies. Unfortunately I have found a lot of them to be pretty bland and, more often than not, they do not really tell the public anything they do not already know.

I had a very modest career as a lower-league footballer and you could label me the proverbial 'journeyman' as I went from one modest footballing backwater to another, despite starting at the top. I thought my story was pretty unremarkable until, over the last year or so, I wrote a blog about my thoughts and experiences that was well received by the small group of people I interact with via social media.

As a result, I decided to write this candid book about my experiences within the football industry. People who know me well will already be aware that I find it hard to express my feelings openly, but I will use this book as a channel to give an honest and balanced view of my working life and the people I came across during a career punctuated with a few highs and many lows.

Here we go…

Ben Smith
Witham, Essex, 2012

CHAPTER 1

THE END

It is a late Sunday evening and I am, without wishing to sound too dramatic, at a crossroads in my life.

My professional football career is officially over.

I've known this has been coming because I have endured a drawn-out divorce from the game over the past twelve months. The 2011/12 season was personally an unmitigated disaster.

Last summer I signed a new one-year contract at Crawley Town after a successful season that saw the club crowned Conference Premier champions. Not only that, but we also set a new record for the highest ever points tally (105), plus added joint records for most consecutive games without defeat (thirty-one), fewest defeats over a season (three) and biggest goal difference (sixty-three). I had a good season and secured a £12-a-week pay rise – more about that extravagance later! – but deep down I knew maybe it was time to move on. Crawley had huge financial backing and it was clear the owners would invest heavily to strengthen the playing squad. As one of the elder statesmen within the team, I knew I was ripe for replacement.

As any professional sportsman will tell you, however, total faith in your own ability is a pre-requisite and I was confident I could have remained a regular member of the first team if given a fair chance to do so.

Unfortunately that scenario did not happen, with some of the reasons down to me and some not … anyway, I digress.

I have always been pretty level-headed and appreciative of how fortunate I've been to earn my living from playing football, but the transition from footballer to 'employee of the real world' has proven to be more challenging than I could have ever imagined.

I have become a business and ICT teacher. This came about after I volunteered at a local school (the one I had attended as a youth) on my Wednesdays off throughout 2012. The aim of this was to simply gain some work experience. I was working with the school's football academy because coaching is something I really fancy doing, but unfortunately there wasn't a full-time role within the academy so I've taken this teaching job in the hope a sporting opportunity will come up in the future.

But I constantly feel like a fish out of water. I soon found out the Year 7 pupils know more about ICT than me and the sixth-form students look at me as if to say: 'What does he know about business?' They do not vocalise it but I can see it in their eyes – and they're right.

This is a horrible situation to be in.

I am also used to being a well-respected member of football club dressing rooms whereas I am an 'unknown quantity' within the school staff room.

Another reason I took the job is because it's local. The last thing I want to do is move house again after leading such a nomadic life to date.

I was offered three different roles within the football industry over the summer of 2012. Two were as a coach and one was as a manager. I rejected them all because I still had a burning desire to play and did not feel ready to make the move to the other side of the touchline. That seems pretty ironic now, though, as I could not feel more unprepared every time I stand at the front of my classroom.

But, being fair, my desire to continue playing has begun to dwindle as well. After being part of a club that had been promoted in consecutive years I thought I would be, if not inundated, then at least sought-after by semi-professional clubs.

But I was wrong and that was one of many mistakes I made over the summer.

Billericay Town wanted to pay me £160 per week – the same money it pays to twenty-year-olds who have played only a handful of non-League games at best. When I was twenty I was certainly not getting the wages of experienced professionals. Needless to say, I rejected that particular offer.

I've eventually ended up at AFC Sudbury, which means playing in the Ryman Division One North. By the end of last August we were already out of both the FA Cup and FA Trophy competitions. Being honest, I didn't even realise these tournaments start so early in the season.

Sudbury is a nice club, however, and Chris Tracey (the manager) is a decent guy. I do not personally think he is cut out to be a manager, though: he's put together a good squad of players for this level of football, but we're a crap team.

Since I've joined I've played terribly. It's strange. I thought playing at this level would be easy for someone of my experience, but I was wrong. I have always had to play with my brain to make up for my lack of pace, but I am not on the same wavelength as some of my teammates. At this level, the things I do well on the pitch can look bad when, for example, my colleagues make the opposite run to the pass I play.

Players also do not show for the ball as much and I end up pirouetting, looking around for options until I get dispossessed. Maybe I should just lump the ball down the pitch like everybody else, but my principles will not allow for that. I think people expect me to go on mazy runs but I've never been able to do that at any level.

I also find it hard to comprehend that in 2011 I was playing at Old

Trafford, home to Manchester United, in front of 75,000 people, while just eighteen months later I'm playing – quite poorly – against the likes of Ilford and Heybridge Swifts.

It is amazing how quickly a career in football deteriorates. At this moment, I would be happy never to kick a ball again but I know, deep down, things will improve and that I cannot keep playing so badly.

Although it might not sound like it, I do feel I am one of the better-prepared players for the move into the 'real world'. I have earned a degree (a 2:1 in business management), studied for my UEFA B coaching badge and FA Youth Modules 1 and 2, and have been learning Spanish for the past two years.

This all sounds fine on paper, yet none of it has prepared me for the emptiness I feel at the moment. People tell me things will get easier and I hope they are right. I would give anything to be able to have a few more years back in the safety of a dressing room with my teammates – somewhere I've always felt comfortable.

Another problem I have is I find the money I'm earning at Sudbury really useful. I will not be put on the breadline if I don't get it, but I want to protect my savings. As a teacher I earn just over £21,000 a year, which is half what I earned in 2011 and only a quarter of what I was earning during my best days at Hereford United. This wage alone nowhere near covers my monthly expenses.

The £210 a week after tax that Sudbury pays me makes life a lot easier but, for the first time in a long while, I am not enjoying playing football. I feel like I'm stealing money off the club because my performances are so poor. I will be very surprised if I'm still playing for them by the time I finish writing this book. Some of my time on the pitch has been so inadequate that, at this rate, I will honestly be surprised if I see out this month.

CHAPTER 2

THE BEGINNING

I was right: Sudbury did not last. Chris Tracey rang me today and told me a tale of how the 'chairman' is going 'mad' about needing to cut the playing budget.

I believe that is just football talk and, roughly translated, means: 'You have been playing rubbish and this is my way of passing the buck in an attempt to sugar-coat the decision to release you.'

Chris seemed apprehensive when he broke the news but he should not have worried because I felt more relieved than anything – I no longer have to toil through tedious matches. In every single game I played for Sudbury bar one, I paled into the landscape as just another mediocre player in a mediocre team in a mediocre league. Chris appreciated the grace with which I took the decision and I hold no grudges. Ultimately I did not perform and, if I'm honest, I just could not motivate myself to. It's strange because I didn't lose my motivation for training. I still enjoyed going to the gym and working hard but, when I pitched up on a Saturday, I just could not convince myself the game was important. There was no fear factor and no public humiliation if I had a stinker – whether I played well or not, my performance would generally be forgotten by 5 p.m. and I certainly never got rated out of ten in a national newspaper.

It's not surprising the gaffer has to trim down his playing staff. According to one of my former teammates, the playing budget is £1,600 per week — yet I believe the club is running at double that. I think this is the economic model used by many football clubs, unfortunately.

So I've decided I'm done with playing, unless something comes up in the higher echelons of part-time football. I fancy concentrating on coaching or maybe even trying my hand at scouting. I have always been pretty analytical regarding football, so I believe that role could suit me. I could call in a few favours to try to compensate for the loss of wages from football. Hopefully in a few years I will regard my conversation with Chris as a blessing. I'm confident my transition from playing to coaching or scouting will happen at some stage.

On the plus side, I just received my first pay packet from the school. I'm meant to clear around £1,400 a month but I've somehow been paid £2,375. Suffice to say, I'm not telling anyone, although with this sort of fiscal management it's no wonder the government is effectively bankrupt!

Anyway let's crack on with my story.

· · ·

I AM GOING to start right from the beginning but, as I typically always find the bit about the player's formative years in any autobiography quite boring, this will be short and to the point.

I was born and raised in Witham, Essex. It is a pretty unremarkable place. I do not mean that in a derogatory respect, but the best way I can describe it is that if you – or family or friends – do not live there, then you have no real reason to visit.

Witham started off as a small town 30 miles from east London, but in the

1960s it became an overspill town for Londoners who wanted to live in the country. My dad and mum were two such people, so Peter and Margaret Smith moved to Essex in the mid-1970s. I joined them on 23 November 1978 and my brother Joe completed our family at the start of 1981.

My upbringing was that of a typical suburban family. My dad worked as a London fireman (and as anything else he could find to make ends meet) while my mum looked after the house, my brother and me. Dad would regularly work a night shift at the fire station, do some kind of skilled labour the whole of the next day and then go back for another night shift.

I used to wonder why he would come home and sometimes snap at me when all I wanted was to talk or play games with him. Now I am working in a 'proper' job I really appreciate how tired he must have been, but the vast majority of times he would submit to my demands and stand in goal while I smashed footballs at him.

I have no real gripes about my upbringing. The only sad point I can think of was when we all struggled through a couple of years of stress because my mum and dad were wrestling with the decision of whether or not to split up. They tried to hide it from my brother and me, but the tension and frostiness were clear to everyone and made our house an uncomfortable environment for a while.

In fairness they were only doing it to try to keep the family together. In hindsight, and I have discussed this with both of them, it would have been in everyone's interest to have two happy parents who lived apart than two miserable ones who were living together for their children's sake. I do not think the former ever works but, in the mid-1990s, there was much more of a stigma around divorce than there is now.

My memories of my early years are quite vague but I remember not starting to play football until about the age of eight. That might not sound old but I know kids these days who start going to soccer schools and other such organisations as soon as they can walk.

My dad loves telling a story about us walking through our local park when I was five. He wanted to stand and watch a football match but, according to him, I said, 'Daddy, I don't want to stay here – football is boring!'

A couple of my friends always used to try to get me to go football training with them and I eventually succumbed aged eight and joined my first team – the Witham Nomads.

I do not remember being particularly good in those days, or even having any real passion for the game. But I continued with it and, as I got older, I became obsessed about practising. My dad had to regularly rebuild the wall outside our house as I used to continuously kick my ball against it.

I used to go over to the park with my pals pretty much every day after school to play 'headers and volleys'. If nobody wanted to play I would go and practise ball-juggling non-stop. My record was once 10,000 touches without dropping the ball. When I go on different coaching courses I now realise that kind of exercise is the reason for my good touch. Those hours of repetition trained my brain to know exactly how hard or soft to hit the ball depending on where I wanted it to go.

I also have to thank my dad for the fact I can play with both feet. He used to spend hours making me kick the ball with my left foot and it got to the stage where the majority of people who watched me play thought I was left-footed. I also developed a pretty unique style of predominantly using the outside of my foot. I haven't got a clue how I created this technique – it was not something I consciously worked on – but I always took it as a massive compliment when I read scouting reports saying that I could use both feet.

Within a year of joining Witham Nomads I moved on to Witham Youth Football Club and then Valley Green. Little did I know this was an early indication of the nomadic lifestyle I would lead nearly twenty years later – that first team name was very prophetic!

I played for Valley Green between the ages of nine and fourteen. Joining them was, I believe, the first piece of good fortune that contributed to my becoming a professional footballer.

Ryan Oates, still one of my best friends, played with me there, and his dad Gary was the manager – a man who had trodden the footballing path I wanted to follow.

Gary had been an apprentice and professional footballer at West Ham United. Unfortunately his career was curtailed by what nowadays would be a pretty insignificant injury – he had the cartilage from one of his knees removed. That sadly ended his professional career at the age of twenty.

I cannot remember if he was a brilliant coach but he was an excellent player whenever I watched him play for my dad's Sunday team, or even when he joined in training with us youngsters. He was a cultured left-footed midfielder and maybe in hindsight this was where I developed my dominant left-sided style.

I am a big believer in the theory put forward by the likes of Matthew Syed, in his superb book *Bounce*, and Malcolm Gladwell, in his equally impressive *Outliers*. These authors argue that excellence is nurtured and not something we are born with. I believe being coached by Gary Oates was one of those strokes of luck they refer too. It put me in contact with someone who knew what was required to have any chance of succeeding in the professional game for the first time. This, in my opinion, gave me an advantage over any peer being coached by an enthusiastic but less experienced volunteer.

That Valley Green team was all-conquering. We won our league every season as well as the majority of the cup competitions. At the end of our first season we went into summer five-a-side tournaments and won all eight we entered. We had five or six really talented boys who made us a formidable side in that form of the game.

I enjoy looking back on those days playing for Valley Green. I used to look forward all week to training on a Saturday and games on a Sunday, although there is one tragic episode that will stay with everyone who was involved with the team forever.

We were playing an away game against Stony Stratford in the East Anglia Youth Cup. They were based in Milton Keynes so it was a long trip for us. When we arrived at the venue we went to inspect the pitch.

To get to the grass we had to walk across a couple of others that contained moveable goals. My memory tells me they were full-size goals, but I'm not sure eleven-year-olds could have touched the crossbar. Anyway, some of the lads did what boys tend to do and jumped up to hang from them. Again, my memory tells me there were at least three or four lads who successfully did this.

Their combined weight made the goal unstable and it toppled over, pinning them to the floor. Most of them were unharmed but Jonathan Smith was not so fortunate. The impact of the goal frame had broken his neck and he died almost instantly. My dad, being fully qualified in first aid, was on the scene at once and gave Jonathan mouth-to-mouth. He managed to resuscitate him on more than one occasion but he tragically couldn't keep him alive.

This may sound strange to some of you but, as a youngster, you do not really understand the enormity of such a tragic accident. Young boys can be pretty resilient. It is only now that I reflect on the impact this must have had on the adults within our club. I know that my dad and Gary especially were hit really hard for a long time as they felt a responsibility to Jonathan. I can only imagine the pain his mum and dad, Peter and Brenda, went through – and no doubt still do to this day.

I remember the funeral being a hugely emotional day. The whole team was inconsolable as the magnitude of what happened became a reality. Jonathan was a huge West Ham fan and they were great with regard to the funeral – former Hammers midfielder Stuart Slater was in attendance.

That devastating incident aside, my days playing for Valley Green were brilliant. The success of our team meant we started to generate a lot of interest from professional clubs. By the age of nine I had been spotted by local professional club Colchester United. I trained with them for a year before then attracting interest from West Ham and Ipswich.

West Ham wanting to sign me was especially exciting as my dad had grown up in the area and been a lifelong fan. Obviously, with him supporting them, I had the dubious privilege of doing the same – I say 'dubious' because I seem to remember not having a great deal of choice in the matter!

Initially I trained at both clubs but, after a while, it became clear that I would have to make a decision. As much as we loved West Ham, my dad and I felt that the club had an approach of quantity over quality. At every training session there were twenty or thirty players in each age group. I felt like just another player – nothing special.

Ipswich was different; I felt really wanted and appreciated there. Even at the age of ten that was important. During my time at the club there were some players who went on to become stars in the Premier League. There was Kieron Dyer and defender Matthew Upson, who both trained in my age group, as well as goalkeeper Richard Wright, who was in the year above.

One incident involving Kieron Dyer really sticks in my mind. We were doing some kind of small-sided game and Kieron ran at me with the ball. He twisted me up to the point where I ended up on my backside before he went on to score a goal. The coach was kind enough to stop the session and get Kieron to re-enact the incident in slow motion, including putting me on my arse. It was embarrassing enough once, let alone twice!

After twelve months there I had another decision to make as Arsenal began showing interest in me. Steve Rowley, who is now the chief scout, started regularly attending our games and eventually he invited both Lee Boylan and me to train with them. I enjoyed it straight away, plus it felt a lot more selective – training sessions would often have fewer than ten players involved.

I was in a bit of a quandary. I was perfectly happy at Ipswich but this was the start of the 1990s. Arsenal had just won the First Division championship (now the Premier League) by beating Liverpool on a memorable night at Anfield. At the time they were arguably the biggest and best club in the country and they potentially wanted to sign me!

Signing young players was different in those days. You signed a 'centre of excellence' form for a year and the agreement was re-assessed at the end of every season until you got to fourteen, at which point you could sign a two-year contract called a 'schoolboy' form. This was the holy grail as it meant you were eligible for free football boots from the club, although slightly tempered by the fact Arsenal handed out very unfashionable Gola-branded boots to their schoolboys. I doubt this is still the case but it didn't even bother me as Ian Bishop, my favourite West Ham player at the time, wore Gola.

I was just starting senior school when Arsenal wanted to sign me, so I was eleven years old. Ipswich did their best to persuade me to stay once they became aware of the interest. Tony Dable was the youth development officer at Ipswich back then and a nice man. He gave my dad and I the normal advice about Arsenal being a big club and how tough it would be to be a success there. Bearing in mind the future success of the Ipswich lads I mentioned earlier, maybe he was right. I definitely felt equal to those players at that time, but his advice fell on deaf ears and we came to the decision that I had to take this opportunity.

So that potent Valley Green squad stayed together until we all went our own separate ways to embark on the next part of our careers. I joined Arsenal while Lee Boylan, who was our star striker, went to West Ham. Gary's son Ryan joined Ipswich and a couple of other lads played regularly for lower-league professional clubs.

I trained initially at Arsenal's regional training centre in Grays, Essex. It was a small indoor ball court at Grays Athletic FC and, as I mentioned previously, it was a really select group. The sessions always involved players from my own age group (the under-12s) and the year above. This was the first time I came up against players I knew were better than me. One player, Lee Hodges, was especially brilliant.

Lee was one of the older players but he was head and shoulders above everyone. He reminded me of Gazza as he had such quick feet and was brilliant at dribbling with the ball. He finally left Arsenal and went to West Ham but never fully broke into the first team and eventually played in the lower divisions for the likes of Bristol Rovers and Scunthorpe United. I think his career was curtailed prematurely by a persistent knee injury, but Lee is the first example of many players you will read about in this book who, for whatever reason, did not go on to realise their full potential.

Joining Arsenal put me in contact with the next big influence on my career. My coach at Arsenal was a guy called Andy McDermid. He was superb – everything a player could want from a youth football coach. He was enthusiastic, energetic, outgoing and, most importantly, knowledgeable. Without a doubt he was one key person who helped mould the football philosophy I hold to this day.

As I recall those training sessions, I remember we did not do anything groundbreaking. Often we would only have six or eight players and we would just play knockout competitions in pairs with Andy in goal. But, whatever we were doing, there would always be a theme to the session and he would drop in pieces of advice and information. As there were so few players you got loads of contact time with the ball. The philosophy of small-sided 4v4 games that everyone preaches now is what we were doing twenty years ago.

I specifically remember learning what a third man run was and how to do it. We practised it for weeks on end until everyone got it. For the uninitiated, a third man run is when two players combine to then play a pass through to a third man making a late forward run, hence the name.

As much as I enjoyed Andy's sessions, I also really liked him as a person.

He was always teasing us and telling us about his own football career. Apparently he played in goal for England under-16s and he even brought an England cap to training once. I was never convinced it was his though as he was about 5 ft 7 and not a particularly good goalkeeper, but he was adamant. Whether it was true or not didn't really matter as it inspired us to try to show him what good players we were.

After a couple of years at the Grays training centre I progressed to training at Arsenal's old Highbury Stadium. The club used to have an indoor training facility under the old Clock End called the JVC Centre and I would go there a couple of times a week. I cannot remember who the coach was but I remember continuing to enjoy the training. Among the other players was one Frank Lampard.

At that time Frank was a decent player, but not someone who really stood out – and definitely not someone you'd have predicted to go on to have the wonderful career he had with Chelsea. However, even at that age he had a great attitude towards training. I think Arsenal knew that his loyalties were always with West Ham but they had a go at taking him on anyway.

So, at the ripe old age of fourteen I played solely for Arsenal and everything was going well. I always felt like one of the stronger players in my age group. By the time I came into my last year at secondary school I had been with the club for five years. I had been one of only a couple of players who had signed those precious schoolboy forms two years previously, so I was relatively confident I would be offered an apprenticeship. In those days an apprenticeship was through the YTS scheme and would last two years.

However, the one fly in the ointment was the strength of the players in the age group below. My team only had about seven regular players and, in hindsight, that was because the year below was so strong. There were about twenty players in the younger age group with some really talented boys. We would regularly play against them in school holidays and, more often than not, lose.

Arsenal eventually made a decision just after Christmas to offer me a contract. Leading up to that time I also received interest from Leyton Orient and Cambridge United. You may think that there was not a choice to be made there but I do often look back and wonder whether I made the right one. Yes, at Arsenal I would get the opportunity to train with world-class players and coaches and use top-level facilities but, realistically, would I ever get anywhere near the first team?

However, if I were to join Leyton Orient or Cambridge, I could quite realistically be in and around a first team within a year. If that happened, and I impressed when given the opportunity, then it may not have been long until another big club showed an interest in me.

On the flip side, I was also conscious of the fact that if it did not go well at one of the smaller clubs then where do you go from there? I would've had to rebuild my fledgling career in non-League football. Even if it didn't work out at Arsenal, I was at least pretty confident I would get another opportunity lower down the League. Every coach knows a person has to be of a certain standard to have been at a club like Arsenal for the amount of time I had been there so they would, as a minimum, give me an opportunity to impress.

So, after about five seconds' thought I put my fears aside and accepted Arsenal's offer of an apprenticeship. I do not think you would have found many sixteen-year-old boys who would have passed up such an opportunity, and the kudos I received at school was enough justification (let alone all the other positives).

Signing the contract was my first of many career mistakes, however. I instantly decided that signing guaranteed me superstardom and riches beyond my wildest dreams and, as a result, there was no need to concentrate on my GCSEs, in my opinion. I just downed tools at school.

I still took all my exams and picked up some decent results (five A–Cs and five Ds) but I could and should have achieved so much more.

Not that this bothered me in the slightest at the time. In a display of arrogance I did not even go and pick up my results, confident in the misguided idea that I would never need them. I was busy preparing for the next chapter of my life and conquering the world of professional football. It did not quite go according to plan…

·   ·   ·

29 OCTOBER 2012

I have somehow managed to make it to half-term at the school. Teaching is so much harder than I imagined. That extra £1,000 in my last pay packet was a tax rebate, by the way – just another illustration of how far I have fallen financially.

Currently I am teaching ICT, maths, philosophy, citizenship, science and a little bit of football. It seems ironic to me that the one area in which I am an expert is the one in which I do the least.

I pretty much resigned last week. The headmaster asked me to a meeting and said he wanted to retain me after my one-term contract expired. He asked me how things were going and, as he'd caught me in between my worst couple of days, I told him exactly how I felt: 'I'm teaching lots of stuff I know nothing about.'

He seemed to sympathise with me but I was warming to the theme, going on to say I did not think teaching was for me and that I wanted to resign as soon as possible.

As I have no other job lined up, was that a brave or stupid thing to say? Over the past month I had applied for five jobs and not been asked to even one interview! It seems, worryingly, that I am over-qualified for most of the positions I have been pursuing.

However, I've decided being unemployed is better than my current reality – I simply do not look forward to going into work. I know in my previous job I was lucky enough to get paid to indulge in my passion, but I also loved going in for training. There were plenty of times when things were not going well personally or professionally but as soon as I got onto the training pitch all those problems dissipated and I felt free. Working at the school is so different, probably because I am absolutely winging it. I'm frustrated that the school has got me in this position. How can they put someone who has never taught before, or had any formal training, in charge of a classroom? I used to think I was a resilient and focused person but now all I think about is quitting.

Having written that, I do think in the back of my mind I could actually become a good teacher within a year or two. The real question is: do I want to go through all this shit to get to that point?

I recently had one of my lessons observed by a senior member of staff who graded me on criteria set by teaching governing body Ofsted. You can be marked as either 'outstanding', 'good', 'requires improvement' or 'inadequate'. I also looked for 'crap' but apparently that is not one of the options.

Anyway, I surprised myself by earning an overall 'requires improvement' grade with some elements of 'good' thrown in. The person who graded me said she was really impressed, considering I only had three weeks' experience. I do like building relationships with the pupils too, which helps, although sometimes I probably blur the line between friend and teacher by engaging in some of the classroom banter.

A couple of days after that meeting with the headmaster I told him I would at least see out my contract and re-assess the situation nearer Christmas. I am sure I can do this now and, more importantly, be good at it. I just need to keep reminding myself to be patient.

Meanwhile, like an ageing journeyman heavyweight boxer, I have been lured out of football retirement for a few extra quid.

I was convinced, after being deemed surplus of requirements by AFC Sudbury, that I was hanging up my boots for good, so I made no attempt to find another club and was instead looking at coaching and scouting options. However, the reality is you have to work much harder doing either of those things to earn less than you would through playing, even if it is at a low standard in front of one man and his dog.

A couple of weeks into my 'retirement', Mark Stimson, the manager of Ryman Premier League side Thurrock FC, rang me and asked if I would come and play for him. He offered me £200 per week after tax plus £25 an appearance and £25 a win. Considering they were bottom of the League with one win all season I was not banking on the win bonus too much!

I was not in a position to turn down that sort of money from a manager I really respected. I'd spent a month on loan at Kettering Town with Mark in the 2011/12 season – the club itself was a shambles but I took to him straight away. He's a brilliant coach who simplifies the game and paints pictures for his players in training sessions. We also share similar footballing philosophies, which is important when you become a stubborn senior player and are less likely to submit to managers who can be, especially at this level, less qualified than yourself.

Only two weeks into the arrangement, however, and I'm already struggling to motivate myself – so let's see how long it lasts. I need to regain my full love for the game; there is still opportunity to earn good money playing in the lower leagues but I have got to want to do it. Money has never been my main motivation to play football, but it is at the moment – and it's not enough.

CHAPTER 3

IN THE BIG TIME

SEASONS: 1995/96, 1996/97
CLUB: ARSENAL
DIVISION: PREMIER LEAGUE
MANAGER: PAT RICE (YOUTH TEAM)

WITHIN A MONTH of finishing my GCSEs in the summer of 1995 I was embarking on my first ever pre-season as a full-time player alongside David Donaldson, Lee Richardson, Jason Crowe and Mark Thorogood – all of whom had also signed two-year YTS contracts. It seems like another lifetime ago, but I can recollect some memories vividly.

The then assistant youth development officer Steve Rowley gave me a lift to my first day of training and I bounced into the training base at London Colney confident in my own mind that I was going to be a superstar.

My first day also coincided with the first for new manager Bruce Rioch. He had the unenviable task of taking over from the hugely successful George Graham, who had been relieved of his duties after being found guilty of receiving illegal bungs. I had grown up watching Graham's team (youth players were given complimentary tickets to every home game) and although the style of football was not aesthetically pleasing, the team was superbly organised and built on strong foundations, with sprinkles of genius from the likes of Ian Wright, Paul Merson and Anders Limpar. But, being honest, Arsenal under Graham did not play my kind of football.

We were not the only new boys on that first day either. Arsenal had also signed two undeniable superstars who were massive heroes of mine: the mercurial Dennis Bergkamp from Inter Milan for £7.5 million and David Platt from Sampdoria for £4.75 million. I used to watch Bergkamp every Sunday afternoon on Channel 4's coverage of Italian football and Platt was the sort of box-to-box attacking midfielder I had tried to base my game on.

I will let you judge who you think was the most successful of all these new signings arriving at London Colney that day, although what I will ask is this: did Bergkamp or Platt ever grace the hallowed turf at Hereford's Edgar Street?

My youth-team manager was Pat Rice, the legendary ex-Arsenal right back. He was the ideal youth-team manager – a tough man who would come down on you like a ton of bricks if you stepped out of line but would also build up your confidence when he felt it necessary. I have never really feared authority and have always been pretty cheeky, which I think he quite liked, but he often gave me a bollocking when I crossed the line between being confident and gobby.

In those days at Arsenal, everyone (first team, reserves and youth-team players) trained together during the first week of pre-season. There were a total of sixty players. I remember this as I was number fifty-eight – I believe it was sorted out via alphabetical order, not ability!

We were then mixed up into several groups to work at one of the different stations spread around the training ground for thirty minutes at a time. These stations included a body weight circuit, the dreaded perimeter run (around the outskirts of the whole training ground), shorter shuttle runs and head tennis.

The late George 'Geordie' Armstrong was in charge of my group and, while I cannot remember everyone in it, I can recall defender Nigel Winterburn's behaviour. We were doing some simple weaving in and out of poles but Nigel decided he would just run through them and clothesline them all like a WWE wrestler. I was stunned! All the senior players just laughed at him and Geordie did not say much. I bet he was pissed off though.

In those days, pre-season was not taken very seriously, especially for the first couple of weeks. A lot of players came back overweight so the first priority was to shift that excess via lots of running – not like it is nowadays where footballs are often incorporated on the first day.

Having said that, there were balls used for head tennis, of course. It is called 'head' tennis but you can use any part of your body to get the ball over the net. I had gone from playing 'headers and volleys' with my friends in the park to playing it with experienced Premier League and international players. Suffice to say I was a nervous wreck and my sole aim was to ensure I was not the one to make a mistake.

Paul Dickov, the fiery Scottish striker, was in my group and prided himself on his head tennis expertise. He could not care less if you were an established player or a spotty teenager – if you made a mistake he deemed preventable, he gave you both barrels. Luckily one of my strengths has always been my first touch so I managed to get through that unscathed.

On one of those early days my group had just completed its perimeter run and we were waiting for our turn on the head tennis court. Dennis Bergkamp was playing in the group ahead of us and produced a piece of skill that left me open-mouthed. The ball came over the net from about 10 metres in the air, but Bergkamp cushioned and caught it on his foot in one motion and then nonchalantly flicked it back over the net. Everyone went mad! It was amazing and my words probably do not do it justice. Even in those early days it was starting to dawn on me just how good you needed to be to make a career for yourself at the highest level.

The first few months were a real learning curve. My adolescent body was struggling to adapt to the rigours of full-time football and I had gone from being a top player in every team I had played in to being one of the weakest. Physically and mentally I was still a boy and I soon realised I had a massive challenge on my hands to make a career for myself at any level of professional football, let alone playing in the Premier League.

My home in rural Essex was geographically on the cusp of Arsenal's club-run accommodation boundary. As a result, they let me make my own choice and I decided I wanted to stay with my family and friends.

This was another mistake.

I should have moved to north London and immersed myself in trying to be a professional footballer. Instead I spent a lot of time on the train commuting to and from Highbury.

As an apprentice footballer in those days I was paid the princely sum of £29.50 per week in my first year. On top of that, the club also paid my dad £60 a week to look after me and they covered my travel costs too. As you can see, this was long before the pampered lifestyle of young scholars nowadays.

My week consisted of training Monday and Tuesday, attending college in King's Cross on a Wednesday, more training Thursday and Friday and then a game on Saturday mornings. When the first team was playing at Highbury, our week would finish by watching them in the afternoon. However, these were only half of our responsibilities.

Every player was in charge of looking after three professional players' match day and training boots. The players who had the dubious honour of me cleaning their boots were David Seaman (at that time the England national team goalkeeper), Ian Selley (who I thought was a brilliant central midfield player before his top-level career was ended prematurely by injury) and Matthew Rose (a young professional who went on to have a good career with the likes of Queens Park Rangers). The best memory I have of Rose is that he had a very attractive girlfriend!

Now I say it was a dubious honour mainly because I took no pride in cleaning my own boots, let alone anyone else's (even if they were a current England international!). I have been criticised throughout my career for having dreadfully dirty boots – often having it cited as a lack of professionalism. However, I like to argue that my boots were always dirty because I loved football so much and was always using them.

To make matters worse, Seaman was very particular about the preparation of his boots. He insisted the Nike logo on each one be painted with a well-known paper correction fluid and that there be no black polish on the logo at all. Now this probably does not sound too taxing but you have to factor in that I am not artistically gifted. Seaman was thankfully one of the more laid-back professionals, however, and would show any displeasure with a loud, deep laugh, accompanied by a headlock. We mutually parted ways early in the New Year of my first season and his boots were passed on to another apprentice who took more pride in his responsibilities. However, this still gave Seaman the opportunity to illustrate his displeasure with me via his Christmas tip.

At Arsenal there was a tradition where you had to sing a Christmas carol to the whole playing staff in order to get your tip – no song equalled no money. As I am sure you can imagine, this was a pretty daunting prospect for anyone, let alone a seventeen-year-old fresh out of school.

Legend has it that when Ray Parlour was an apprentice he sang 'Little Donkey' to Tony Adams. The defender allegedly showed what he thought of the song by chasing Ray around the training ground – but I never found out whether he caught him or not!

I got the Cliff Richard classic 'Mistletoe and Wine' to murder – and that I did. I am one of those unfortunate people who is tone death but thinks they sound good until they witness the quizzical look on the face of any onlookers, who often cannot tell if I'm being serious or taking the piss. I can't even compensate with some eye-catching dance moves as they are arguably just as embarrassing.

So the first team and reserve players would be watching and baying for blood with buckets of freezing water, saliva and God knows what else. If you were good the players would sing along until you finished and you'd escape a soaking. If you were terrible you would get booed off and covered in whatever inhabited those buckets. Needless to say, I suffered the latter.

Now, if I knew the size of the tip coming my way from England's No. 1 I do not think I would have bothered at all. I could not believe it when he handed over £50 … £50?! A conservative estimate would say he must have been on £10,000 a week. Probably more. We have established that I was not the best boot boy in the world, but surely he could have given me a couple of hundred quid. Other apprentices were getting bundles of £50 notes, new boots and as much sports clothing as they could carry. Maybe he was teaching me an early lesson?

Selley gave me £30, which, considering he liked to clean his own boots, was acceptable, although still a little tight in my opinion. Rose gave me £25 – another paltry amount…

On top of boot-cleaning, we apprentices also had other duties to carry out. Chores included taking all the training kit from Highbury to the training ground, preparing all the equipment for said sessions, packing the players' boots for away games, cleaning Highbury before and after games and keeping the youth-team bus clean.

I remember early in my apprenticeship, we had packed the kit and boots for an away youth-team game, arrived at the venue and started to unpack the huge metal skips, and realised one of them seemed really light. Turned out it was empty. The lads on duty that day had picked up the wrong skip and left the kit at home. Laurence, the youth-team kit man, went apoplectic. The lads responsible got a right bollocking. As it was nothing to do with me I found it hilarious, although I'm not sure those sentiments were shared by those involved!

Highbury would always have to be cleaned on a Thursday before a

Saturday home game and, on such days, I would leave home at 7 a.m. and not get back until 9 p.m. – not exactly what I had signed up for. I soon realised that a lot of apprentices are taken on as glorified cleaners. Back then I believe a lot of clubs, especially lower down the leagues, recruited enough players to play in their youth team and carry out all menial jobs, knowing full well that the vast majority of them had absolutely no chance of making any type of career in football.

That first year as a full-time footballer was a huge learning curve. I could not break into the youth team in my favoured position of central midfield but, due to the fact I was comfortable with both feet, I managed to nail down a place on the left. My performances in the first half of that 1995/96 season were very up and down, though, as I struggled to find any real consistency.

I either played really well and would be one of the best players on the pitch or play horrendously and be the worst. Unsurprisingly, the latter resulted in me being on the wrong end of Pat Rice's hairdryer treatment on more than one occasion. This was the first time I had been on the end of such aggression and I was not too sure how to handle it. You have to quickly realise that it is not personal and that at some stage of the season everyone gets a kick up the backside. I just managed to get more than most.

My most memorable dressing-down came when we played an FA Youth Cup match at Highbury against Wimbledon. Leading up to the game I had been struggling with a hip problem. It was not enough to stop me playing but it was causing me discomfort. The coaching staff was undecided about whether I should play or not, but I insisted I was fit and they took my word for it. In hindsight, I definitely should not have played as the game was a complete disaster, but it was my first opportunity to play in such an iconic arena and the best ground I had played at before then was Colchester United's Layer Road in an under-10 cup final for Valley Green.

We were totally outplayed in the first half and were getting comfortably beaten by half-time. I had been at the club long enough to know that a rollicking was coming our way and that there was every opportunity I would be one of its recipients.

I was not disappointed. Rice initially went mental at everyone and then I had the misfortune of catching his eye. He exploded, saying how I had let him down as I clearly was not fit.

He was pretty much foaming at the mouth and saliva was going everywhere as he launched into the finale of his dressing-down, which involved him thumping his fist on the treatment table in front of me. He did it with such ferocity that his watch broke and fell onto the floor. Even in my petrified state I had to suppress the laughter swelling inside me. He did not find it amusing and it was the end of my participation in that game.

It always made me chuckle when I used to hear Arsenal fans on radio phone-in shows saying there seemed to be nobody on the coaching staff giving out criticism when the team was underperforming. Pat Rice, who spent sixteen years as first-team assistant manager until the end of the 2011/12 season, would have had no hesitation in letting his thoughts be known – believe me!

At that age, such setbacks had a detrimental effect on me. After that game, my form suffered for quite a while, which did not go unnoticed by some of my teammates. Generally in football there is very little sympathy handed out and this case was no different. Players would come out with comments such as, 'Where were you Saturday?' or 'Shock, you gave the ball away again.' Sometimes it would be under their breath but always loud enough for me to hear. In the long term it spurred me on to improve, but in the short term it made life tough. I remember sometimes during that first year, especially in the early days, dreading going into training.

The situation was not helped by the fact I also had to handle the embarrassment of getting subbed before half-time in a youth-team game once. It was after that game that I first learnt managers will sometimes be conservative with the truth.

Thanks to the ever unpredictable British Rail I had missed training on the Friday before the match. The ritual in the youth team on a Friday was to do functional work, which consisted of working on the formation we were going to play, trying some set-piece situations and finishing with a small-sided game. I had missed all this.

The next day I threw in one of my worst performances and was dragged off after about twenty-five minutes. I thought I was going to get another dressing-down, but Pat must've realised how low my morale was and made up some cock-and-bull story about me not knowing the formation we were playing. We were playing 4–4–2, which, even at the age of seventeen, I had played hundreds of times before. I suppose it was his way of protecting me, but I was intelligent enough to know the real reason.

However, as the season wore on, my confidence both on and off the pitch did begin to grow. I started to feel at home with my teammates and slowly won the respect of the group. I had found a niche for myself in the team on the left side of midfield and began to add some consistency to my play.

Bruce Rioch seemed to take a liking to me as well. He was a regular at youth-team games when the first team was playing at home. One particular game, I cannot remember the opposition, he seemed to take a real interest in my performance. It may just have been that I was playing on the side of the pitch where he was standing, but he was giving me lots of advice that I attempted to take on board.

I was amazed the manager knew my name, let alone took any interest in my performance, but it gave me a lot of confidence and I felt I was making progress.

I had always been technically gifted with a football and, even in the youth team at Arsenal, I knew I was one of the better in the group when in possession. In those days I thought that being good with the ball was enough, so, unfortunately, I did no extra fitness work and would regularly cheat when doing the bodyweight circuits. Pat Rice would refer to me as

'Fatty Arbuckle' – he said it in jest but it was a dig and I knew it. In those days one of my heroes was Paul Gascoigne and, in my mind, I thought that if Gazza could get away with being a little chubby then so could I. Obviously I was wrong. My diet was terrible too, but I do not blame the club for that. My education on such matters was and always is my responsibility.

Putting my physical deficiencies aside, I was definitely making progress – although I was acutely aware of the strength of the age group below who were due to be first-year apprentices in the 1996/97 season. A lot of the names will not be as recognisable to you as they should be, but the likes of Andrew Douglas, David Livermore, Julian Gray, Tommy Black, Greg Lincoln and Paolo Vernazza had the ability to become mainstays in Arsenal's first team. I do not think it is an exaggeration to say those boys could and should have had the same impact as the famous Man United class of '92. To be fair, the likes of David Livermore and Julian Gray went on to have good careers, but that batch as a whole underachieved.

The biggest problem I had was that the best of the bunch, in my opinion, was Paolo Vernazza – and he played in my position. When he came to train with us in the school holidays he would do things with the ball that would just make me go 'wow'.

Now, anyone who knows me will know that I am my own biggest fan, but even I could not put a convincing argument forward to say that I was a better player than him. In those days I saw things as being very black and white. I thought someone was either better than me or they were not. I did not think about other factors such as desire, determination or attitude – all key ingredients required to become a top player.

Putting these fears aside, I was relatively happy with my progress in my naïve mind. In that first season I played the most games out of anyone in the youth team. However, if I knew then what I know now, I would have realised I was not doing anywhere near enough – either on or off the pitch – to be a successful player at any decent level.

At the end of that 1995/96 season I got my first taste of how a change of management can have a huge impact on someone's career.

Pat Rice was clearly wasted working with the youth team and, although he was doing a fantastic job with us, he deserved to be working with international players and not chubby teenagers like me. With him moving on, I was going to get my first experience of the so-called managerial merry-go-round. The man who eventually got the job was Tom Walley, who had a great pedigree in youth football with the likes of Watford and Millwall, including winning the FA Youth Cup with the latter. During my career I came across lots of players who spoke very highly of Tom, but, unfortunately, I cannot share their sentiments.

He was very strict. Now, I can understand the phrase 'If you give footballers an inch the vast majority of them will take a mile', but Tom took it to the next level.

By the end of that first season, the apprentices fortunate enough to have signed professional contracts were training with the reserves and the others were off trying to win contracts at other clubs. This was Tom's cue to run the legs off us 'little fuckers', as he would say. The season was about to end and I could not understand why we were doing athletic work and not technical stuff.

I do not think my sharp tongue and sarcasm impressed him. I remember on one morning he was telling us where to put the equipment for the reserves and first team. There were four stations – three were a few hundred metres away and one was about 5 metres from where we were standing. I thought it would be funny to just move the equipment to the nearest station. Well, that went down like a lead balloon and got me the first of many Tom bollockings!

Even though our relationship had not got off to a great start, I put any fears to the back of my mind and went away for the summer looking forward to the new season – though I was aware that with the quality of the players coming through I would have a real challenge on my hands to earn a place in the team.

Stupidly, however, I did not really work hard over the break to gain an advantage over my teammates. Instead I took it as an opportunity to continue my inappropriate lifestyle.

As ever, the break flew by, and next thing I knew I was back at London Colney preparing for my second season as a full-time player. Going back as a second-year apprentice gave me a lot of confidence: I was no longer the new boy and I knew what to expect.

That pre-season training was as intense as any I had ever done. Anyone who knows anything about youth football will know that lads going from school to training every day have to be treated very carefully. Not only is your body still growing and going through changes but it is adapting to the demands of professional football. This was not a philosophy shared by Tom and, over the course of the 1996/97 season, many players suffered from stress fractures. One or two could have been a coincidence, but not the amount we encountered.

His aggression continued and I saw him on more than one occasion make players cry. This hostility did not seem to have much of an effect on me. In fact, I found it quite amusing although I know a lot of my teammates did not see it that way.

As that season wore on, my initial fears about the talented group joining our team were confirmed: fifteen of them had been signed as apprentices. Considering they only took on five from our age group, it was clear how highly they thought of this pool – and rightly so.

I was beginning to get frustrated because I was struggling to get into the youth team, let alone push for the reserves like I needed to doing be at that stage of my development.

The club must have sensed my disappointment as, out of the blue, I got the opportunity to train with the first team on a couple of occasions. This was brilliant as I got the chance to work alongside the likes of Adams, Berg-kamp and Ian Wright. I seem to remember performing pretty well on those occasions, but it didn't change anything.

The sessions were not really any different to those we did in the youth team, but the speed and intensity was of a different level. Strangely I do not remember being overly nervous either; I suppose at that age you just take it all in your stride. I remember the senior players being welcoming but giving us no extra leeway once the session started.

Around October of that season I made the decision that I did not want to hang around until May to be told I was not being offered a contract. Instead I went to speak to Liam Brady, who had been appointed as the new head of youth, and asked for permission to try to win a professional contract elsewhere, which he agreed to. In hindsight, this might have been a rash decision as it was still early in the season, but I didn't want to waste time at a club where I didn't seem to have a future, even if that club was Arsenal.

I also thought that being associated with Arsenal would have clubs queu-ing up to sign me and that it was just a question of which one I wanted to sign for.

Again I was very wrong…

Clubs invest a lot of time and money in their youth players and become emotionally attached to them. This means that if you go to a new club and attempt to win a contract already earmarked for one of their established players, you need to be head and shoulders above your competition.

I sent my CV out and waited for the avalanche of phone calls. There was not exactly a deluge but eventually Southend United took the bait. Peter Johnson was the youth-team manager there and asked me to come down for a couple of weeks. This was ideal for me as, at that time, South-end was in what is now the Championship – and only thirty minutes from my family home.

The initial trial went well and they asked me to stay until Christmas. I was playing regularly in both the youth team and the reserves and felt I was good enough to earn a contract. Unfortunately, I think the main reason they wanted me to stay was that I was better than the apprentices they already had and they just wanted to use me for as long as they could get away with.

The situation eventually came to a head just before Christmas as my frustration was getting the better of me. During one Friday training session we were playing a small-sided game where you were restricted to a maximum of three touches every time you had the ball.

Someone took too many touches.

Now I know it sounds petty but I have always been a stickler for the rules of these games. I complained loudly to Peter and made my feelings known when he did not make, what I believed to be, the right decision.

He clearly did not like that as, when I went to see him after training to find out what time we were meeting for the game the following day, he told me I was not required for the game – or indeed ever.

I hope that doesn't make me come across as a troublemaker because I am definitely not. However, I have always been opinionated and I do not think there are many managers who like players with an opinion – especially players who have just turned eighteen.

I was still not learning lessons off the pitch either. During my spell at Southend I regularly went out with friends at inappropriate times. At that stage in my life it was more important for me to go out with my friends than concentrate on what had the potential to be a successful career.

I was now back to square one. I had burned my bridges at Arsenal and was deemed not good enough for Southend. This was a real wake-up call as I realised clubs were not desperate to sign me. I had a battle on my hands to find a club that would give me an opportunity to progress.

As I have done many times throughout my career, I sent out letters asking for a trial to all the local professional teams. The first club to respond this time was Brentford FC. At that time they were riding high at the top of what is now League One and were managed by ex-Chelsea player David Webb (who ended up managing me at two different clubs during my career).

The manager of the youth team at Brentford was a guy called Bob Booker and I initially went there for a couple of weeks. As soon as I arrived I knew I would be one of the better players and I felt comfortable when training with the younger professionals as well.

What really struck me during this entire phase of my career was that it seemed even lower-league professional clubs signed apprentices as a form of cheap labour. It was clear the vast majority of players in the Brentford youth team had no chance of forging any kind of career in football, but they were being used to do an abundance of totally unrelated tasks dressed up as 'learning your trade'. Surely the best way to do that was to be out on the training pitch working on technique rather than cleaning kit and painting dressing rooms? The one bonus of being an apprentice on trial was that I didn't have to do any of these jobs.

I ended up staying at Brentford for about a month and the end result was the same as Southend: they told me I was not good enough. My star was waning and I was dropping down the leagues rapidly. I found it really hard to believe that I was not good enough to sign for either of these clubs and, for the first time, I became a bit disillusioned with football.

I was still contracted to Arsenal so should have returned there, but I knew that there was not much communication between Arsenal and Brentford so I just decided not to go to training.

In hindsight, that was a ridiculous thing to do. My assumption that there was no dialogue between Arsenal and Brentford was also misguided, as proven by the phone call I got from a very irate Liam Brady, who had realised I was no longer training at Brentford. He basically said if I was not at London Colney the next day I would be sacked. I decided I did not want that on my CV and sheepishly returned to Arsenal.

When I returned, Tom Walley took great pleasure in telling me that, according to Bob Booker, I had been poorly behaved during my time at Brentford. He said that I did not listen and frequently juggled the ball when he was talking. I was furious about that because, although I was no angel, my behaviour and respect towards other people is impeccable, drummed into me from an early age by my parents. Whether this was true or something Tom had made up I do not know, but it had a galvanising effect: it wound me up and made me more determined to prove people like him and Bob Booker wrong.

I stayed training at Arsenal until another opportunity to go out on trial presented itself. After about a month, and another round of CVs being sent out, Steve Kean, the youth-team coach of Reading FC, asked me to go over to train and play a couple of games with them.

At that time, Reading were competing in Division One (which is now the Championship) and, as soon as I went there, everything seemed to fall into place.

I felt really comfortable and my performances were good. I was playing for the youth team and also getting regularly selected for the reserves, which is always a good barometer of how things are going as a second-year apprentice. The reserve-team manager was Kevin Dillon, who had played for Newcastle United and Birmingham City among others. He seemed to take an instant like to me and the feeling was mutual.

The first-team management set-up was pretty unconventional, however. Instead of having just one manager, Reading had joint managers in Mick Gooding and Jimmy Quinn. Not only that, but they were both player managers. Mick was an industrious midfielder and Jimmy was a traditional target man. This was a pretty unique situation – I remember Charlton Athletic had Alan Curbishley and Steve Gritt as joint managers once, but I cannot recall any clubs having joint player managers. Also on the coaching staff was West Ham legend Billy Bonds, which, with me being a Hammers fan as a kid, was especially thrilling.

Initially my main point of contact was Mick. He seemed to take an interest in me and I presumed this was due to the positive reports he was getting from Steve and Kevin. It was at Reading that I got my first taste of regularly training with the first team. I remember the squad being pretty small and, after a couple of weeks, I was called up to train with the big boys frequently.

Although there was only one division between Arsenal and Reading, the gulf in class between the players was instantly clear. I was initially nervous during the sessions but soon realised I could compete with these guys. A lot of the senior players seemed to take to me and I was made to feel really welcome. It probably helped that Darren Caskey, the club's record signing, was based in Essex and banned from driving, so I drove him in on almost a daily basis.

After a month or so of being on trial I got called into a meeting to get the news I had always dreamt of: Reading wanted to offer me a professional contract. I was ecstatic, especially after rejections from both Southend and Brentford. I had started to doubt whether this day would ever come.

The club offered me a one-year deal, which started immediately. However, as it was late March 1997 at that point, in effect I had a fifteen-month contract since all Football League contracts run until 30 June. I was offered £200 per week, plus £80 a week payable to whoever was my landlord. The club had allowed me to do the commute from Witham – a 200-mile round trip – while I was on trial, but I was now expected to move to the area.

I just sat there open-mouthed and nodded in acceptance.

As a youngster with no experience, that was the full negotiation – you just took what you were offered. There was no agent involved; it was just you and the manager – or, in this case, managers. I think it would have been frowned upon if I had started to barter over an extra £50. Even someone as clueless about the business side of professional sport as I was back then realised this was a wonderful opportunity.

CHAPTER 4

THE DECLINE BEGINS

THERE WAS STILL a month of the season left and I trained with the first team pretty much every day. I had not officially signed until after the transfer deadline, which I believe was the last Thursday in March, and Reading had already secured their place in the division for another season. Man City could only finish fourteenth, irrespective of the result on the last day of the season, so I was given special dispensation by the authorities to play a part in the game if selected.

We travelled up to play Manchester City, who were not the force they are now but still attracted crowds of over 25,000 every other week. On 3 May 1997 I was named on the bench at Maine Road in front of 27,260 fans. An inconsequential last game of the season often produces a carnival atmosphere and this was no different; Manchester City and their fans had designated it as a day to convince the Georgian midfield genius Georgi Kinkladze to sign a new contract. He did not play, unfortunately, but he did partake in numerous laps of honour to milk the applause.

I was named as a substitute and went on to make my League debut in the seventieth minute of the second half. My main recollection of that day is us not having enough pairs of shorts, so I had to change into Lee Nogan's (who had come off ten minutes earlier) in the tunnel. The steward patrolling the area seemed to find this especially amusing!

I remember playing pretty well when I came on and really enjoying the occasion. Playing for Manchester City were both Eddie McGoldrick and Paul Dickov – two players who just a year earlier had scared the life out of me every time I put a foot wrong while training with the reserves at Arsenal. Now I was competing against them in a 'proper game', although we lost 3–2 after leading 2–0. The negative turnaround was nothing to do with me, I hasten to add!

Paul and Eddie seemed pretty surprised to see me but I had always got on well with Eddie – he had christened me 'Curtains' due to my 1990s Jason Donovan-inspired mop. Eddie had an especially cutting and harsh sense of humour but I liked him and often tried to give him some back if I was feeling especially brave.

As I am sure you can imagine, I was thrilled to get on the pitch and I had adrenalin coursing through my veins. I was everywhere, trying to both support the attack and supplement the defence. My performance was more than acceptable and I felt comparable to the players I was competing against.

Suddenly I had gone from someone who had struggled to earn a contract in lower-league teams to making my League debut at the age of eighteen in front of over 27,000 people. I went away at the end of that season confident I could compete to play regularly next term for Reading in Division One.

However, during the summer break, there were the early signs that I was getting a little carried away with myself. At the end of the season, most clubs will go on a small jaunt, which can take the form of 'official' or 'unofficial' club trips. Either way, they are normally four or five days for the players to 'let off some steam' after what is a physically and mentally demanding season. This normally includes a lot of drinking – day and night.

Now, some people may frown at the fact professional sportsmen can behave in such a manner but personally I do not see a problem with it when you have participated in a fifty-plus game season. However, I am not so sure you earn the same privilege after playing twenty minutes of the last game of the season! That fact did not stop me though – in my head I was now a fully fledged professional footballer with £200 burning a hole in my pocket every week. Why would I not accept the offer of a free holiday to the Cypriot resort of Ayia Napa?

In hindsight I should have been at home working on my fitness and physique and preparing to compete for a place in the first team the following season – not getting drunk every day for a week. Admittedly it did help integrate me into the group, but more as a good socialiser than a good footballer.

This is not a criticism, more an observation. It is the sort of situation when I would have benefited from having someone in my family or close to me who had been involved in football or a professional sport themselves – someone who could have reined me in. My dad and I were both novices in this world and we were learning together. I might not have appreciated any such advice at the time, but it could well have made a difference in the longer term.

It was during the summer of 1997 that I first realised how decisions out of my control could have a direct effect on my career. At the end of that season, Reading had finished eighteenth and comfortably avoided relegation. This seemed, to me, a respectable position for a club of their size at the time. John Madejski, the club's owner, did not concur, however, and promptly relieved both Mick Gooding and Jimmy Quinn of their duties on 9 May 1997. I was gutted as I knew they both thought highly of me as a player. But, after the trip to Ayia Napa, I soon got over the disappointment and enjoyed my summer.

Just before we were due to report back, Terry Bullivant, who had previously managed Barnet, was appointed the new manager. I knew nothing about him and I was pretty sure he knew even less about me.

After my ill-advised decision to go on the end-of-season 'holiday' I made my next big mistake at the start of the 1997/98 season. As I mentioned previously, I was now expected to move to the area so, about two days before pre-season was due to start, I rang Steve Kean and asked him where I would be staying that year. Unsurprisingly I had not been at the top of his list of priorities and he said he had no idea. In those days, I don't think the club had a network of people who offered lodgings for young players, whereas now a club can put you in touch with families who make sure you are leading the lifestyle befitting a professional athlete.

I initially travelled to training with Darren Caskey, Trevor Morley and Ray Houghton as they were all based in Essex – although in slightly more luxurious surroundings compared to mine. They used to laugh when we discussed what we had for dinner the previous night and I told them about the large doner kebab and chips I had dismantled.

Steve Swales, one of the northern-based players, was looking for a lodger at his place. This seemed perfect to me as it meant I did not have to stay with strangers. I could have my own space without someone looking over my shoulder every five minutes and reporting back to the club.

What I wanted and what was best for me were two completely different things, though. Surprisingly, the club allowed it – probably because the new manager didn't know anything about me – so Steve and I began our new working/living relationship.

Swalesy is a brilliant guy. I found his self-deprecating northern humour hilarious and I loved sharing a house with him, although I don't think he was the best role model for an impressionable eighteen-year-old who had never lived away from home. Our place became a drop-in centre where players who lived a long way away, such as Martin Williams and Martin Booty, would stay overnight if it was either too late or they simply could not be bothered to go home.

These guys were all regular first-team players and being around them helped me become part of the group. However, the problem was I was living my life like a first-team player without doing any of the work that enabled someone to achieve such status. Most of the players would go into Reading town centre after a Tuesday night game. They always had Wednesday off so what time they got home and where they ended up was pretty irrelevant.

Now, it was one thing to go a bit wild if you had been playing, but it was quite another to go out after just sitting in the stand watching them. When you add this to the fact that every other weekend, when the first team played away and I wasn't involved, I was back in Essex on all-day drinking binges with my friends, I was not exactly in peak condition.

All the good will I had built up under the previous management was irrelevant under the new regime. Terry Bullivant brought Alan Harris, brother of the infamous Ron 'Chopper' Harris, as his assistant, plus the recently retired Alan Pardew became reserve-team manager. With me being one of the youngest members of the professional players I was very much at the bottom of the food chain and so I spent much of my time with Pards.

The job of a reserve-team manager seems a strange one to me. You have an eclectic mix of players and personalities: from the eager to the not-quite-so-eager young professionals like me; from the out-of-favour established first-team players to players coming back from injury; plus the experienced older players whose careers are winding down. All have to be treated and motivated in different ways.

The reserve-team manager may often not have a clue until about an hour before training who or how many players he will have for his session. One day they could have twelve; the next only four; or halfway through a session, the first-team manager could come over and say he needs to take three of the players. Reserve-team managers have to be really adaptable.

I liked Pards from the start. He was, much like he is now, very confident, sometimes crossing over to arrogance. His sense of humour was 'big time' and by that I mean he would regularly refer to his past success – whether to take the mickey out of someone who had achieved less or to put someone in their place. I have always found this sort of banter really funny, although only when someone can back it up. There is nothing worse than blatantly insecure people who talk loads but cannot deliver on their words (incidentally, they are very common in the world of football). Alan was not one of these people, though; he gave it all the talk but could clearly back up any of his promises both on and off the training pitch. He especially liked shooting competitions as he had an unerringly accurate right side foot that always seemed to find the bottom corner, irrespective of the power behind it.

I think Pards liked me too. My cheeky, sarcastic personality could rub some people in authority up the wrong way, but he seemed to enjoy it. He had also been a central midfielder and this was good for someone like me – every coach, however knowledgeable, knows their own position better than any other. Pards was continuously giving me pieces of advice.

I remember one training session when I gave the ball away once, twice, three times in a row (the only time that ever happened in my career!). By that stage, as I am sure you can imagine, I was getting plenty of abuse from my more experienced teammates so Alan pulled me to one side and said:

> If you are playing first-team games you can get away with giving the ball away once. If you do it twice in a row then the crowd will start getting on your back. If you do it three times too often you will soon get dragged off by the manager.

This may seem like simple advice but it really stuck in my mind and became something I would often reflect back on throughout my career on those rare occasions I did give the ball away!

At that time I probably was not mature enough to take on board all the advice offered. At a young age it can feel like people are constantly criticising you when, in fact, those offering good advice normally think a lot of you and want you to progress. As my standing at the club deteriorated during the year, I soon realised what happens when you are no longer seen as a viable first-team prospect…

Nothing.

The silence is deafening, and people could not care less if you play well or not.

Initially, even though my lifestyle was disgusting for a young athlete, I made some sort of positive impression on the management. I came on for a fifteen-minute appearance against a full-strength Chelsea team in pre-season. During my cameo I produced a lovely piece of skill and hit the crossbar, which was greeted with a nod of approval by none other than Gianfranco Zola and made my day. Then, straight after, I nearly gave a goal away when Gus Poyet nicked the ball off me.

As the season progressed I was regularly appearing for the reserves and generally bounced around with the naivety and confidence you tend to have at that age. I remember scoring for the reserves against Rushden & Diamonds, only to get a bollocking from Pards after the game for not doing my defensive duties – a common theme throughout my career. I followed this up with a couple more positive performances and suddenly I was more involved in the first team.

Every Friday the match day squad – the sixteen wanted for the following day – trained with the first-team management. Up until early September I found myself left with those not selected, doing a mixture of technical and fitness work with Pards and looking longingly over to the big boys. On 12 September 1997, however, my name was called out to go join the first team. I was as surprised as anyone after the stern dressing-down I had received just a couple of weeks earlier. Pards had told me, with expletives, that I was nowhere near the first team.

We played Oxford United the following day and I was a substitute. It always felt like I was on the bench simply as a reward for the respectable performances I had put in over the last few reserve games more than because I had any actual chance of getting on the pitch.

This was another period where, again, I wish I'd had an experienced football person around to advise me. Rather than being thankful that I was in and around a Division One first team at the age of eighteen, I felt frustrated it was only a seemingly token involvement. Obviously, in hindsight, Terry Bullivant was going to take a lot more persuading than a couple of above-average performances in the reserve league, especially considering my ability to throw in some very erratic displays. I managed to keep my place in the first-team squad for another game before returning to the shadows.

I do not think it did my career prospects at Reading any good when I accidentally broke the once club record signing's leg in training either.

I was meandering along at Reading, going nowhere very quickly, and I became one of those players you get at every club: someone in love with being a professional footballer. I enjoyed the fact I went into training at 10.30 a.m. and was either back home by 1 p.m. or wandering aimlessly around town. It never dawned on me to stay behind and work on my technique or go down to the gym and improve my physical strength and fitness. It was not 'cool' to do that and I was not strong enough to go against the grain. I did not want to put the work in required to enhance my current lifestyle or even continue it.

I like to think of myself as being relatively intelligent but, the more I look back, the more I realise people at the club were trying to tell me I had a real opportunity to carve out a successful career. Kevin Dillon was always supportive and really believed in me, and he was not the only one. I remember on one occasion, Phil Parkinson – a stalwart of the club and a very combative midfielder – invited me to do some extra running after training. It was not really my cup of tea but I accepted his invitation. In between the work-out we chatted about how football was changing and

Phil kept stressing to me that players of the new era, players like me, could go on to become millionaires from football. I took what he said with a pinch of salt; instead of taking his advice on board, it just passed me by. At that time Phil was not the sort of person I admired – he didn't go out partying all the time and was a very limited player, although he made the most of the ability he had. Nowadays, players of his ilk are exactly the type for whom I have the most respect. Any player can waste his ability, but very few go on to overachieve.

I was more interested in going out and enjoying myself with the likes of Swalesy, Michael Meaker, Darren Caskey and the rest of my more dubious role models. They, or the legendary former Reading player Robin Friday (who was the local equivalent of George Best), were who I wanted to be like. I'm not criticising them, though – they had, after all, earned the right to enjoy the fruits of their labour. I had not. I'd done nothing in the game but I behaved like a fully fledged first-team player. If I had idolised someone like Phil Parkinson who knows how things could have turned out?

Being a stalwart in the reserves during the 1997/98 season, I often had conversations with Alan Pardew regarding my progress. He was a lot more forthright than most and told me, in no uncertain terms, that I was wasting my ability. I remember, on one occasion, I was having a great day in training and modestly decided to compare myself to Dennis Bergkamp. To my surprise, Pards agreed with me – although he did qualify the statement by saying I was normally more like the old comedian Denis Norden. This slightly took the wind out of my sails.

Pards regularly questioned my attitude and asked me how much I really 'wanted it'. I always assured him I was desperate to become a success. I thought at the time I was telling the truth, but I obviously wasn't and he knew it. That dawned on me over time.

He always told me about a player he knew called Peter Garland. He said

Garland was exceptionally talented but wasted his ability by being over-weight and lazy. Pards warned me I would end up like him, straddling the lower leagues rather than showcasing my talents at a higher level. Unfortunately, I managed to prove him right.

As my first full season as a professional player progressed, the gap between the first team and myself was getting bigger. No longer was I having the friendly chats with the senior professionals or receiving the bollockings from management.

I was training more with the youth team now and was constantly overlooked when Bullivant was calling players over to make up numbers for the first team. Even at my tender age I could read the script: my days were numbered. I had managed to fuck up a great opportunity, and it was only ten years later, as I struggled to make a living in the lower leagues, that it dawned on me what an opportunity it had been.

By the start of March 1998 I was only honouring my contract and counting down the days to go. There had been no conversation between the management and myself regarding the future, but from the way I was being treated it was clear where my future lay – and it was nowhere near Elm Park.

In those days, before the transfer window was introduced, the last Thursday in March was the final chance for players to move clubs before the end of the season. Pards pulled me to one side earlier in the month and informed me that Yeovil Town, who played in the then Conference Premier, wanted to sign me. He told me he had played at the club at the start of his career and said it was a good opportunity to reignite a fledgling career that was already stagnating before I'd hit the age of twenty.

I had no idea about Yeovil geographically, let alone the football club, but I agreed I had nothing to lose from going down to the club to have a look around and chat with the manager Colin Lippiatt. My advisor – by which I mean my dad – and I made the long journey to Somerset a few days before the transfer deadline.

When I got there I was pleasantly surprised at the quality of the ground: it was a proper football stadium. I had also carried out some due diligence and discovered that Yeovil were well-known FA Cup 'giant-killers', who commanded attendances of 1,500-plus. Of course, it was no 27,000 like I'd faced at Manchester City less than a year earlier, but it felt like a big step up from playing in front of a handful of people for Reading reserves.

When I met the manager he told me all the right things and what he thought about me as a player. It turned out he lived in Bracknell, which is near Reading, so regularly took in our reserve games and had seen me play on quite a few occasions. As always, the reassurance a manager had seen me play live and could specifically talk about my game, rather than give some generic bullshit, appealed to me as I think my style of play is an acquired taste. I have always had definite strengths and weaknesses that are not everybody's cup of tea.

After a period of deliberation in the Reading branch of TGI Friday's, my dad and I agreed that it was time I started to play regular first-team football. Yeovil offered me £250 a week and a £50 win bonus, both after tax, to sign on a non-contract basis until the end of the season. As I was on a League contract at Reading I was entitled to get paid until 30 June, whereas Yeovil, a semi-professional club, only paid their players until the last game of the season. On this occasion, however, Yeovil agreed to honour that part of my contract and paid me through the off-season too.

At the time I did not realise what a risky move this was. When you sign as a non-contract player there is no job security and the club can let you go whenever they want. When I told Alan Pardew about the deal he was especially angry and said that he had only allowed the transfer to go through on the understanding I was given a two-year deal – although he was not bothered enough to take it any further!

I was oblivious to the gamble I was taking and pretty happy with myself really. I had effectively dropped three divisions but managed to negotiate myself a pay rise. Moreover, Yeovil only trained once a week so I was getting paid more money for less work.

. . .

27 DECEMBER 2012

Another anticlimatic Christmas has been and gone. I have decided Christmas Day is what Sundays would be like without football – very boring. I thought I would enjoy my first Christmas being a 'normal person' but it did not really turn out that way. I'm still playing for non-League side Thurrock FC and my football mindset did not allow me to kick back and relax, but the Boxing Day game eventually got rained off anyway so my restraint was wasted.

I did manage to somehow negotiate a full term at school, however, although I'm not too sure how. Even more surprising is the fact I've been offered an extension to my contract. I did not want to stay initially as I found myself doing too much of what I knew very little about – as illustrated by the fact that I recently found myself teaching a business studies class to Year 7s and 8s while the school caretaker was taking a football lesson!

The school's headmaster is a really good guy and had a frank discussion with me about the situation. He asked me whether I would stay if my time-table were based around both business studies and football – which was what I'd been led to believe was going to happen in the first place.

I agreed and my contract has been extended until the end of the school year. I received my new timetable just as we broke up for Christmas. It's not quite as I expected but I have come to realise that what you are told in the education industry and what actually happens are often two different things (a bit like football). I now have football all day on Fridays, so I'm at least moving in the right direction.

I was still seriously considering moving on, though. I even contemplated starting up my own business or just doing something completely different, but it's funny how hard it is to take your own advice. If one of my friends came to me and said they're struggling with a new career, I would tell them:

1) It's going to be tough.

2) You need to persevere.

3) Keep in mind why you wanted to do the job in the first place.

Yet when people I respect gave me similar advice, I tried to find as many reasons as possible to disagree and justify the urge to give up.

However, in a rare moment of clarity I realised that although I've managed to get myself into a situation where I'm not doing enough of what I like, I'm gaining experience working with children that will be invaluable in the future. This period in my life has confirmed that I want to coach children in a professional environment. I just have to work out how to go about doing it.

The beauty of being a teacher is, of course, the holidays. School doesn't restart until 7 January and, to be honest, I'm not particularly looking forward to going back. This is a strange feeling as I loved going to training when I was a footballer. Even on the low days I still managed to see the bigger picture.

This scenario is different – it is not a feeling of dread but it is also not a buzz of anticipation. I need excitement and am determined to find it again. It is not all doom and gloom as there are some parts of the job I enjoy. I've started mentoring some Year 7 boys from different backgrounds, which has been really enjoyable so far, and I also like building relationships with the students It's only when I need to get them to do something that the problems start – motivating teenage boys can be tricky.

I've also enrolled on an assessor course, which will help not only with the teaching but also in my quest to improve my future for the better.

CHAPTER 5

THE DECLINE GATHERS MOMENTUM

SEASON: 1998/99
CLUB: YEOVIL TOWN FC
DIVISION: CONFERENCE PREMIER
MANAGER: COLIN LIPPIATT

I SIGNED FOR Yeovil at the start of March 1998 and made my debut on the 7th at home against Morecambe. Unbeknown to me, I made that debut alongside others the club had signed at the same time, including Sammy Winston (a robust striker), Steve Parmenter (a versatile left-footer from Bristol Rovers) and Dave Piper (a right back from Southampton who had a hairline that belied his young years and who became a close friend of mine).

We lost that game 3–2, despite Morecambe going down to ten men in the first half. Not the most auspicious of starts but I really enjoyed playing and was subsequently named 'Man of the Match'. I went into the game having no idea what to expect and with no respect for my teammates or the opposition – I had come straight from a Division One club so obviously this was going to be easy and I would be the best player on the pitch every game.

On this occasion that happened to be the case, but little did I know that my new level of football was littered with talented individuals who, for whatever reason, had ended up playing below their potential. I was just another example.

Initially I was playing with a freedom I had not exhibited since playing in the park with my pals. I had an arrogance to my game that all players have when they are playing to the peak of their capabilities. I also had the advantage of being parachuted in from a full-time professional environment to a semi-professional one.

In the late 1990s the only full-time teams around at that level were those who got relegated from the League (and only one team got relegated back then), plus the odd ambitious club like Rushden & Diamonds. So I had the advantage of being in a much better physical state than my peers, even taking into account my dubious lifestyle and the benefit of not having to work another job all week.

We only trained one day a week – on a Wednesday evening – so I had plenty of spare time. Initially I stayed living in Reading with Swalesy. It made some sense: I had no ambition to move to Somerset, and Berkshire was a lot closer to Yeovil than my family home in Essex. Also, while I had a driving licence, I did not own a car, so my new boss Colin Lippiatt, who was based in Bracknell, kindly gave me lifts to training and games.

After the personal triumph of my debut, my progress continued on an upward trajectory. The team's results were not overly impressive but I remember, without blowing my own trumpet too much, being one of our standout performers.

After Morecambe we drew away to Kettering and then beat Stalybridge Celtic at home 2–0. In the next game we beat Telford United away 4–1 and I scored my first two senior goals. This landmark was followed by a boozy Wednesday at the Cheltenham horse-racing festival with my former Reading colleagues, ending up in the Utopia nightclub where one of the lads performed the greyhound (an act of pulling his trousers and pants down, putting his cock and balls between his legs and roaring around on all fours) while Gareth Davies earned a 3-inch carpet burn on his forehead after being rugby tackled to the floor by one of his teammates. This was pretty much in line with how I spent the majority of my days off.

With the confidence of my first senior goals still coursing through my veins, things continued to go well. Apart from a narrow away defeat at Northwich Victoria, we remained unbeaten for the next month. Part of that unbeaten run was a 1–0 victory over Hednesford Town, which included a spectacular effort from the halfway line by myself. Although it ended up being scrambled to safety by the Hednesford goalkeeper, subsequent CCTV footage showed that the shot had actually gone over the line. I believe this was when the clamour for goal-line technology really started!

I was building some good relationships with my teammates on and off the pitch. Dave Piper and I became great friends. On the pitch he would give me the ball whenever he could and off it he had the same outlook on life as me: enjoy yourself as much as possible, even to the detriment of your football. I also struck up a great understanding with Warren Patmore, who was a strapping centre forward and won everything in the air. I played as an advanced central midfielder so would regularly feed off his knockdowns or play off him in and around the box. Before the end of this season we became travelling partners as I moved back to Essex and he was based in Watford.

Warren was one of many players I came across during my lower-league football career who could have achieved so much more if he had been more disciplined. In his defence, I don't think he ever really had any ambition to play higher. He was a shrewd man who did very well out of non-League football and he had an abundance of interests off the pitch that have subsequently resulted in him doing very well for himself. He was and still is a Yeovil Town legend.

The club was obviously happy with the impact I had made because they wanted to sit down and discuss a proper contract, like the one Alan Pardew had assumed I was initially signing. We arranged to have a conversation after the home game against Hereford United on 18 April. I had no one representing me and no real idea what everybody was earning, so I didn't really have a figure in my head regarding what would be acceptable.

We beat Hereford United 2–0 and I scored both goals in the first half. Even I realised this would do my negotiating position no harm at all.

The meeting itself illustrated just how unprofessional both the club and I were back then. On that particular weekend the players had arranged a team night out so we were enjoying a few pre-drinks in the bar at Yeovil's ground. I was not the only one discussing a new contract so, by the time I was called for my chat, I had consumed at least three pints.

I went to speak to the chairman John Fry with – and I still cringe thinking about this – a full pint of beer in hand, which I promptly slapped on his desk. He opened discussions by saying how happy the club had been with me and how it would like to tie me to a contract. He explained this meant I would be protected and guaranteed to be paid every week. Moreover, if another club wanted to sign me, they would have to pay a fee unless Yeovil agreed to let me go for nothing.

I was more than happy to do this. I had scored four goals in my first nine games, with a few assists thrown in for good measure. Whether it was slightly drunken bravado or my own self-importance I thought I should be the highest-paid player in the team, as, at the time, I thought I was the best player. The club initially offered me £275 per week, which, if memory serves me correct, also included a small signing-on fee of about £1,500. The problem was all this money got taxed so, in effect, I was worse off than my current £250 a week after tax. There may have been a few little add-ons thrown in, such as appearance money and goal bonus, but nothing significant.

John was not impressed with my claims and was not really budging on the offer. A few of the players who travelled a long distance also had cars paid for by the club so I decided I wanted a club car in my deal too. I did not feel this was unfair as I was now commuting from Essex, although it may have been a little cheeky as I was still only nineteen and had done nothing in the game.

We did not come to an agreement that night and decided to talk again on Monday. I didn't mind – I had a big night out planned and did not want to waste time discussing matters that could wait until the following week.

The club seemed keen to get the contract sorted out as soon as possible, however. I was flattered by their attentions but what happened during that week may have been the reason for their haste.

Right on cue I got a phone call from the club on Monday enquiring about my thoughts regarding the contract. I had spoken to a few people about my situation and decided that Yeovil was the best place for me to continue my football education, but I wanted to squeeze a little more money out of any deal. I told them I would sign if they raised my basic wage to £300 a week and included a pay rise in the second year of the contract if certain performance-related conditions were met. Yeovil agreed.

So the final deal was £300 per week, rising to £325 in the second year on the condition we finished in the top six of the League in the 1998/99 season. I also received a signing-on fee of £1,500 paid in instalments, a sponsored car and a goal bonus. This new deal would kick in straight away but meant I would, after this summer, no longer get paid through the close season.

The day after the agreement was made we were due to play Rushden & Diamonds away. When I arrived at the ground I was ushered onto the coach to sign my contract before the game, which I did.

The game itself was an exciting 2–2 draw. I scored one and set up the other to follow on from the two goals I had scored against Hereford the previous Saturday. That made it five goals in my first ten games.

It was by far my best game thus far for Yeovil and I tormented the Rushden defence throughout. They were a big-spending team at the time, backed by Max Griggs (founder of Dr Martens), who was willing to do whatever it took to get the club into the League. They had a wonderful stadium with top-class training facilities and, for the standard we were playing at, a team to match.

I was really happy with my performance and had that brilliant adrenalin buzz you get after an exhilarating game. I got home at around 11.30 p.m. and almost straight away my phone started going off. An agent, whose name escapes me but who I do remember was northern, rang me and asked if I had signed my contract with Yeovil. I told him yes, I had, thank you very much. He went silent on the other end of the line. I asked him what the problem was.

He went on to tell me that he had just spoken to Brian Talbot, the manager of Rushden & Diamonds, who wanted to sign me immediately.

He said the deal would be two years with a basic salary of £500 per week and a £25,000 signing-on fee. Back then, £25,000 seemed like a lottery win and would have surpassed any individual signing-on fee I would receive in my entire career. Suddenly the buzz I had felt after the game had gone.

I felt sick.

The deal was worth a guaranteed minimum of £75,000 over the two years without contemplating any add-ons for success, which, considering the team they had, seemed a given. It was also a 52-week contract, meaning I would get fully paid over the summer break. Aside from the finances of the deal, Rushden were also full time, which meant I would be training every day again.

The agent believed we could get out of the Yeovil deal as it would not have been lodged with the FA yet. He insisted that I speak to the manager and tell him I had made a mistake.

But I refused to do this.

History shows that many players have used this strategy successfully, but it did not sit comfortably with me – especially when suggested by a man

I hardly knew. He insisted I was making a mistake but I refused to budge and, after all, I hadn't even spoken to Brian Talbot so I didn't have any confirmation that what the agent was saying was true.

This agent, like a lot of middlemen, was very persistent and said he would speak to the Rushden hierarchy to ask if they would be willing to pay a transfer fee for my services. After a couple of days of going backwards and forwards it was relayed to me that Max Griggs, much like myself, was not keen on making enemies of other teams and that Rushden's interest in me would not go any further. I never actually spoke to any club representative so I will never know how strong their interest was, nor how true the figures the agent quoted were, but from what I subsequently heard, I am pretty sure they would have taken me on a free transfer.

After that fiasco I continued with the rest of the season. We still had four games left, which turned into two away defeats (against those big, horrible northerners Leek Town and Southport) and two home victories (including ten goals scored against Dover and Gateshead). We finished the season eleventh – perfect mid-table mediocrity – with fifty-nine points. I hadn't scored another goal so finished the season with five in fourteen games.

Yet again I spent the summer abusing my body.

I was still friendly with a lot of the Reading players and as soon as my season finished I joined them on midfielder Paul Holsgrove's stag party. I spent three days drinking non-stop and never made it back to our apartment during the whole trip. I did make one aborted attempt to return for some sleep, but was so disorientated I had no clue where the apartment actually was. I should probably take this opportunity to apologise to the taxi driver who toured the outskirts of Magaluf trying to find my accommodation. As the meter kept going up, it dawned on me that we were never going to find where I was staying and I had no money to pay my increasingly irate chauffeur. We briefly stopped in traffic next to a backstreet and I took my chance to escape. I jumped out of the car and headed for the alleyway but, as I did, the driver got my shirt and ripped off half the buttons. It was not enough to stop me, however, and I was away.

Unfortunately, I was then left wandering around Magaluf with no money and a half-ripped shirt. This was before most people took mobile phones abroad so I couldn't easily contact any of the lads. It was FA Cup final day so I pitched camp at a Linekers Bar, reasoning that my colleagues would eventually turn up there. They did but, unsurprisingly, not until about 9 p.m. I hate to think what I looked like that day!

It took me a good four days to recover from that 'holiday'.

Some may argue that this was immediately after the season ended so there was no real harm done. Nobody could say that about my next decision, however. As I had dropped into 'non-League' football, I surmised that pre-season was no longer important and I could go on holiday whenever I wanted. Along with some of my non-footballing friends, I decided to take a two-week holiday in Ibiza in early July.

Pre-season training pretty much always begins around 1 July, give or take a couple of days. So, even though I'd just had two months off, I thought it wise to have another two weeks at an all-inclusive resort drinking and eating as much as I could rather than preparing for a new season. Admittedly I did get the blessing of my manager, but that is irrelevant. It was a ridiculous thing to do and during the 1998/99 season I paid for it in a big way.

I re-joined the Yeovil Town squad for training a couple of weeks after everyone else. Except for bringing up the rear during the running in my first training session, I actually seemed to be getting away with my lack of preparation. I performed relatively well in my first pre-season game against Plymouth and continued that form to be selected for the first game of the season away at Kettering Town.

My manager and his staff were still talking really positively about me before the game and referring to me as one of the 'go-to' players in the team – this satisfied my ego. We won the game 2–1 and I remember performing fine, but I missed a great opportunity to score in the first half. The ball had sat up perfectly and all I had to do was lift it over the stranded keeper from around 20 yards. I did that part expertly, but I also managed to clear the crossbar and the chance was gone.

The good start sadly did not continue as we lost at home to both Kingstonian and Hednesford Town. I remember learning a footballing lesson against Kingstonian. They had Gary Patterson and Geoff Pitcher in midfield, both really experienced midfielders who complemented each other perfectly, treated me like the nipper I was and totally dominated the game.

Those two losses were followed by a draw at Hayes and then a win at Dover, where I played poorly and was substituted. We then beat Kidderminster Harriers 3–1 at home on the August bank holiday and I played a more advanced role just off Warren Patmore. I got my first goal of the season and, more importantly, my club car.

I did not stipulate what type of car I wanted but I cannot say the green Seat Ibiza, complete with tow bar, was what I had envisaged. I was a young eligible bachelor and this was not the sort of transport a 'man about town' should have been driving – not in my opinion anyway. It was probably very cool in rural Somerset, though, and it was in club colours.

I was hoping that bank holiday performance would kick-start my season and bring on a consistent level of performance after a so-so beginning. Our next game was at home to Rushden & Diamonds and it was the first time we'd meet after their rumoured interest in me the previous season. I was determined to impress.

We lost the game 1–0 but I felt I had been our most effective attacking player throughout. You can imagine my surprise therefore when, with fifteen minutes left and us chasing the game, I was taken off. I could not believe it when my number came up and I showed my anger by telling the manager what I thought of his decision as I left the pitch. He was a lovely man but I was really frustrated. We were playing with three central defenders and had two defensive-minded midfielders on as well. The general gist of my argument was that he should have taken one of those defensive players off and left me on as we needed a goal. I had a strong case but my reaction was unprofessional and must have looked terrible to the supporters, not to mention the manager in the other dugout who I was trying to impress.

I felt vindicated though when, with five minutes to go, the sponsors named me 'Man of the Match'. Quite often the announcement of the sponsors' player of the game is met with bemusement, but I obviously agreed this time.

After the game Colin took me into the office and gave me a bollocking, which he was totally entitled to do. He told me he 'couldn't care less who I thought I was' and that I had 'no right' to question his decision. I accepted that point but still could not agree with his rationale for the substitution.

On this occasion we had to agree to disagree. I wonder what he thought of me after that meeting – some chubby nineteen-year-old who had only been playing first-team football for six months telling a man of vast experience what he should be doing.

Colin did not hold a grudge though and continued to play me. In return, my performances were acceptable … until the end of September when we played Woking away. I put in the kind of performance that far too regularly punctuated the season. We drew 0–0, which was a good result considering we played the first fifty minutes with ten players. No one had been sent off, it was just that my performance was nothing short of horrific. I was anonymous other than when I was giving the ball away and was relieved to be put out of my misery in the early part of the second half. I was so embarrassed I just wanted to get off the pitch as quickly as possible.

I had gradually lost the trust of Colin and unsurprisingly found myself on the bench. With hindsight, it was obvious what happened: after coming from the professional game and full-time training, I was now a part-time player who lacked the discipline to keep my fitness levels at the required standard.

In those days I was very much of the opinion that I did not need to be fit, I just needed to be good on the ball. One problem was that Yeovil only trained on a Wednesday evening and my favourite local club night in Chelmsford was on a Tuesday. The now defunct Dukes held a '70s night and all drinks were 70p, so, more often than not, I was in no shape to train to any decent standard the next day.

I trained religiously every day at the park by myself, but I was just working on my touch and it had no physical benefits. As a result, I was putting on weight, which led to me feeling lethargic on match days and contributed to my erratic performances.

It was a full two months later, in mid-December, before I managed to get myself back into the starting eleven.

The break seemed to benefit me as I came back into the team and performed closer to my potential. This was a good time to find my form as we were still in the FA Cup and had drawn a big third-round tie against Cardiff City at their old Ninian Park stadium.

Cardiff were only a Division Three team then (which would now be League Two) but it was a big game and relatively local, too. My focus during this Christmas period was to ensure I started in that game.

I managed to achieve that goal.

We drew the game 1–1 in front of over 13,000 people. Anyone who has played or watched football in south Wales knows how fanatical the supporters are. The atmosphere was intense and aggressive – some may say intimidating – but I had always relished such occasions. Former Cardiff player Carl Dale put us in the lead early in the second half and it looked as though we were about to add another chapter to Yeovil's illustrious giant-killing history. Unfortunately we were pegged back with fewer than ten minutes to go so just held out for a draw.

I was really happy with my performance and felt that, after a poor few months, I had managed to re-establish myself. We took Cardiff all the way in the replay, but eventually lost 2–1 in extra time to a bizarre goal that has subsequently been replayed many times as a 'football blooper' clip. Our goalkeeper Tony Pennock – ironically a lifelong Swansea City supporter – had rolled the ball out ready to hit a long goal kick, while Cardiff's Kevin Nugent pretended not to be interested. As soon as Tony put the ball on the floor, however, Nugent turned and attempted to win it. This totally caught Tony out and they got embroiled in a fifty-fifty challenge; Tony got to the ball first but it ricocheted off Nugent and flew into the goal.

With the Cup run over, our focus was back on the League. Unfortunately those games against Cardiff turned out to be the highlight of my season as I reverted back to being a peripheral player. By mid-April our season was petering out and I was not particularly focused on the upcoming games as I had no idea if I would be playing from one week to the next.

On 22 April we played Cheltenham Town away. I knew they were top of our league but didn't realise they could win it if they beat us. I was expecting to rock up and play in front of the usual couple of thousand hardy souls so you can imagine my surprise when I got there and learnt the game had sold out. We lost 3–2 and Cheltenham scored the winning goal in about the eighth minute of injury time to gain promotion to the League. Cue pitch invasion and the usual race back to the safety of the dressing rooms for the players and officials.

As a club we enjoyed a successful season, finishing a very creditable fifth with seventy-one points from forty-two games and getting to the third round of the FA Cup.

Personally, on the other hand, it had been a really disappointing year. What was even more disappointing was that all my problems were self-inflicted. I had gone from being a key player to a bit-part squad member.

I managed a total of forty appearances (twenty-eight starts and twelve subs) and scored three goals. You could say that's not too bad as there weren't many twenty-year-olds playing regular first-team football, but I knew I had seriously underachieved. The only positive was that I had met the terms of my contract triggering my £25-a-week pay rise. I had not done a great deal to earn it, but I was not going to look a gift horse in the mouth.

It was not just me who was disappointed with my overall performance, though: Colin was not happy either. If I had been out of contract I would definitely have been released. Thankfully I had another year to go, because who would have taken me after failing at Arsenal, Reading and Yeovil?

Colin wanted to move me on, however, and put me on the transfer list. I do not think either of us expected an avalanche of offers, but he was going to see if anyone would take the bait. This gesture galvanised me and I was determined to prove Colin, and anyone else who had endorsed that decision, wrong.

CHAPTER 6

A RENAISSANCE ... OF SORTS

SEASON: 1999/2000
CLUB: YEOVIL TOWN
DIVISION: CONFERENCE PREMIER
MANAGERS: COLIN LIPPIATT/STEVE THOMPSON/DAVID WEBB

DESPITE BEING LISTED for transfer, there was very little interest in my services. Yeovil made me aware that Stevenage Borough had made a tentative enquiry regarding my availability but, for whatever reason, did not take things further. So, whether it was desired or not, Yeovil was lumbered with me for another year.

However, for the first time in my fledgling career, I embarked on my own fitness regime over the summer break. During pre-season training for the 1999/2000 season I saw the benefits of this hard work.

It was evident immediately; I scored a hat-trick against an admittedly weak local side called East Coker and then an excellent half-volley against Gillingham. I surpassed myself in this game as I managed to enrage pretty much the whole Gillingham team with my antics. After my recent hat-trick and this early goal I was really full of myself and showboating at every opportunity. Predictably, I became a marked man as the game wore on, attracting attention from Gillingham's senior professionals in particular. Their captain Paul Smith tried to scythe me in half, but I cheekily nudged the ball through his legs and watched as he nearly slid out of the ground! Next I tried to nutmeg Andy Hessenthaler, who looked at me with contempt, took the ball and said, in no uncertain terms, what he thought of my attempt. Finally Barry Ashby, a big centre half, made it clear what he was going to do to me if I came anywhere near him.

After these kinds of friendly games, Yeovil always put food on for the players. You can imagine how sheepish I felt as I wandered upstairs for my post-match Lucozade and pasta while rubbing shoulders with players who wanted to kick seven bells out of me – thankfully they all saw the funny side and left me alone.

Pre-season continued to go well and the highlight was a resounding 5–3 victory over a youthful Manchester United side, which included Danny Webber and Michael Rose (a future teammate of mine).

It seemed like I had managed to re-establish myself in the Yeovil first team and things were going well off the pitch too. During the summer, the club had signed Terry Skiverton from Welling United. Terry was based in east London so would commute with Warren Patmore, Dean Chandler and myself to Somerset. Terry and I hit it off from the start and began a bromance that culminated in my becoming his landlord.

Summer had gone as well as I could have imagined and I was convinced I would be in the team for the opening game of the season – the almighty trek to Scarborough. We travelled up to Yorkshire on the Friday before the game and Terry and I shared a room.

Colin Lippiatt did not name the team until a couple of hours before kick-off but Terry got a phone call at 11 a.m. on the Saturday. It was the gaffer and he wanted to see Terry in his room. Now, any professional will tell you that you only get a phone call like this before a game if: a) You normally play but will not be selected today; or b) You do not normally play and, out of the blue, you are in the starting line-up.

Considering Terry had played nigh-on all the pre-season friendly games, I guessed it was the former reason. After he hung up we shared a knowing look and off he went. Upon his return I said: 'I'll have two sugars in my tea please, Terry!' to insinuate I was the senior professional and he had to wait on me.

As expected, I was in the team, but unfortunately that was the highlight of my day. We lost 5–0 and I was subbed at half-time while we were 3–0 down – although, on this occasion, I'm not sure my performance deserved it.

Terry was one of the subs who came on and, as he got ready, whispered in my ear, 'I'll have two sugars in my tea please!' Touché, I deserved that. Even in my depressed state I still had a little chuckle to myself!

All that early season optimism disappeared and I returned to my default position on the bench. My pre-season form had not done enough to gain Colin's trust; considering some of the dross I had served up for him last season that was understandable.

Yeovil had a good start to the season following that initial hiding, though. For the rest of August my contribution was restricted to one start and a smattering of cameo appearances as a substitute. I was frustrated after working hard to get myself into good shape, but I also had to accept there was nobody to blame but myself.

There was real competition for places in central midfield with experienced players such as Steve Stott, Steve Thompson, Jamie Pitman, Dave Norton, Paul Tisdale and Matt Hayfield in front of me. While not capable of the sort of displays I could put on at my best, these players were a lot more consistent and reliable.

Everything seemed to be going swimmingly for the club until, unexpectedly, Colin Lippiatt resigned from his managerial post just before October. Normally if you're out of the team, such news can make you quite happy (even if you don't admit it). However, on this occasion, this was not the case.

Yes, I was frustrated about my lack of playing time but I really liked Colin as a person. I never came across anyone, at the time or since, with a bad word to say about him. Apparently he quit because the club wanted him to become the full-time manager and he didn't want to give up his day job. How true this was, I don't really know.

Steve Thompson was given the post on a six-week trial – an intriguing development for me as Steve and I had an interesting relationship. Sometimes we got on well but other times things were a little strained. There's no doubt Steve rated me as a player but I think he was frustrated by my lack of application and thought I was wasting my talent. I wasn't sure how much playing time I was going to get under him.

A game against Tonbridge Angels in the previous campaign illustrated our somewhat erratic relationship. We had laboured to a 1–0 victory against our lower-ranked opposition in the FA Trophy second round. At the next training session, Colin carried out a post mortem and Steve offered his opinion, stating that the reason we were so poor was because we were playing with ten men – the insinuation being that carrying me in the team was like playing with a man down. This was not a comment I appreciated in front of my peers, but bearing in mind my performance level around that time it was probably fair.

I should not have worried, though, as Steve showed a lot of faith in me. He actually seemed to be going out of his way to get me playing at my best. Before we played Sutton United away he said, in front of the whole team, that he thought I was the most talented player he had seen at Conference level. I repaid him by going on to score the only goal in a 1–0 win.

Moments like that were tempered with some disappointments too, however. I was left on the bench for an FA Cup first-round game against my former club Reading at their new Madejski Stadium and had to settle for a ten-minute cameo.

I continued my good form regardless and scored in a 5–1 demolition of Rushden & Diamonds. I also had a goal wrongly chalked off in a draw against Weymouth in an FA Trophy tie.

After that initial six-week period, Steve was given the job on a full-time basis. This seemed the right decision by the club and definitely something I was happy about as I continued to play a prominent part in the team. Everything seemed to be going well and, at the end of January, we were third in the League and only four points off top spot.

Results began to tail off, however, and by the beginning of March we had dropped to fifth and were fifteen points off leaders Kidderminster Harriers.

Seemingly out of the blue, Steve Thompson was relieved of his duties as manager and replaced by ex-Chelsea legend David Webb in early March. Steve was demoted to his assistant.

David embarked on a revolution; his brief was to oversee the transition of playing staff from part time to full time. Nobody's position was safe, irrespective of any current reputation or standing. The majority of the squad's higher earners and older players (mostly one and the same), as well as those not willing to commit to full-time football, were dispensed of ruthlessly.

Every player had a short introductory meeting with the new manager at his first training session. In my meeting he asked me what position I preferred to play. I went into great detail about how I liked to play in a midfield three as the advanced midfielder, just behind the striker. He listened patiently and then, in his very matter of fact way, said he did not play that way and our formation would be 4–4–2. I quickly backtracked and said I also liked playing central midfield!

In a strange twist of fate, we had played Doncaster Rovers at home just before David was appointed and we then had to play them away for his first match in charge. Considering we had lost the home game 3–1 with an experienced team, it was with a sense of trepidation that we embarked on the long trip to Yorkshire. David's match-day routine was a lot different to what we were used to. He named the team just before 2 p.m. ... and that was it. We did not see him again until about fifteen minutes before kick-off, when he just moved around the dressing room and gave short pieces of tactical information to individuals.

To my amazement, not only did we hold our own, but we comfortably won the game 3–0 and produced an excellent all-round team performance. I really enjoyed the game and put in a good shift. Like the majority of the squad, I would be out of contract come the end of the season, so it was important to impress the new manager.

I went on to play every minute of the new manager's first eight games. We only lost one and I felt I had played well even then. After those eight games, the manager arranged meetings with everyone to discuss their futures at the club. I bounced into my meeting extremely confident I would be offered an improved full-time deal. The manager's face, however, told me that maybe my confidence was misplaced.

David went on to say that he 'really wasn't sure' about me and had actually been prepared to let me go until an incident the previous Saturday – a 3–0 home win against Hednesford – had changed his mind. He'd seen me lose the ball on the edge of the opposition box and then work back to deny Hednesford a shot on goal with a tackle on the edge of our own box. The manager said this made him think he could turn me into what he called a 'proper' player.

I was a little crestfallen but also relieved.

However, the deal he offered was only a one-year contract on the same money – and I lost my club car. David said he was amazed players even had club cars.

It was not overly surprising that I lost the car – just a month earlier I'd managed to get through three in a week! I'd been upgraded to a Vauxhall Corsa from my vulgar green Seat, but it broke down and had to be replaced. The local garage temporarily gave me a scruffy old Volvo, but that subsequently broke down on the way home too. Skivo, Glenn Poole and I had to be towed back to Yeovil and the garage reluctantly gave me a Ford Mondeo so we could get home to Essex. You can imagine how happy they were when, two weeks later, I returned the Mondeo with a cracked front bumper and half the back bumper missing. I was not responsible for either misdemeanour but, as I was the person insured, I had to take the rap. To be honest, as it was not my car, I cannot say I took a great deal of care of it and I regularly lent it to any member of our travelling party who wanted to use it.

I was still disappointed with the club's offer though. Obviously I was going to incur some extra costs as I needed to find myself somewhere to live, so I didn't think it particularly fair for them to ask me into full-time training on the same salary.

I told the manager I would have to think about it.

That Saturday we drew away to Altrincham in a League game. It was a May Day bank holiday weekend though so we had another game on the Monday, which gave me another opportunity to demonstrate my lack of professionalism: I played five-a-side on Sunday with my mates and managed to injure myself. I then had to ring Steve Thompson on Monday morning and say I had picked up an injury in the Saturday game. As we were part time I managed to get away with it, but I dread to think what the manager would have said if he'd known the truth.

David pulled me into his office before the Monday game and I thought he was going to question my injury. Thankfully he just wanted to enquire about my thoughts on the offer. I told him I wanted more money. He said he had been really impressed with my reaction in Saturday's game after the initial meeting and he upped the offer to £350 per week.

My current contract was due to end straight after the last game of the season and any new offer would not start until 1 July so David also agreed to give me £1,000 relocation money too. Officially this money was to cover the costs of moving to the area and was not taxed. However, in reality, it was money to get me through two months of no pay. My contract would run until the last game of the 2000/01 season.

I accepted the offer as I had nothing to keep me in Essex and I knew this was a great opportunity for me to get back into full-time football. I also saw the way the gaffer was culling experienced players and realised there was every chance I could become an important member of the squad. I wanted to be one of his blue-chip players.

I enjoyed playing under the new manager. He was really strict and exactly the sort of character I needed to keep me under control at that time in my life. He could scare the shit out of you without even raising his voice and one incident illustrated this best.

We were playing away at Stevenage Borough. It was a pretty nondescript game destined to end in a 0–0 draw. Glenn Poole got substituted midway through the second half and rather petulantly walked straight down the tunnel. At the end of the game the gaffer made a beeline for him straight away and, in a very aggressive but controlled voice, told Glenn: 'If you ever do that again I will hang you up from the fucking floodlight and you'll never play for this fucking club again!'

I was only sitting next to him and I was petrified, so I can't imagine how Glenn felt!

After fleetingly being top of the League a couple of times during the season, we eventually tailed off and finished seventh on sixty-four points. I made forty-five appearances, including thirty-seven starts – a big improvement on the previous year, although I only scored five goals.

Due to the fact we had released so many experienced players, there was a subdued vibe among supporters in anticipation of the following season, but I was optimistic and could not wait for the start of 2000/01.

CHAPTER 7

A SECOND CHANCE

SEASON: 2000/01
CLUB: YEOVIL TOWN
DIVISION: CONFERENCE PREMIER
MANAGERS: DAVID WEBB/COLIN ADDISON

AFTER JUST TWO years away from the professional game I had been given a second opportunity to be a full-time footballer and I was determined to make the most of it. Terry Skiverton, Dean Chandler, Dave Piper, Adrian Foster, Warren Patmore, Glenn Poole, Tony Pennock and myself had been retained from the previous season and we were joined in pre-season training by a mixture of young players from the reserve team and some trialists.

We had a young, vibrant team but I can honestly say I did not have a clue how we would do during the 2000/01 season. It was very much a journey into the unknown.

On the first day of pre-season training the management took us over to a rather large hill called Nine Springs, which was located next to the dry ski slope in Yeovil. We just ran and ran and ran until a few players were physically sick. The highlight of the day was when Paul Steele, one of the new players, was found lying under a tree exhausted, claiming he could not do any more.

That was a sign of things to come. Without a doubt it was the hardest pre-season training camp I was ever part of during my career and my days quickly became a routine of train, eat, sleep, repeat.

Our training base was at RAF Yeovilton, which, unfortunately for us, had a running track around it. We did double training sessions every day and would spend most afternoons doing some sort of athletic work on that track. I guess the manager, having such a young team and only just converting to full-time football, wanted us to be the fittest team in the League.

It was not all hard work though. As part of pre-season we went down to Plymouth for a few days to play a couple of games and do some team bonding. We played a game on the Friday and were then given free rein in the evening. The gaffer was not staying at the hotel so there was no curfew, although Steve Thompson told us not to get back in too late. I'm not sure what he made of bumping into a returning James Bent, who was just getting into the lift to go to his room when Steve came down for breakfast at 8 a.m.!

It was a heavy night but a great way for everyone to get to know each other in more relaxed circumstances. The after-effects of the night out took me more than a couple of days to recover from so, thankfully, I was ruled out of the game on Sunday as 'injured'.

Pre-season was going well personally, though. I was playing in all the important friendlies and it seemed I was going to be a player the manager would rely on. During a break between one of our double training sessions David pulled me into his office and asked me how I felt things were going.

I told him I had always felt like a peripheral player but was now ready to be one of his main men. To my surprise he agreed: he said he wanted to build his team around me. I was to be the playmaker and take all the free kicks, corners and penalties. This was a great piece of man management and I left his office feeling 10 ft tall.

Pre-season could not have gone better and I couldn't wait for the first game of the season. I was, without doubt, in the best physical shape of my short career.

The curtain-raiser for the 2000/01 season was against Kettering at home. It did not quite go according to plan initially as I managed to have a penalty saved and Roy O'Brien (a debutant and one of my former Arsenal colleagues) got sent off – all in the first ten minutes! What pleased me though was, unlike in previous seasons, I did not let my penalty miss affect my performance and I went on to play an important part in our 2–0 victory.

The season continued encouragingly as we beat Woking away 3–2, after being 2–0 down. I managed to score the winner with a dipping volley from just outside the box.

At this time however I'm not sure which was more exciting – my social life or my football career.

Almost everyone in the team was either in their late teens or early twenties and single. After the majority of games, be it a Saturday or Tuesday, we would meet up for a night out. This helped bring a great sense of spirit and camaraderie to the team and, in my opinion, definitely contributed to our success. Playing away at Woking on a Tuesday night held no difference to us; we rushed straight back to Yeovil and caught the last couple of hours in 'Gardens', our favourite midweek haunt.

People in rural outposts such as Yeovil do not get to see many celebrities, other than the odd nightclub appearance from luminaries such as Paul Danan (of *Hollyoaks* fame) or ex-*EastEnders* man Dean Gaffney. As a result, and it felt strange, we used to be looked on as minor local celebrities.

Now I know as well as you do that myself and my fellow lower-league footballing friends were absolutely nothing special but it did not stop us suddenly getting a lot more opportunities on a night out with the opposite sex than maybe we should have been used to. Suffice to say I was now enjoying the fruits of my labour both on and off the pitch – our formerly untainted rented accommodation was now becoming quite the opposite!

The early season optimism was tempered slightly by a 3–0 spanking in our third game of the season at Haig Avenue against Southport – never a happy hunting ground for me. The result was compounded by the fact I managed to strain a medial ligament in my knee, which ruled me out of the next game.

Any feeling that the wheels were falling off was removed by the fact we bounced straight back and won our next four games. Even more pleasing for me was, even though I lost my place for one game through injury, the manager was desperate to get me fit and put me straight back in the side. No manager had ever been so eager for me to play and it made me feel great.

What I really liked about David Webb was that he simplified the game. Training took the same pattern most days: a warm-up and then some sort of possession or small-sided game mixed in with some organisational work when we got closer to a match day. Even though the pattern of the sessions was repetitive, they were never boring. In fact, I'm not sure I'd ever enjoyed training so much. It wasn't anything revolutionary, but the difference was in the intensity. The manager didn't let anyone slack off, irrespective of how well we were playing.

He made it clear what your job was as an individual and did not ask any player to do something they were not capable of. My job in his team as a central midfielder was to go from box to box: when we had the ball I had to always be available to receive a pass; when we were out of possession I had to compete with my opposite number to win it back. I also had to take all the set plays.

No grey areas.

If you were not doing what he asked of you, he told you what he thought in no uncertain terms. I got my first real taste of that treatment after a sloppy performance at home against Chester in early September.

We won 2–1 but I had not put in one of my best displays and had generally been guilty of wasting possession. In injury time I had tried to keep the ball in the opposition's corner to try to wind the clock down. Unfortunately they'd managed to nick the ball off me, break up the other end and hit the crossbar. We'd got away with it but the gaffer was not happy. In the dressing room after the game he began to have a go at me. I raised my hand, acknowledged that it was my fault and apologised, but, in his very matter-of-fact way, he said: 'Don't fucking apologise, just don't fucking do it again!' That may not seem like much, but the way he delivered it was enough to focus my mind and ensure I raised my level of performance.

After that game we were top of the League, which was quite a sight considering the low expectations held at the start of the season.

A spanking away to Boston United aside, we continued our excellent form until the club was hit by a big blow at the end of September.

We'd laboured to a 3–2 victory at home to Morecambe and had been working with the manager long enough to know that he would not be happy. We were expecting a rocket – except the rocket never materialised. Instead the manager told us how proud he was of all of us but he was resigning with immediate effect.

The silence was deafening.

I, for one, was devastated. My career finally looked like it was going somewhere, but the man making it happen was leaving.

It transpired that Southend United, where the manager was a legend after taking them to what is now the Championship in a previous spell, wanted to give him an opportunity to manage back in the Football League. To me it did not seem like that much of a forward step as we were arguably in better shape at the time, but David had made his mind up. He left us in a great position – second in the League and only two points behind big-spending Rushden & Diamonds – but that was not much of a consolation. I am still convinced that if he had stayed we would have won the title.

The manager leaving had no effect on us on initially. Steve Thompson took his default position as caretaker manager and we continued with the same form. We spanked Dover Athletic 4–0 at home (a game in which I scored) and then grabbed a good point away against a strong Hereford United team at Edgar Street.

The rumour mill had identified our new manager correctly and everything was confirmed after the Hereford game, where he had been watching in the stands.

Colin Addison strode into the club with the attitude and look of someone a lot younger than his sixty years. His style was a lot different to David Webb's – he was a lot more laid-back – but I instantly liked him. Being the experienced and intelligent football man he was, Colin quickly identified that very little needed changing and he ensured that we continued as we had done.

His match-day style was very different to the previous manager's as well. David Webb was very detached before a game, saying nothing about the opposition and just letting us get on with it. Colin, on the other hand, was very thorough. I guessed this was from his European background as he had previously managed both Celta Vigo and Atlético Madrid.

Before our first game under his stewardship, away to Northwich Victoria, we had a lengthy meeting to discuss the strengths of the opposition. I finished the meeting a nervous wreck – Colin had talked one of their players up so much I thought he was Zinedine Zidane! Turned out I needn't have worried because we won 2–1 and I scored our equaliser with an acrobatic volley.

During the early part of Colin's reign there was plenty of speculation in the local press that David Webb wanted to sign a host of Yeovil players. The morning after that Northwich win I was in bed nursing my customary post-game hangover and scanning the papers when I had a phone call from Mr Webb. He politely enquired how I was doing and then said he was interested in signing up six Yeovil players. I was one of them.

I was really flattered. Only six months earlier he hadn't been sure whether or not to offer me a contract and now he was willing to pay money for me. I told him I would definitely consider it and he said he would be in touch. I'm guessing he got short shrift from Yeovil, though, as that was the last I heard of it.

Despite this distraction, both the team and my own impressive form continued. It seemed I was finally achieving the level of consistency I had been lacking in my career to date.

We suffered a slight hiccup by needing a replay to dispose of Horsham in the FA Cup after a stuttering draw at home in the first game, but other than that everything was going swimmingly.

Our first big test came at the start of November when we played our big rivals Rushden & Diamonds away. We won the game 2–1 in front of over 5,000 fans, the ever-reliable Warren Patmore giving us the lead before Darren Way calmly converted a penalty with five minutes to go (Darren had assumed penalty-taking duties from me after I had fluffed my lines in the first game against Kettering). This result sent out a message to every team in the League that Yeovil were serious title contenders. The result put us four points clear at the top with a game in hand.

We then faced Colchester United at home. This was a great draw as far as I was concerned because I had been born and brought up just fifteen minutes from our opponents. Before the game Colin had decided to take us down to Bournemouth for a team bonding exercise. Translated, it meant we went on a three-day piss-up – not something recommended by the modern-day sports scientists, although it was a great trip. As I alluded to earlier we had a brilliant team spirit where everyone socialised together. Normally you get a few players who do not like socialising with the group but not in this team. Everyone got on like a house on fire. I have been a part of some really strong groups and this compared favourably to any of them.

But, despite not really needing it, Colin was brilliant at pulling everyone together and, even at his age was in the thick of the action. I would not say I came back from that trip refreshed but it definitely had the desired effect.

Not only did we beat Colchester, we thrashed them out of sight 5–1. As you would expect, with a result like that, the whole team was in imperious form. Warren and Barrington Belgrave ran them ragged up front, Darren Way and I dominated the midfield and Skivo marshalled the back line expertly. A new, tougher tackling style led to me ending ex-Ipswich Town man Jason Dozzell's participation in the game early – although fairly, I should add – and the scoreline flattered Colchester if anything. I was delighted with my own performance as I assisted three of the goals.

My form was starting to attract some attention and I got called up for trial games used to select players for the England non-League team (England C as it is currently known). Warren had played in it a few times and I was keen to get at least one cap. Every time he came back from a trip I questioned him about it, asking him everything from what the other England players were like to the standard of the opposition. Unfortunately for me, my game got cancelled and was never rearranged – that was the closest I ever got to a call-up.

In our next game we drew 2–2 away to Scarborough and I scored a free kick. Around this time Colin pulled me into his office and we had some informal talks about a new contract since mine was due to expire in the summer. He wanted me to stay and asked what sort of contract I was looking for. I still had no agent so conducted the discussions myself.

I told Colin I wanted a two-year contract with a £5,000 signing-on fee and £500 a week in the first year, rising to £550 a week in the second. I felt this was fair considering my standing in the team and Colin did not seem to baulk at the figures, although he said he would have to speak to the board.

Colin came back to me a week or so later saying that the board would not agree to that level of contract at the time so we would discuss it again nearer the summer. I was comfortable with that as I was playing well and I knew

Southend was interested in me, which probably meant there would be interest from other clubs too. Colin said my contract would go up immediately though – from £350 per week to £400 – to put me in line with my peers.

Coming up to Christmas we sustained our League form and also continued to progress in the FA Cup. We faced Blackpool away in the knockout competition and it was shown live on Sky. At that time they were a Division Three team (now known as League Two) and we beat them 1–0 with a goal from Nick Crittenden, but I don't remember the game with much fondness…

The pitch was heavily waterlogged and the game would have been cancelled were it not live on television. My first pass got stuck in the surface water and I was not happy with my performance in general. The highlight for me was when I cleaned out one of the opposition players with a poorly timed tackle in front of the Blackpool dugout and their manager Steve McMahon, who played at Liverpool in his prime, called me a 'fat cunt'. I wouldn't have minded if he'd said it a year before, but I was in good shape at this point, thank you very much!

We listened to the third-round draw on the coach on the way home and I was slightly deflated when we got Bolton Wanderers away. They were a Premier League team at the time but it was not the 'glamour tie' we were dreaming of.

On New Year's Day 2001 we beat Forest Green Rovers at home 2–0 and sat at the top of the League with fifty-four points from twenty-two games. We were seven clear of Rushden & Diamonds with two games in hand.

We played the Bolton game at the Reebok Stadium on 6 January and narrowly lost 2–1 thanks to an added-time goal from Michael Ricketts.

The team as a whole played brilliantly to run a Premier League team so close on their own pitch, but I was a little disappointed with my own performance. I had played well in the first half but my contribution deteriorated during the second and was not up to the high standard I had set for myself. It was a great experience contending with Per Frandsen, who was an excellent ball-playing midfielder, but this was the first indication my form was tailing off and a sign of things to come.

My off-field activities and drinking were beginning to catch up with me. I was not training with anywhere near the same intensity as I had been at the start of the season. Yes, the atmosphere around the club was a lot more relaxed than under David Webb, but it was not affecting anyone else's performance. I was still not mature enough to take responsibility for my own fitness levels.

I knew my quality of performance was slipping but I did nothing to try to rectify it. I did not work harder in training or curb my inappropriate off-pitch lifestyle; I just buried my head in the sand.

I got away with it through January as the team was still picking up positive results – if a team is winning it can hide a multitude of individual sins. I even managed to nick another goal at the start of February in a 4–2 victory against Wakefield and Emley in the FA Trophy.

However, by mid-February the results started to reflect my form. We lost away to Chester (I played like crap), lost at home to Dagenham (my performance was even worse) and got knocked out of the FA Trophy by Burton Albion in a poor personal and team performance. I was now only staying in the team through the credit I had built up earlier in the season.

During this period there was one funny moment that did help lift the mood, though. Skivo received an anonymous card on Valentine's Day. For a large ginger man with an abnormally sized head this was quite an occasion. I noticed that the postmark on the card was Hereford. Knowing that the gaffer was from there and his daughter was a regular visitor to the club I put two and two together. I did not actually think it was from her but thought it would be funny to bring it up.

The gaffer was giving one of his usual speeches during training, which every now and then could drag on a bit. When he finished I brought up that Terry had received a Valentine's card from someone in Hereford and put forward my theory. Everyone laughed and I thought nothing of it after we finished the session.

After training the gaffer pulled me to one side and started interrogating me about it. It turned out that she *did* send the card as she had a soft spot for our devilishly, yet slightly unorthodoxly, attractive captain.

Unfortunately this story did not have a happy ending. They went out on a date but Terry said her mannerisms were too similar to her dad's and he found this a little off-putting!

The team had a terrible time from 10 February to the middle of March – we only won one game. During that time we had managed to turn a three-point lead into a seven-point deficit although, admittedly, we still had two games in hand. I also completed my fall from grace with a disgusting performance at home to Nuneaton Borough, which the local press very fairly described as 'anonymous'.

I held on for one more game – an uninspiring goalless draw at Christie Park against Morecambe, where ironically my performance had improved – before Colin put me out of my misery and left me off the team for the first time that season.

Little did I know that I would hardly kick another ball for Yeovil Town after that. The incident that proved to be a massive contributing factor to that fact happened during a game against Dover Athletic a week later – but it did not happen on the pitch.

Having been dropped from the team previously, Dave Piper, James Bent and I were dropped from the playing squad for the Dover trip altogether. At the time, the Crabble (where Dover play their home games) had a bar that overlooked the pitch and stayed open throughout the game. In a display of poor judgement, three very disappointed players decided to watch the game through the bar window while enjoying a few Budweisers.

A group of Yeovil supporters were in the bar too, and they bought us a few drinks and talked football. We spent the whole game like that and were pretty drunk by the end of it. At one stage, one our players got injured near our touchline and play was stopped. I started banging on the window to get the lads' attention to show them what we were doing.

After the game, the guys who'd played came into the bar and we bought a few beers to drink on the way home. I went to the back of our coach and kept a low profile but, unfortunately, some supporters rang into the club to say how disgusted they were that players were getting drunk while their colleagues were playing. They had a point – it was ridiculously unprofessional. But I didn't think like that at the time.

Steve Thompson came to the back of the coach and told James Bent and myself (Dave Piper had made his own way home) that the gaffer was not happy and we had to report to the ground first thing in the morning. You may think this would've been my cue to go home and get an early night, but I wasn't finished yet. I continued my bender until the early hours of the morning once we returned to Yeovil.

The gaffer dragged me into the office the next day and questioned me about the allegations. I didn't try to deny anything until he mentioned the knocking on the window and the flashing of beers at the lads while the game was going on. He said he did not believe I would do something so disrespectful and I said of course I would not.

He believed me. I hated lying but I had to – I think if I'd admitted to it he might have sacked me. He eventually fined all three of us a week's wages and got Steve to run the bollocks off us. That was an expensive afternoon's drinking – I reckon those Buds worked out at about £40 each!

This was not the end of my punishment though as I was banished to the reserves for the next week. Apart from the odd substitute appearance, I played no further part in the season and our results were up and down. We had to beat Rushden at home in early April to have any chance of winning the League. In front of a crowd of just under 9,000, we could only manage a goalless draw and, even more unfortunately, I was one of the people watching.

Our failure to win promotion was confirmed in the penultimate game of the season when we lost 3–2 at home to Hereford United. Again, I was sitting in the stands.

After that game, Michael McIndoe and I had a heated exchange. I came into the dressing room and started joking with Dave Piper about a wonderful diving header he had scored. This probably was not the wisest move considering the circumstances, but I did not mean to offend anyone. Macca was not best pleased and started going off on one about how gutted he was. I told him to fuck off as he had only been at the club five minutes.

In reality our title challenge had slipped away weeks ago and that defeat just confirmed the inevitable. Michael and I sorted the situation out the next day but maybe in hindsight we needed some more intense characters like him to help get us over the line.

We eventually finished the season in second place on eighty points – six behind champions Rushden & Diamonds. This was before the introduction of play-offs so our season ended there. I'd made forty-five appearances, including forty-two starts, and scored five goals. Again, these statistics weren't bad for a 22-year-old – if I had started the season out of the team and made that many appearances it would have been a good year. But the way the season ended for me was a disappointment – even more so considering my problems were self-inflicted.

Colin Addison immediately resigned from his post as manager of the club. It seemed there had been a difference of opinion between him and the board. I was really disappointed as, even though the season had finished poorly for me personally, I had nothing but the utmost respect for Colin. I felt like my performances at the back end of the season, and the way I'd behaved at times, had let him down. I'm not sure whether it would have made a difference to our season if I'd stayed in top form, but it definitely wouldn't have done us any harm.

I was now in limbo.

I'd verbally agreed a new contract with the club but they were now saying I had to wait for the new manager to be appointed before anything could be sorted out. I was not happy and argued that after my 140-plus appearances, the club should be well aware of what I was capable of on the pitch.

Unfortunately the board stuck to their guns. As my contract was due to expire immediately after the last game they agreed to extend my contract on a month-by-month basis until the new manager, whoever that would be, could make a decision.

After a poor end to the season I felt it was a risk to leave my career at the whim of one man. I decided to take matters into my own hands and called David Webb directly to ask if he was interested in signing me for Southend United. He said he would talk to his chairman and get back to me. A couple of days later he offered me a one-year contract on £450 per week. I went down to Roots Hall, had a chat with him and accepted the offer.

As Southend were in League Two, I got a standard Football League contract, meaning my new deal would run until 30 June 2002 rather than the last game of the season. They also started paying me from the beginning of June seeing as Yeovil would stop my wages as soon as I left. Normally a new contract would not start until 1 July.

As I was under the age of twenty-four, this move would normally have entitled Yeovil to a transfer fee for my services. However, for this to be the case, Yeovil would've had to offer me a new deal on at least the same wages and for the same length of contract. Since all they did was offer a monthly extension, I was entitled to leave for free.

It was a strange situation because I had loved my time at Yeovil and settled in the area. I was leaving behind a lot of friends, including Skivo. We had built up a really good relationship and I could not have asked for a better lodger!

Ciderspace, the unofficial club website covering everything Yeovil Town, wrote the following about me when I left the club: 'Ben can be a hugely frustrating player to watch, but at the same time is blessed with more natural talent than most players. When motivated he is good enough to play at a much higher level.'

I think this quote summed me up pretty well.

As disappointed as I was to leave Yeovil, the Southend move meant a chance to play at a higher level, with the added bonus that I could move back to Essex. I made 144 appearances and scored eighteen goals in just over three years at Yeovil.

· · ·

16 FEBRUARY 2013

I have made it to the next half-term at school. My situation as a whole is not improving though. Every morning when I wake up the first thing my subconscious tells me is to quit. It is the same every evening when I go to sleep. Surely this cannot be right?

It does not feel like it's getting any easier and I'm not enjoying it. I have decided I am definitely leaving at the end of the school year – or before, if I can secure a new job. The way I'm feeling at the moment I might quit anyway, irrespective of any other employment.

I've been suffering from a headache all week and had an outbreak of mouth ulcers too. I never get headaches, not unless they're self-inflicted.

I think it might be stress, although I don't feel any more worried than I have done for the last five and a half months. I do feel under pressure, though, as an inspection from Ofsted is looming. I'm worried my teaching isn't good enough and I'm going to let everyone down.

I sit in meetings listening to teachers talking about grades and the data required by the Ofsted inspectors. I do not have a clue what they are talking about. I pass on my concerns to my fellow teachers but they don't seem bothered – not about me, anyway. It's very much an 'I'm all right, Jack' culture. I think, in their defence, it's because everyone is so busy.

My main worry is the ICT lessons I am teaching. I say teaching – it's more a case of me standing up in front of a class and waffling. I know nothing about ICT. Never have. More importantly, I have no interest in it. I was assured by the headmaster when I agreed my new contract that I would no longer teach ICT.

In reality, I got an extra lesson of it.

Over the course of the term, my lessons have deteriorated to the point of shambolic so, out of courtesy, I went and told the head of ICT how I'm feeling. She didn't seem too fussed and was more worried about re-iterating how much support she'd given me.

I then went and saw the vice principal and told her in no uncertain terms that my ICT lessons are a shambles, I don't know what I'm doing, I have no interest in the subject and I'd been promised by the headmaster I would no longer be teaching it.

I emphasised my fears regarding Ofsted because, as an absolute bare minimum, I wanted to flag up the situation in case shit hit the fan. The vice principal seemed really concerned and, within an hour, managed to offload two of my lessons to ICT teachers. It seems strange to me that I've been teaching ICT when two fully qualified ICT teachers were available all along.

On the Friday before half-term I sent the vice principal a cheeky email asking if she'd managed to 'dispose' of any of my other ICT lessons. Her helpful demeanour had disappeared and she sent me a curt reply:

Ben, I have removed two and that is all I can do as no other teachers available. Spoke to the head, this is your current timetable and contract. If this isn't what you want, then that is all we can do from this end. You should be teaching 44/50 lessons (this is over a two-week timetable).

Shit! I've gone from trying to get rid of lessons to getting my whole timetable changed and having to teach a lot more lessons – that backfired.

I think the vice principal was just passing on what the headmaster had said, which made it even more disappointing as we clearly discussed this in our meeting. At least I now know where I stand and it's clarified my thoughts on the future.

Turns out it is not just the world of football where people are economical with the truth.

CHAPTER 8

BACK HOME

SEASON: 2001/02
CLUB: SOUTHEND UNITED
DIVISION: LEAGUE TWO
MANAGERS: DAVID WEBB/ROB NEWMAN

THIS CHAPTER SHOULD not take long to read because my move to Southend was an unmitigated disaster pretty much from day one.

Yeovil eventually appointed Gary Johnson as manager and went from strength to strength. From what Skivo subsequently told me, I think Gary would have offered me a contract and given me the opportunity to be part of their success. Players from the team I played in went on to have great careers, as did players Johnson brought in.

I was now residing on the Essex Riviera.

Everything started off fine. I came back to pre-season training fit and ready to prove myself at this higher level. However, in one of the early pre-season games against local Essex team Heybridge Swifts, I managed to injure myself, despite scoring the only goal of the game. It was pretty innocuous but it set the tone for my time at Southend United.

If injured, as is the case in most clubs, you have to turn up early to be assessed. This allows the physio to report to the manager regarding the severity of your injury and decide whether or not you can train. At Southend, you had to be in by 9.30 a.m., but I didn't care much for these rules and rolled up at about 10, pleading ignorance. Unfortunately John Gowans, the rather aggressive and uptight Geordie physio, did not take kindly to this and tore an absolute strip off me.

I was slightly bemused by his anger and thought it was a bit of an overreaction, although I can now understand how unprofessional and disrespectful my attitude was.

It turned out I had only severely bruised my foot, putting me out for a couple of weeks. That does not seem much of a blow but, as any player will tell you, when you join a new club it is so important to make a positive impression straight away. It also meant my fitness levels dipped below everyone else's.

I regained my fitness just after the start of the season and had to bide my time while waiting for an opportunity in the first team. Unfortunately, that opportunity never really came. After a couple of decent reserve outings I managed to sneak onto the bench for a home game against Halifax Town on 25 August. We won 4–1 but when I say my two-minute substitute appearance was the highlight of my time at Southend, it should tell you all you need to know about this part of my career.

Before I could challenge for a starting place in the team I managed to pick up a really bad injury that disrupted my whole season.

We were playing a small-sided training game of 'one touch'. I was poised to shoot as a pass was played across my body but my studs got caught in the ground. I felt a sharp pain and went down in agony. I looked down expecting to see the bone popping out of my right leg. Thankfully it wasn't, but I instantly knew I had a bad injury.

In their wisdom, the club decided they were not going to send me for a scan straight away, preferring to wait and see how the injury settled down.

I was not too pleased about this but, as a new player, I kept my opinion to myself. I was sure if I'd been an established first-team regular a scan would have been done at once.

My injury had not improved after two months of rest and recuperation so I was finally sent for a scan. It showed, as I suspected, a meniscus (cartilage) tear to my right knee and a chipped bone in my right ankle. A foreign body within the ankle had also created a cyst that had to be removed. The recuperation time was three months, which didn't seem too bad until you factored in the two wasted months the club had gambled on sorting it out.

It always makes me chuckle when football clubs try to 'save' money on MRI scans. I think the price back then was around £300 to £400 per scan; the wait actually cost Southend around £4,000, which was what they paid me while 'assessing' the situation. If they had paid for the scan immediately, I would have been available to play by Christmas.

To make matters worse, David Webb left the club as I recuperated. During October he had been away from the club and it transpired he was suffering from a heart complaint. He could not take a risk with his health, fair enough, but it didn't help me. I was now stranded; injured at a new club where none of the management staff knew my qualities.

After our rather inauspicious start, John Gowans and I started to build a good relationship. To be honest, we didn't have much choice as I spent the vast majority of my time in his physio room. John worked me hard and it was the first time I took any real interest in training in the gym.

At Southend's training ground (Boots and Laces), the club had a decent gym area and I used it every day. If you were injured you trained seven days a week, bar the odd day off, so I had plenty of time to utilise the facilities. This was the start of my love affair with the gym, which continues to this day.

However, my injury was not helping me control my off-the-field activities. Being back home with my friends meant I had plenty of opportunities to go out partying, which, more often than not, I took up.

I managed to endure John's wrath again when I called in sick one Sunday morning. I had been out drinking heavily the night before and, when I got up the next day, I got in the car to drive to training and realised I was still so pissed it would have been dangerous for everyone. Before starting the car I rang John, left a message telling him how ill I was and turned my phone off, knowing full well there would be an irate northerner on my voicemail when I turned it back on the next day. He was fuming, but angrier that I'd lied to him. Thankfully he didn't tell the manager, but this was proof that my social life was still more important than what could still have been a promising career.

The change of management happened while I endured my injury-forced sabbatical. Rob Newman, the former Norwich player, was initially given the job temporarily before being appointed on a full-time basis.

When I first joined the club, Rob was the assistant manager and I thought he was perfect in that role. He was very approachable, friendly and had a good sense of humour – an ideal foil for someone like the manager, who could be very detached and quite intimidating.

Unfortunately this all changed when he became first-team manager. I'm well aware that when anyone becomes a manager they need to change and keep a certain amount of distance from the players, but Rob changed too much, in my opinion. He went from being a really affable character to the exact opposite. He would regularly have little digs at me for being injured, as if I was happy being on the treatment table every day.

By February 2002 I was starting to get fit and I spent two of the hardest weeks of my life with John doing aerobic work once I was clinically given the all-clear. The next step was to join in with the team. I got right back in the swing of things and raised a few eyebrows with some of the senior boys who didn't know much about me as a player.

I was confident I was good enough to play at this level but not quite as confident I would get an opportunity to showcase my ability in the first team, since Rob and I were not getting along. In hindsight, he was obviously struggling with the pressure that went with the job – something I can now relate to.

He would try to dig me out in front of others and I would snap straight back with a sarcastic comment. I remember after one reserve game, my comeback against a youthful Norwich side, I was doing a bit of shameless self-publicity regarding my performance when Rob quipped that I had only been playing against Norwich's youth team. I retorted with I could only do it against the players he put me up against and 'if you want me to do it against better players then put me in the first team!'

I do not think he made much of comments like that but I was not really bothered.

Other than the underlying tension with the manager, however, my comeback was going well. I played in a few second-string games and was doing everything expected of me. After a long spell on the sidelines it was just a buzz to be back on the pitch. The first team was pretty average and I sensed I was close to getting an opportunity, whether from the start or off the bench.

But the adrenalin was subsiding as my comeback progressed and I started to feel new aches and pains. My right knee and ankle felt fine but, as often happens after a long-term injury, my body was subconsciously protecting the affected areas, which had led to a soft tissue injury.

In early March we were doing a shooting session and I could feel my left quad tightening up. Now, in a normal situation I would have stopped training immediately but, after being out for so long and desperate to impress, I kept going. Eventually the inevitable happened and I pulled my left thigh properly. To add insult to the injury, I subsequently found out that they'd been strongly considering me for the local derby against Leyton Orient on 12 March.

I was devastated as this new injury meant I was guaranteed to be out for at least three or four weeks. It pretty much meant the end of my season.

I was out of contract and, in my mind, I had little or no chance of earning a new one.

I did manage to get back for the last couple of reserve games but I was nowhere near fit enough to compete for a place in the first team. The season had been terrible. What had looked like a great opportunity had been nothing of the sort. My sole contribution, if you can call it that, was my two-minute substitute appearance in early August. Southend finished right in the middle of the table on fifty-eight points.

Obviously this highly successful personal season meant I was due an end-of-season piss-up, so off I went with the Southend boys on a three-day bender to Dublin. I made the schoolboy error of going out in Chelmsford the night before the trip and, after an excellent first night in Ireland, I was a wreck for the last two days.

I was now out of contract and it seemed pretty obvious that I would be on the move again if I could get a new club. However, after a poor end to my last season at Yeovil and a non-existent year at Southend, I was far from confident that someone else would take me.

To further complicate matters, the Football League had agreed a £315 million deal with ITV Digital to broadcast League and Cup matches on its then-new paid TV channel. Unfortunately the new broadcaster went bust without fully honouring the contract and ended up owing a total of £180 million to Football League clubs. With football being the industry it is, where clubs spend money before it's earned to guarantee future success, this was a big problem. Clubs knowing they were entitled to a certain chunk of the TV contract had used the money to offer players more lucrative contracts. Anyone out of contract, like me, was in a very vulnerable position. Best case scenario: you got a sizeable pay cut. Worst case: you got released. This debacle ended a lot of senior players' careers prematurely and a lot of younger players' before they began.

I was convinced I was going to be one of the victims of the situation. As usual in these circumstances, I had a one-to-one meeting with the manager to discuss the previous season and my future. Our chat did not last long but, to my surprise, he didn't immediately release me. He gave me the normal spiel about how the club had no money and I had contributed very little to the season, but he then went on to say he thought I had ability and he was willing to give me an opportunity to prove my fitness. He offered me a three-month contract on £300 per week. My wages for the previous season had been £450 per week so this represented a big cut. He was basically proposing a paid trial on the understanding that, if I proved my fitness, my contract would be extended for the season.

I was surprised to get any sort of offer, but it was not the sort I in any rush to sign. I was also put off by the fact Rob wanted us to train through four of our eight weeks off. I told him I would have to think about it.

When a Football League club makes you a contract offer, and it is in writing, you have twenty-eight days to either accept or reject it. During that time the club cannot retract the offer and they have to honour it if the player accepts. Again, as at Yeovil, this new contract offer was lower both in terms of salary and length of time, which meant, if I did move on, there would be no fee involved for my services.

All the signs were pointing for me to start packing my bags again.

. . .

23 FEBRUARY 2013

Former Prime Minister Harold Wilson said a week is a long time in politics and I'm sure someone slightly less important has said the same thing about football. Well, it turns out this is also the case in the world of education. Half-term is coming to an end and I do not want to go back. I have thought long and hard about it and teaching ICT, science and maths is not for me. I have written my resignation letter ready to hand in on Monday:

Dear Sir,

After much deliberation I am handing in my notice as I intend to leave my position at Easter.

I appreciate the opportunity you have given me but I have not enjoyed teaching such a wide range of subjects. After giving it six months I don't envisage this changing and, as a result, I don't think secondary school teaching is for me.

Once again, thanks for allowing me to experience working in the industry and good luck for the future.

Ben

I've even printed it off and put it in an envelope ready to go. My mind is made up.

. . .

9 MARCH 2013

Well, I thought it was … until I got a phone call that made me think twice. Alan Bailey – the man who got me into teaching, has been my mentor and was, incidentally, my PE teacher when I attended as a pupil – was taken very ill.

He told me he was going to be away from school for a prolonged period of time and asked if I could come and see him at his house. He said that he won't be returning until Easter at the earliest (though probably not until the end of the school year) and that I am the only person with the expertise to do his job: he wanted me to take over from him, at least on a temporary basis.

So I went and saw the headmaster and told him I'd been intending to leave until I heard about Alan's condition. I said I didn't want to take Alan's job, but I did temporarily want to take over his timetable, teaching football, PE and business. I also said I didn't want to go back to my old role if no job was available for me when Alan returned, in which case I would just have one month's money before moving on.

The head appreciated my honesty and was good enough to change my time-table completely. He got rid of all the lessons I hated teaching and I'm now just left with subjects I actually know something about. Once again, my fledgling teaching career has been extended.

My fears about the Ofsted inspection were realised as well, though. At the start of this month we were notified of a surprise inspection. Everyone went into panic mode – me as much as anyone.

On the second day of the inspection I was out of school coaching the sixth-form football team, so I really only had to get through the first day of it. I managed to negotiate myself all the way to fifth period unscathed. By then I was quite relaxed, talking to one of the sixth-formers in my business studies class and telling him how I was only small fry so there was no chance anyone would come in and observe me.

Right on cue the lead inspector, who was a former business studies teacher, walked in and sat down. After the initial shock I just got on with the lesson and even cracked a couple of jokes. I thought it went quite well, all in all. I was lucky he came to a sixth-form lesson where there aren't too many behav-ioural issues, as opposed to some of the younger year groups where I can spend the majority of the lesson trying to get them to shut up.

I had a PE lesson in football earlier in the day with a group of Year 7s, which was absolute chaos. One of the lads was desperate for a wee and wanted to go up the fence. I told him I did not care how desperate he was he had to cross his legs. I could just see it now, him urinating up the fence while one of the inspectors strolled round the corner.

Thankfully they did not come to that lesson. That would have been really embarrassing, being told my football session was inadequate.

At the end of the day I bumped into the inspector and asked if I could get some feedback. I thought I would get it in straight away that I'm new to the job and have only been doing it for six months. He asked if I'd received any formal teacher training – which I haven't, so he said in that case he was impressed by my potential. He marked me as three out of four, which means 'requires improvement', though he also said there were a lot of 'good' features (a mark of two) within my lesson.

I think this was a fair assessment. Apparently the inspector was very complimentary about me in the end-of-day briefing: two vice principals and the headmaster all came and told me as much. I really appreciated their comments and it's made me feel more positive about the future.

CHAPTER 9

HEREFORD'S NUMBER EIGHT

SEASON: 2002/03
CLUB: HEREFORD UNITED
LEAGUE: CONFERENCE PREMIER
MANAGER: GRAHAM TURNER (GT)

I WAS IN limbo and loath to take the offer Southend United had made. I was not keen on Rob's management style and even less keen on the 33 per cent pay cut. I booked the whole of May off, gambling on the fact I would have a new club by then and thus not need to come in and train in June.

I had a big problem, however: I'd hardly kicked a ball the previous season and I hadn't been a regular first-team player since March 2001. I'd resorted to sending my CV out to every League Two and Conference National team yet again and was awaiting their responses. You never know when you'll get a reply to such letters as the season close can be a strange time. Managers go away on holiday or work from home and therefore may not receive any CVs until weeks later. I imagine the vast majority of applications get thrown in a bin. I often thought Football League managers had a wastepaper bin full of my letters and would laugh about me with their secretary every year – 'Ben Smith has sent in another one!' – before asking for my application to be put in that 'special place'.

However, out of the blue late one evening I got a phone call from Ron Jukes, chief scout of Nationwide Conference side Hereford United. He seemed to know a lot about me and asked why I hadn't been playing. I explained my injury situation and, after a long intake of breath, he told me that manager Graham Turner liked me and wanted to know how much money I was earning.

As always in these situations, I added a bit on and said I was earning £500 a week. Ron replied that was big money for Hereford and he would have to speak to GT, who was actually the owner, chairman and manager all rolled into one. After a couple of days he rang back and asked if I would come to the Midlands to have a chat.

I was delighted. I'd been involved in some good battles against Hereford during my time at Yeovil and always thought they would be a good club to play for. A week later I met GT at the Hilton hotel in Bromsgrove – mainly because it is an unwritten rule that all contract negotiations take place in either a hotel or a motorway service station! As I had no agent, I turned up by myself in my ill-fitting Yves Saint Laurent suit (which I had bought from a catalogue and was still paying off). I think GT liked the fact I did not have a representative and, for an hour or so, we just talked football; discussing players at Hereford, how he liked to play the game, players I had played with and those at our level in general. GT came across as a good, honest football man.

We never at any stage talked about money. I think GT just wanted to chat and see what sort of person I was. He'd spoken to Colin Addison, my former Yeovil manager and a good friend of GT's, who'd told him I was a good player but a handful off the pitch – a fair assessment of me at that stage.

GT finished the meeting by saying he was interested in signing me and would be in touch. A day later we arranged for me to go to Edgar Street,

Hereford United's home, to have a medical and try to agree a deal. This time I brought my dad with me for some advice.

I sailed through the medical so all that was left was to agree a deal. I told GT I was not particularly bothered about the money – I just wanted to play every week. He said if I signed then I would be Hereford's number eight. That was good enough for me. I wanted to be a key member of a first team again.

GT explained Hereford could not give me the £500 per week they thought I was on at Southend, but they could offer £450, plus £50 appearance money – which meant, if I was playing, I would be earning my desired amount anyway. Strangely this appearance money was not per game but per week, whether I played one game or four. That didn't bother me though as the sneaky £50 added to my basic wage meant I'd be getting the same as at Southend, with the opportunity to earn an extra £200 per month if I played full time.

I agreed and my new contract was due to start on 1 July and run until the last game of the season – although if I agreed a new contract at the end of the season I would get paid through the summer. Despite being in the Conference Premier, Hereford United was still a full-time club that trained its players every day – another bonus.

It was late into May when I agreed the deal and I took great pleasure in calling Southend United on the way home to say I was not accepting their offer. Unfortunately I could not get through to Rob Newman, so I left a message with Steve Tilson. I didn't hear anything from Rob but was not bothered in the slightest.

As with most football clubs, pre-season training started on the first day of July. Hereford had disappointingly finished seventeenth in the previous season and, as a result, there had been a large playing staff turnover. I believe only five or six players were left from the year before's squad. Not great for team spirit, admittedly, but it did make it easier for new players to settle in as everyone was in the same boat.

I initially stayed in digs with Michael Rose – another new player – and Matt Baker. We were lodging with John and Joan Criasia, who were very hospitable and made me feel welcome. Michael enjoyed the hospitality so much that he eventually married their daughter!

Matt Baker then bought his own house. So, after about six weeks, I moved in with him in Credenhill, just outside Hereford, which incidentally is where the SAS are based.

For some reason I seemed to attract big, ginger roommates – firstly Skivo at Yeovil and now Matt. I quickly took up the role of 'unskilled labourer' within the house. I got a pretty good deal because in exchange for whipping the Hoover around the house a couple of times a week and doing the washing up, Matt knocked up a gourmet meal for us every night.

Even though Matt was a year or two younger than me, maturity-wise he was streets ahead – which made us an odd couple. He would do or say things that I would just ignore or laugh at, but then started doing myself a year or so later. For example, who in their twenties reads the *Sunday Times*? Matt did. He was not a typical footballer and got plenty of stick about it, although he didn't seem to care.

If I were to look up 'stubborn Yorkshireman' in the dictionary I would expect to see a picture of Geoffrey Boycott, closely followed by one of Matt Baker. Matt revelled in the fact that a scout from Manchester City once said of him that he 'exuded confidence, which bordered on arrogance'. I think he would like this on his gravestone!

His more sophisticated and professional approach was good for me as, while he couldn't totally eradicate my more laddish side, Matt did help suppress it. He was teetotal, for one, so I didn't have him egging me on to go out drinking every few days. I still had regular Saturday night blasts on the town with the boys, but my midweek sessions were now few and far between.

Joining Hereford also put me in contact with Richard O'Kelly, who had joined the club over the summer as assistant manager/physio/kit man – basically anything that needed doing – and I loved everything about him straight away. He had no ego whatsoever and was a brilliant coach – the best I had ever come across. He was so enthusiastic and loved football more than anyone I'd met. Even now when I'm coaching, I try to base my style on Richard's. I'll be delighted if I turn out to be half the coach or man he is.

I had done some work over the summer and came back to training feeling sharp. I must have impressed as, during one of our breaks, GT said he knew I was good, but didn't realise just *how* good. Now, anyone who has worked for him will know these compliments are rare. During my four and a half years with GT I think I heard maybe two more 'well done's. He was very old-school and reminded me of David Webb in that you normally knew you had played well when he said nothing at all.

I was well off the pace in our first friendly against Tranmere Rovers, but I suppose that was to be expected after not playing for nearly eighteen months. We had another game against Swindon a few days later and I felt a lot better in that one. It was also the first time I played with a striker by the name of Steve Guinan – we instantly built up a good relationship both on and off the pitch.

But then disaster struck…

We had an away game at Bromsgrove Rovers. I was on the bench but came on for the last thirty minutes. During this time the ball fell to me in the opposition's 18-yard box but I could see an opponent coming towards me at the same time. My plan was to nudge the ball away from the oncoming defender, anticipate the contact and, once I felt it, go to ground and win a penalty. This was something plenty of players do time and again.

Unfortunately the contact was heavier than I anticipated and it sent me high in the air. I landed on my elbow, which took the full force of the landing and levered my right shoulder out of its socket.

The pain was instant and unbearable and I was rapidly taken to hospital. The journey was more painful than I envisaged as, when the ambulance approached the hospital, we had to go over speed bumps and my damaged shoulder was moving all over the place.

In casualty, I was injected with a horse tranquilliser to help put the shoulder back into place. I remained conscious but have no recollection of it being done – only coming around with my arm in a sling.

Unfortunately I had not suffered a straightforward dislocation. Not only had the shoulder fully come out of the socket, but I had also severely damaged the nerve in the right deltoid. For the next six months I had no feeling in that muscle, and yet a specialist decided I didn't need an operation. He also told me there was a very good chance the shoulder would dislocate again, which didn't exactly fill me with confidence.

It was a huge blow after missing so much football the previous season. I seemed to be changing my reputation from 'good-time guy who goes out too much' to 'injury prone'. I didn't want to be perceived as either of these, let alone both, so I decided I could either whinge about the situation or I could just get on with it. In some ways I was lucky it was an upper-body injury as I could continue working on my fitness throughout the recuperation period. I was determined to be physically better than I'd been before and ready to play as soon as the physio gave me the all clear.

During the rehabilitation period I did lots of work in the gym and with the physiotherapists at Lilleshall, which, at that time, was the national sports centre.

A couple called Phil and Pauline had, in conjunction with the Professional Footballers Association, created a centre where professional sportspeople could go to recover from long-term injuries. Recovering from such injuries can not only be a long process but a rather lonely one too, so it was nice to get a change of scenery and work alongside other players in the same situation. As well as other footballers, there but also some top cricketers there like Mark Butcher and Andrew Flintoff, who were also on the way back from long-term injuries.

My recovery went well and, by the beginning of November, I was back in training with Hereford. I eventually made my full League debut against Barnet at Edgar Street on 30 November 2002. Steve Guinan stole the show by scoring a hat-trick but I also managed to get on the score sheet in a 4–0 win. I was running on adrenalin and delighted to play my first senior game in eighteen months. Scoring made all the hard work even more worthwhile.

I kept up my personal promise of hitting the ground running and went on to score two goals in my next game – a 5–0 hammering of Woking at home. I was really enjoying my football and was playing with some really good players. Matt was nearly as good a goalkeeper as he thought he was, while in defence we had Matt Clarke, Michael Rose, Tony James and Andy Tretton. I built up a good relationship with Jamie Pitman in midfield – he carried the piano and I played it! Left winger Paul Parry was clearly going on to big things and Steve Guinan was my type of centre forward, intelligent and a good finisher.

My recovery took a bit of a setback in my third game, though. We beat Chester 1–0 away but I caught tonsillitis leading up to it and, as a result, put in a crap performance. A combination of the tonsillitis and my initial adrenalin surge subsiding meant my performances tailed off after that; I found myself struggling to complete games and was regularly substituted.

That pattern looked set to continue when we played Telford at home on New Year's Day, however, in the sixty-third minute – around the time I was normally being replaced – I somehow ghosted past a Telford defender and smashed a right-foot shot into the top corner of the goal from just inside the box. That goal prevented my substitution and went a long way to helping recapture my form.

I scored again in a 2–1 defeat against Yeovil in the FA Trophy. I received plenty of stick from the travelling fans for being – how can I put it? – 'cuddly' (a fair comment a couple of years previously maybe, but not at that point!).

My place was now cemented in central midfield playing alongside Jamie

Pitman. Our qualities complemented each other well: his discipline allowed me to break forward into the box regularly and his defensive strengths covered up my frailties.

The team was playing well and we were making a late push for the play-offs in the process. The goals mostly dried up for me after that one against Yeovil – I only scored one more against Kettering – but I was pleased with my overall form.

I loved going into training every day too. The combination of a great set of lads – all around my age – and brilliant training sessions with Richard meant we were really improving as a team. We were only a couple of additional players away from being a very good team.

Unfortunately we didn't quite make the play-offs but we were involved in a few eventful games before the end of the season. We got spanked 4–0 away to Yeovil at the start of March – a game that also saw us have two players sent off. Yeovil dominated us all over the pitch and Skivo took great pleasure in giving me lots of stick for it, both during and after the game.

We played Doncaster Rovers at home for the last game of the season. They had already secured a place in the play-offs and asked if they could play their chairman Jim Ryan at some point. Jim was named as a substitute and came on for the last five minutes. I do not think he touched the ball and it was a good job for him that he didn't. Apparently it had always been his dream to play for Doncaster but a few of our players, myself included, found it disrespectful that he thought he could come and play against professionals. I'm sure he wouldn't have liked it if we'd gone it to his boardroom and started working with senior industry professionals.

Jim could sense our hostility because he kept saying on the pitch how he would buy us drinks in the bar afterwards. We did not care about that; we were more interested in 'welcoming' him to the game. Unfortunately none of us managed to and he negotiated those few minutes unscathed. To top it all off we lost the game 4–2 and did not receive any drinks either.

We ended up finishing the season in sixth place on sixty-four points – a little disappointing after flirting with the play-offs during the latter part of the season, but a massive improvement on the previous season's seventeenth. I'd ended up playing twenty-five games and grabbed six goals. Considering I hadn't made my debut until the end of November, I felt it wasn't a bad return.

GT then had individual meetings with each player to discuss the future. I was apprehensive because, although I had done OK, I often drifted in and out of games. I was confident I would be a lot better next season if given the opportunity. Thankfully GT agreed, but an indication of how tight the finances were was the way he haggled over £50.

As I mentioned earlier, you only got paid through the summer if a new contract was agreed with the club. GT explained, however, that a lot of pressure was being put on the cash flow as there was little money coming into the club. He was willing to offer me a new one-year contract on the same money as before (£450 per week), but I would only receive £400 during the close season. I agreed the offer was fair considering I'd been injured for half the season, but I was not keen on the pay cut through the summer.

We eventually settled on £425 over the close season, with my wages going back to £450 on 1 July when we pre-season training began. I was also to receive £50 an appearance, which was again paid weekly not per performance, and £50 for each goal I scored.

In hindsight it seems strange that we were haggling over such small amounts of money but, particularly in lower-league football clubs, these seemingly insignificant sums can make a difference. Most important to me was the fact I had been signed on for another year, though. I was delighted and genuinely felt that Hereford had potential to improve.

I was not expecting what happened next.

CHAPTER 10

WE HAVE LIFT-OFF!

SEASON: 2003/04
CLUB: HEREFORD UNITED
LEAGUE: CONFERENCE PREMIER
MANAGER: GRAHAM TURNER (GT)

IT FINALLY DAWNED on me that, while I needed some rest and relaxation over the summer break, it was also a great time to give myself an advantage over opponents and fellow teammates. So I began a pattern that I continued for the rest of my career: I had some time off as soon as the season ended, plus a week or two later in the summer when I relaxed again and went on holiday, but for the other four or five weeks I worked hard on my fitness and strength at the gym by myself.

I was really looking forward to the 2003/04 season. I had managed to play twenty-five consecutive games in the previous one and was confident that, if fit, I could be a pivotal part of the team. Not only that, but I knew if I could stay fit then my performances would only get better.

Being the shrewd man he was, GT had managed to keep almost every player he wanted, as well as making a few new additions to the squad. Those that made a real impact on the first team were David Brown, a centre forward from Telford, Danny Carey Bertram, a striker from West Bromwich Albion and Ryan Green who, at the time, was the youngest ever player to appear for Wales.

Ryan's record may seem quite impressive but I have always compared playing for a minor country like Northern Ireland or Wales to me playing for my district team! Although that is not always the view shared by my Celtic counterparts!

This was the first time I witnessed how giving a squad of players time to evolve, really learning each others strengths and weaknesses, could lead to a huge improvement in both individual and team performance.

I picked up an ankle injury in the second of week of pre-season so I missed the first couple of friendlies, but other than that preparation was going really well. I came on as a sub against a youthful West Bromwich Albion team and immediately scored two goals. I also went on to play in the rest of the friendlies.

I was still liable to go off on the odd bender, as illustrated by the 'few quiet drinks' I went for with Matt the weekend before the season started – I cannot recall anything from that night past 10 p.m. and we christened it the lost weekend – but, as a rule, I had calmed down and was living my life a lot more professionally.

Our first game of the season was away to newly promoted Tamworth. It was a scorching hot day, as often seems to be the case on opening day. The temperature at kick-off was measured as 37°C. I am definitely not made for such heat and found myself seriously labouring as the first half wore on. I was not the only one: Tamworth have permanent portacabins (if that isn't too much of a contradiction) as their changing room and, at half-time, their 'thick-set' centre half was overheating in there like an old Ford Mondeo. He didn't make it out for the second half!

I managed to shake off my lethargy, however, and scored twice. One was a stooping header from 6 yards and the other a tap-in as I followed up a Steve Guinan shot. It is amazing what a combination of adrenalin and confidence can do, even in such stifling heat. I went from ambling around to suddenly feeling like I had an infinite amount of energy.

We went on to win the game 3–1 and followed that up with a comfortable 5–1 win at home against Forest Green Rovers. We then beat Morecambe 3–0 at home, where I bagged another two goals (a sliding left-footed shot into the top corner and a tap-in at the far post). Morecambe had finished second in the Conference the previous season and we dispatched them easily. My form was continuing on an upward trajectory.

We got a positive draw 1–1 away to Barnet, but the next game at home to Aldershot turned out to be one of the best games I was ever a part of with Hereford. We went 2–0 down in the first half but pulled it back to 2–2 shortly after the break. We dropped behind once more before eventually winning 4–3, with an acrobatic injury-time volley from David Brown. The goal was celebrated by players and fans as if we had won a cup final. I even found myself intensely embracing an unknown pitch invader!

It is impossible to describe the buzz of winning such a game in the last minute. People often ask which is better: scoring a goal or sex? For me I would go with the goal every time, although that may have more to do with my performance in the bedroom!

Our next game was away to Stevenage and we beat them 2–0 with Steve Guinan and myself scoring. We had both scored five goals in six matches at this point and I felt I was improving with every game. In those first six outings I, without a doubt, put in the most consistent run of quality performances of my career. I had a constant rush – before games, after games, during the week – and I could not wait to play or train. Our daily training did not really differ from a regime of warm up, possession practice, a small-sided game and some finishing, but this seemed to suit me. I was getting lots of touches of the ball and it helped keep my brain sharp. As someone who never had pace, I felt it was really important that my mind was working quickly so I could perform at my best. I was seeing the football like a beach ball and regularly scored in both the small-sided games and the finishing practices.

The training sessions seemed to suit the whole team, in fact, as we took sixteen from a possible eighteen points in those first six games, scoring eighteen goals. I got a personal reward when I was named August 'Player of the Month' – a great honour.

We went into September full of confidence and continued our great run by winning 5–0 away to Farnborough, before beating Scarborough at home. This ridiculous run of form could not continue, however, and it came to a halt when we got spanked 4–1 away to Burton. Any successful team I played in very rarely lost two games in a row, though, and this was no different: we recovered swiftly by winning at home to Telford and followed this up with two home draws to Gravesend (where I scored but played like crap) and Dagenham & Redbridge. I was on the scoresheet in the latter match as well after slamming home a great strike from just inside the box, latching onto a clever pass from David Brown. My performance, however, was overshadowed by my post-match interview. After scoring, I spent the majority of the second half preparing – TV people always choose the goalscorers after all!

Dean Beckwith (Dagenham defender and future teammate) and I were chosen to speak before the Sky cameras. I was determined to come across as an articulate, intelligent footballer and, as Dean came out with the usual monosyllabic answers, I was looking more like Einstein with every question I answered. Then I was asked whether I thought a draw was a fair result. I wanted to say it was an even game and tried to explain it was like 'six and two threes', but unfortunately what I actually did was mumble a mixture of about three different sayings, instantly undoing all the good work I'd put in dispelling the lazy stereotype of footballers. Suddenly it was Dean who looked like Einstein!

When I got home, instead of having a phone full of text messages and voicemails congratulating me on my goal on national telly, I had loads of messages taking the piss out of my interview – typical!

After the Dagenham game we continued our slightly stuttering form with a 0–0 draw away to Chester (but this, in isolation, was actually a good point earned, as they were our main rivals). We then dispatched of Harrow Borough 6–1 away in the FA Cup fourth qualifying round, where I scored a rare header from a corner, and we progressed to the first round proper.

It was now the end of October and I had already scored nine goals from central midfield, all from open play. I had not, perhaps surprisingly, had any direct interest from any other clubs but I was starting to get some interest from agents who were becoming aware of my exploits. I spoke to a few, but I don't really know why – I suppose I just felt I ought to have an agent. I eventually signed to a company that had one of my former Reading teammates Michael Meaker working for it.

That was a mistake.

The company kept telling me about potential interest from other clubs – nothing concrete, just clubs looking for players of my ilk. The same clubs kept cropping up in conversation (Bristol Rovers and Shrewsbury Town, to name two) but it did not dawn on me until later that nearly all the managers or teams they were mentioning were 'friends' of the company.

It's clear, in hindsight, that the agency just wanted me to go to a club that would result in the best deal for them, rather than me. I imagine this is something that happens to a lot of young players.

Don't get me wrong, I am not against all agents per se. Some are very good and give their clients invaluable advice. If you are a young player – jumping up from, say, League Two to the Championship – or a top player with a multitude of areas of earning potential away from football – such as sponsorship or endorsements – then having an expert in the field can prove to be a lucrative decision.

However, there were, and still are, many agents who have only one priority – and it is not their clients' best interests. After all, how profitable is it for an agent when his client extends his contract at his current club? I would hazard a guess at not very. If they move club, on the other hand…

Clearly I did not need an agent and should have just concentrated on my football rather than obsessing over where I might be playing the following season – I couldn't have been happier at Hereford anyway. It all seems crazy when I think about it now.

After securing our place in the first round of the FA Cup, Hereford had two more Cup games in quick succession. For a few seasons the Football League and Conference Premier experimented with the idea of allowing Conference teams to play in the Johnstone's Paint Trophy (then known as the LDV Vans Trophy). This collaboration did not last too long as even Conference teams thought the competition was an unwanted distraction.

To be eligible for the tournament a team had to finish in the top six of the Conference, which we had done the season before. After knocking out Exeter City earlier in the season we had drawn Northampton Town at home where we drew 1–1 and eventually lost 4–3 on penalties. As I have alluded to, I have always hated being substituted and I was replaced midway through extra time. Like a lot of the team I was admittedly tiring, so I accepted the decision with nothing more than a dirty look at the management as I trudged off.

That was not the case, however, when I got replaced in the last minute of our next game, which was away to Peterborough United in the first round of the FA Cup. We lost 2–0 but I had played really well and was really frustrated at being replaced. I had been up against Curtis Woodhouse, who was a really highly rated player, and had given as good as I got throughout.

I mean that only metaphorically of course because Woodhouse subsequently went on to be a professional boxer!

You might say it was only in the last minute but I knew how easily this situation could become a trend. As I walked off Richard O'Kelly said I had played well and I responded by mumbling some obscenities at him as I sat down on the bench to sulk through stoppage time.

After getting knocked out of two cup competitions in quick succession, we had no choice but to focus on the League campaign. After a blistering start, our form was levelling out and, at one stage during November, we dropped from top to fourth.

The eagerly anticipated A49 derby against Shrewsbury Town took place at Gay Meadow at the end of November. Shrewsbury had just been relegated from the Football League and were historically regarded as the bigger club, but we were really optimistic of getting a positive result.

We could not have been more wrong: they beat us 4–1.

The team played terribly overall and I was even worse. I got subbed midway through the second half and scuttled to the back of the bench with my tail between my legs.

When I first joined Hereford the established players had warned us that the manager could, when he wanted to, hand out some aggressive bollockings. Up until that point I had not really witnessed it, but I certainly did in that away dressing room. We had been dismal and deserved everything we got. GT went mad at the team in general – and then I caught his eye. He started hammering my performance, which was fair enough, and then mentioned the fact I'd worn moulded boots and had been sliding all over the pitch. Apparently I was unprofessional for not wearing studs and my lack of professionalism was why I was playing 'at this fucking level'.

I did not agree with everything he said, but I knew he was frustrated and wanted to get it off his chest so I just took it all. I thought once he calmed down he would apologise for his personal outburst.

GT is a legend with Shrewsbury after his previous spell in charge of the club in the late 1970s and early 1980s, so he was clearly embarrassed with the performance his current players had put in.

That weekend was also my twenty-fifth birthday, but I spent it sulking in my room waiting for the apology I was sorely mistaken in the thinking I would get.

GT called a meeting first thing Monday morning to further discuss Saturday's debacle. I expected a more analytical approach this time but he just went off on another rant – mainly focusing on me and my footwear. I was pissed off but took it again. I had no complaints about him criticising my performance, but I didn't think it was down to my choice of footwear.

Looking back, because of the sort of character I am, he may have done it to get a reaction from me. If so, then it definitely worked – I was fuming and determined to prove him wrong as I had been pretty consistent all season.

I did not have to wait long for a chance as we were playing Halifax Town at home the next day. We beat them 7–1; I scored two, set up three and was voted 'Man of the Match', even though Steve Guinan scored a hat-trick.

Was that the reaction you were looking for? I thought to myself. *Not bad for someone who does not even wear the right boots!*

It was by far my best performance of the season and, to make up for the worst birthday ever, I got a £100 cheque as part of my 'Man of the Match' award.

We followed up the spanking of Halifax with a more routine 2–0 victory at home against Farnborough Town and I got the opening goal of the game.

Our challenge to the top of the table continued throughout December, including another 7–1 win away to Forest Green Rovers where I grabbed two goals. That took my tally for the season to fourteen goals from central midfield before Christmas. Surprisingly, despite my new agent mentioning Bristol Rovers again, I still received no interest during the January transfer window.

Then, for me personally, disaster struck. It was the middle of February and we were playing Gravesend away. The game was only twenty minutes old when I twisted away from an opponent with the ball in the middle of the pitch. As I did so, my opposite number pulled my right arm – the same side I had dislocated my shoulder eighteen months before. Instantly I knew what had happened: my shoulder had come out of its socket!

With that type of injury you either need to put it back in the socket straight away or wait for a doctor to do it as the muscles around the injury spasm to protect it. I waited in the Gravesend physio room while they called an ambulance. The pain was off the scale and I asked them if they had any relief. Someone offered me a Nurofen! I didn't think that would quite hit the spot so I politely declined.

I knew the script now – I waited in agony at the hospital until a doctor was free. I received the gas and air and was off with the fairies until they put my shoulder back into place. Once the effects of the drugs had worn off I was distraught, though. I couldn't sleep that night. All that was going through my head was how my season was over – and I'd been enjoying the best one of my career.

After a period of letting the injury settle down, and a consultation with a specialist, it was agreed that surgery was required to ensure this would not become a recurring theme, thus confirming my worst fears.

I spent the majority of my time after that convalescing in Essex. The team did not miss me in the slightest – they went on a Conference record run of winning eleven games in a row including a 9–0 away win at Dagenham.

We finished the campaign in second place on ninety-one points, scoring 103 goals in the process. This was over a 42-game season and it would be interesting to know in how many other seasons that total would have been enough to gain automatic promotion.

My season personally finished on 14 February after playing thirty-two games and scoring fourteen goals.

. . .

30 MARCH 2013

I have got through another term and it is now Easter. My timetable has changed immensely, which has made my life easier, but I am still struggling with teaching and I'm feeling quite low at the moment.

School football is terrible. I want to be in a professional environment and I am miles away from that. Once I familiarise myself with the teaching I'll probably be OK in this comfort zone and do the job for years – but I don't want that. I'd rather really push myself and fail than never know.

To top it all off, I am back playing for Thurrock. While I was unavailable for two months, the club signed another central midfielder so I find myself playing down the right or left flank now. My form has been decidedly average and the team in general is really struggling. I am seriously considering hanging up my boots at the end of this season.

CHAPTER 11

MAKING THE SAME MISTAKES

SUMMER 2004 – INJURED again, but I had been really effective when I was able to play the previous season. I'd had the operation on my right shoulder and was due to be fit for the start of pre-season 2004/05. But, such is the short-sightedness of many football clubs, my shoulder injury did not seem to matter too much as it was 'only' my upper body.

GT had made it clear he wanted me to stay but we were struggling to come to an agreement regarding my wages. Once it became evident we were not getting promoted, he came up with his best offer of £550 per week.

As I mentioned earlier, I could not have been happier at Hereford and everything had gone great from an on-the-pitch perspective. But I was also aware that I was twenty-five. I wanted to play in the Football League and needed to earn some decent money – all my hometown friends were buying their own houses and I wanted to do the same.

Money, in hindsight, should not have come into it. If I had continued to perform well, the finances would have looked after themselves. Plus, what is better: to be a bit-part player in the Football League or a key player in the Conference? I'd made that mistake once already when leaving Yeovil and was about to do the same again with Hereford, with my new agents also pushing me to move as there was obviously no value to them in me staying.

I had to give GT a response regarding my future within a couple of weeks of the season finishing. I had three concrete offers from Shrewsbury Town, Chester City and AFC Hornchurch. All were offering substantially more money so I told GT I could not accept his offer.

I still regret that decision.

A couple of days later I wrote GT a letter thanking him for saving my career. I do not know if he ever received it as he has never mentioned it. I hope he did as I really appreciate the opportunity he gave me.

None of the three teams mentioned above were exactly big clubs – and none of them really excited me – but they were all keen for me to join.

Garry Hill was the manager of AFC Hornchurch and had tried to sign me previously for Dagenham & Redbridge. There was never really any chance of me going to Hornchurch as they were playing in the Conference South, but I met up with Garry and chief executive Gary Calder (though I'm not sure Hornchurch really needed a chief exec). Their first offer was £1,000 per week on a two-year contract. I'm pretty sure if I'd been serious about joining that figure could have gone up, but I had no interest in dropping down a league. This was one of my few correct career moves as Hornchurch went bust about a third of the way through the season. I then spoke to Shrewsbury Town – by far the biggest of the three clubs mentioned. I went to Gay Meadow and met manager Jimmy Quinn, who I knew from our brief time at Reading, and his assistant Dave Cooke. Normally when you go and speak to a manager you get a gut feeling about them and the club – mine was not a good one. Jimmy, rather than speaking to me like a manager, was chatting to me like a friend and telling me all about numerous irrelevant events. I could not have cared any less about all that, to be honest. I had plenty of friends and did not need another one. What I wanted was to find out about the team, where I would fit into it and what they did in training. Jimmy and Dave were clearly good guys, but nothing they told me made me want to sign for Shrewsbury.

I visited Chester City next and met Mark Wright, their manager and former Liverpool defender. The meeting went well. He spoke positively about me and how I would fit into his team, but there were a few problems. I spoke to a few former Chester players and none of them had a good word to say about the club or Wright. These were not bitter players who had been rejected by the club, but people whose opinions I valued. With three or four people saying the same thing, I would have been a fool to ignore the warning signs. I had also heard rumours that players did not always get paid on time and, if the chairman took a disliking to you, wages could be stopped or you could even be forced out of the club. With all this evidence, and the fact I had a well-run and financially stable club like Shrewsbury showing an interest in me, it was not a hard decision to turn Chester down.

This again turned out to be a good decision as Chester lurched from crisis to crisis over the ensuing years before finally going bust in 2010.

Due to this process of elimination, I was left with just Shrewsbury Town as a real option. I tried to drag the situation out, hoping a more attractive option presented itself, but nothing did, so I went up to Shrewsbury to finalise the deal.

I arrived at Gay Meadow with my new agent in tow ready to thrash out the details of my contract. You can imagine my surprise when, in Jimmy's office, my agent just sat there and hardly said a word while I negotiated the deal. I was pretty pissed off with that but relatively happy with my new contract.

We agreed a two-year deal on a basic wage of £800 per week. The club also agreed to pay the first three months of my rent as part of my relocation package, plus a £100 goal bonus. It meant, as this was a Football League contract, I would get paid through the summer during both years.

When I'd agreed to be represented by my new agents, I'd signed a contract entitling them to 5 per cent of my wages. They neglected to tell me that I had to also pay the VAT on that 5 per cent, so that meant £204 a month over the course of my new contract – a total of £4,896. Not bad for making a few phone calls! I wouldn't be surprised if they were paid by Shrewsbury too. You could argue that they had managed to nearly double my wages, but I think my performances really dictated that rise. Moreover, when I really needed them in the final negotiations, I was left to do everything myself.

The contract would run from 1 July 2004 to 30 June 2006. All I had to do to confirm the deal was pass a medical, which I did. Just…

I subsequently heard from Rachel, one of the physiotherapists, that she really hadn't wanted to pass me. Looking back, I bet the club wish they'd taken her advice!

CHAPTER 12

UP THE A49

SEASON: 2004/05
CLUB: SHREWSBURY TOWN
DIVISION: LEAGUE TWO
MANAGERS: JIMMY QUINN/GARY PETERS (GP)

PRE-SEASON STARTED AT the beginning of July. My girlfriend Emma and I had found a house to rent in Telford. Emma was moving away from home for the first time and this was great for me as it was nice to have someone by my side. Moving clubs can often be a lonely experience, especially initially.

Emma and I had first met each other – or, I should say, quite literally bumped into each other – in the luxurious surroundings of the Chelmsford branch of a Yates's Wine Lodge about five years previously. Even then I only frequented top-quality establishments. Somehow she managed to resist my advances over the ensuing three years whenever I managed to track her down. My persistence eventually paid off as we began an on-and-(quite often)-off long-distance relationship during the two years I played for Hereford. With my newfound wealth I managed to convince her to join me on my national tour of footballing backwaters.

Stuart Whitehead, one of my new teammates, owned two houses in Telford next door to each other. He lived in one and was kind enough to allow us to rent the other one while we found somewhere to buy.

My initial thoughts when joining Shrewsbury were confirmed during pre-season training – the environment was very relaxed. I often thought Graham Turner would have been even more gutted about missing out on promotion the previous season if he had seen how unprofessional the environment was here compared to Hereford.

Shrewsbury had some really good players such as Ryan Lowe, Sam Aiston and Darren Moss, among others who went on to better things, but the team as a whole was not playing anywhere near its potential.

What also caught my eye when I got there was the abundance of good central midfielders already at the club. These included former Birmingham City captain Martin O'Connor, Dave Edwards and Jamie Tolley. I was starting to wonder where I was going to fit into the team.

I was still recuperating from my shoulder injury so, for the first few weeks, my participation in training was restricted to non-contact activity.

My first involvement came in a comfortable Shropshire Senior Cup win against Bridgnorth Town. Considering I had not played for five months, I did well. This was quickly followed by a short pre-season trip to Torquay. As soon as we got there we had a night out and I got heavily inebriated.

I have always struggled to train after a night on the booze and this was no exception: I was a shambles. A young Joe Hart, the current England goalkeeper, asked me after that session why I didn't like training. I had to explain to him that, although it may not have looked like it, I actually love it.

We had a game against Truro the next day and I had to ask the manager if I could miss it as I still felt terrible from the night out two days before. We had two games in two days so I played in the second one and got on the scoresheet.

That turn of events probably did not show me in my best light, although the atmosphere was so relaxed at the club I don't think anyone really cared.

The Torquay hiccup aside, pre-season went really well personally. I played in the last game of the tour away at Exeter and got a run-out in all the other important games, culminating in a home friendly against Bradford City. I was confident I had done enough to gain a starting berth in the first proper game of the season.

We started our return to the Football League at home against Lincoln City and I was in the team as an attacking midfielder. We narrowly lost the game 1–0, which was no disgrace as Lincoln had been in and around the play-offs for the last couple of years. I missed a great chance midway through the first half, though, when a recovering defender did just enough to put me off. As the game wore on, my performance deteriorated and I was replaced halfway through the second half.

Not exactly the debut I had dreamt of the night before.

I kept my place for the next game away to Macclesfield which we lost 2–1. Personally the game went a lot better and I scored my first goal for the club with a scruffy shot from the edge of the box, plus I also hit the bar with a long-range effort. Even though we lost, I was really happy with my performance. It is always a relief when you go to a new club, get a goal and prove to your new supporters that you are a good player.

Unfortunately our results did not improve and we lost our third game in a row away at Cambridge United. Not only that, but we were totally outplayed from start to finish. When I tell you Cambridge eventually got relegated after finishing bottom of the League, it probably highlights the challenge we had ahead of ourselves.

Rumours started that the manager was under pressure already. It was strange because individually we had some good players. This was backed up by what they went on to do in their careers. However, in my opinion, there was no discipline at the club. We had a lot of strong characters who needed controlling but I did not think Jimmy was the man to do that. He was a nice enough guy but still wanted to be a player and didn't seem keen to upset anyone.

Being the strange game that football is, we found ourselves under real pressure after just three games. Our next one was at home to Northampton Town and we were trying to reverse an unwanted record of zero points from three games.

We started the game nervously, me as much as anyone, but we went on to win 2–0. This was more down to the fact Northampton were reduced to nine men rather than any great performance from us. The game was in the balance until I got the second goal in the last ten minutes. I was in the thick of the action and got 'assaulted' in one of their sending-offs. If my opponent's tackle had been any higher it could have resulted in a very crude castration!

This revival did not last long as we fell to defeat in the League Cup away to Tranmere Rovers and then lost 2–0 at Oxford United, but we recovered to get a good win at home to Cheltenham and followed that up with three consecutive draws (away against Bristol Rovers and Boston and at home to Bury).

As the team found a level of consistency, so did I. Considering I had been out injured for five months before joining Shrewsbury, I was generally happy with the way I was performing.

Our renaissance came to a crashing halt when we got beaten 2–1 at home by Yeovil. After Luke Rodgers put us ahead with a great strike, we got dismantled by a brilliant opposition who just left us chasing shadows. They even had the luxury of us missing not one but two penalties.

This further confirmed how poor the rash decision I had made three years earlier to leave Yeovil was. I could have been a part of that team as opposed to running around getting nowhere near any of them.

We got a fully deserved bollocking after the game and one of the main points to come out of it was we did not pressure them enough in midfield. With that in mind, we faced AFC Bournemouth at home in the LDV Trophy (as it was then called). In one of the early exchanges, I sensed an opportunity to nick the ball from an opponent. As I slid to win the ball, my right arm got stuck behind me and straight away I was in agony.

I knew what had happened – I had dislocated my shoulder for the third time.

The familiar hospital scenario unfolded as I waited for the doctors to tend to those in a more critical condition. Unlike previous times, I actually had to go to theatre and be put under general anaesthetic so they could put the shoulder back into place. I stayed in hospital overnight.

Bournemouth were being coached by Richard O'Kelly at that time and he visited me before I left the hospital. Little things like that are why I, and many others, hold him in such high esteem.

I was really disappointed with myself once the physical pain diminished. I had only one person to blame for this happening again. When you dislocate your shoulder all the ligaments that hold the joint in place are stretched and therefore leave the joint unstable. You can rehabilitate the injury but never really tighten up those ligaments without surgery, which I'd had in March to make my shoulder stable. However, due to me leaving Hereford and not joining Shrewsbury until June, I hadn't had a rehabilitation plan in place as I was no longer Hereford's responsibility and Shrewsbury just wanted to get me playing. Being honest, I hadn't really fancied spending my summer break at Lilleshall doing rehabilitation either – a terribly unprofessional approach, I know. I was clinically fine after the first operation but I didn't do anywhere near enough work to strengthen the area. It was just a matter of time before the inevitable happened against Bournemouth.

After a brief period of wallowing in self-pity, I had to take the positives from the situation. It was an upper-body injury so, even though I would need surgery again, I could still spend a lot of the convalescence period working on my fitness and getting myself into good shape.

After a relatively good start to my Shrewsbury career I was consigned to the shadows as, once injured, you are of no use to the manager. Some do it consciously, some do it subconsciously, but you are pretty much ignored and forgotten about until you can contribute on the pitch again. A long-term injury is bad at the best of times, but even worse when you are trying to establish yourself at a new club.

The team continued to struggle on the pitch. One incident before a game stuck in my mind and, for me, summed up Jimmy's time as manager at the club.

We were playing Grimsby at home in a midweek League game and I had taken up my customary position in the physio's room. The phone in the room rang and the gaffer answered it with: 'Hello, Chinese takeaway, how can I help you?'

I was gobsmacked and sat in the corner cringing.

This was the manager of a club who was hanging onto his job for dear life. Psychologists may say this was his way of dealing with a high-pressure situation but I just found myself feeling embarrassed for him.

As fate would have it, he was relieved of his duties after the visit of Grimsby since we were rooted to the bottom of the League after fourteen games.

It is always disappointing and unsettling when the man who brings you to a club leaves but I was not overly bothered this time.

The chairman and board must have realised that a firm hand and more discipline were required. As a result they employed Gary Peters, a former player who had appeared for Aldershot, Fulham and Wimbledon, among others. He had also managed Preston North End and, at one stage, took a young David Beckham on loan.

I am going to be honest and say GP and I never really saw eye to eye. Having a lot of success with Wimbledon, where he had earned two promotions in the 1980s, had obviously had a big influence on the moulding of his footballing philosophy as he was an advocate of the very direct style of play favoured by the Dons and others. I hated, and still do hate, this style of play with a passion, though. The whole game plan is based on getting the ball forward and into the opposition's box as quickly as possible, irrespective of the quality of the forward ball/pass/hoof. I will admit this sort of prehistoric, high-tempo approach can have a positive short-term effect as it is quite easy to implement. However, after the initial surprise factor of five or six games, the opposition soon work out how predictable this approach is. They then drop deeper as a team, so there is no space behind to put the ball, and just wait for us to give them the ball again and again and again – which we did.

I also consider it lazy coaching – it is a lot tougher to work with a group of players, improve them tactically and technically, and be brave enough to let them make mistakes. In the long term, this will benefit the individuals and team as a whole; however, I am pragmatic enough to know that time is a commodity very rarely afforded to football managers.

Put GP's style of football to one side though and he was not all bad. He instantly put in place some changes that actually bettered the club, such as improving the changing facilities, getting a groundsman to work on the training pitch, putting up a head tennis court, and – when the training pitches were not up to scratch – finding us alternative venues like the National Sports Centre at Lilleshall. He also started providing regular food before and after training.

These changes may not seem much but they made a big difference when put together, especially the improvement of the playing surface. When you are training on a crap surface, more often than not, you just want to get off it as it becomes frustrating and counterproductive. There is nothing worse than mistakes continuously happening through no fault of your own. I could easily shank a ball off the pitch without any help from an adverse playing surface, thank you very much! When on a good pitch though, the players suddenly wanted to stay out after training and work on their game.

Most new managers bring in their own assistant and GP was no different. Mick Wadsworth joined us, having previously worked in the Premier League for Southampton and alongside the likes of Sir Bobby Robson, Alan

Shearer and Nolberto Solano at Newcastle. I know this because Mick told me approximately eight times a day, every day. I quite liked him, though – he said what he thought and had a very dry sense of humour.

Mick regularly told me how much he admired the technical ability of Solano and other South American players. This, along with the other players we discussed, led me to believe Mick was not a huge fan of the way we played. But, being the manager's assistant, he had to tow the party line. I don't think their combination worked particularly well, though. Normally if the manager is a miserable git then you have a very enthusiastic and upbeat assistant to play 'good cop' to the boss's 'bad cop'. A perfect example of this was Graham Turner and Richard O'Kelly at Hereford; I will leave it to you to work out who was the miserable git of the pair. Unfortunately at Shrewsbury, GP was a miserable git and so was Mick. After a bad defeat and a bollocking from the manager, we then got a look of disgust from the assistant too.

I had very little to do with the new manager initially. I dislocated my shoulder three weeks before GP joined and so, after my surgery, I spent all my time with the physio. I watched all the home games and heard some of the stories from the lads but was not really fazed by what was going on. I was intelligent enough to realise I was probably not going to be his cup of tea as a player, but I knew I had the rest of this season and the next one on my contract so just spent my time concentrating on getting fully fit and not relapsing.

Rachel, the Shrewsbury physio, made me her project and was determined to ensure my shoulder would not dislocate again. I spent the next five months working with either her or the physios at Lilleshall and also used the time to do loads of fitness, which helped drop some weight and improve my body fat percentage.

I also bought my first house. Emma and I moved from our rented accommodation in Telford to a lovely little two-bedroom house in Shrewsbury, just outside the town centre. One of the main motivations for me moving clubs was to buy my own house so it was great when this actually came to fruition – although it was tricky doing the decorating with one arm.

By February 2005 I was ready to join in with the first-team squad again. Since I had been out for so long I was eased back into training gradually. As is always the case, the first week or two with the lads was a struggle. I was miles off the pace and my timing was all over the place. My touch is my biggest asset but, for a while, the ball was bouncing off me like it would a brick wall.

By the start of April my comeback was going OK, aside from a setback in March when I got a small tear in my hamstring (this can often happen after a long time injured). As a team, however, we were still struggling, and the manager made a decision that seemed very brave at the time.

Our main goalkeeper was Scott Howie – a decent enough lower-league keeper who was, like the majority of keepers at that level, a very good shot-stopper. Our reserve keeper, however, was a seventeen-year-old called Joe Hart. It was obvious from training that Joe was going to be a brilliant keeper and I can honestly say I am not surprised in the slightest that he has gone on to have the success he has had. However, it still seemed very risky to put such an inexperienced keeper into a vital game…

The risk paid off. We were playing Oxford United at home and went on to win 3–0. For that decision I must give GP a lot of credit.

Now, if you are an Arsenal fan then the next couple of paragraphs may make you feel sick.

Joe kept his place in the team and, as they say, the rest is history. But a few games into his career I saw a familiar face in the crowd: Steve Rowley – the man who initially signed me for Arsenal and was now their chief scout – was at a Shrewsbury game.

It did not take a genius to work out who he was watching. The game was not sold out (as was the norm), so I wandered over and sat with him. Steve obviously asked my opinion on Joe and I gave him a glowing reference.

Steve said Arsenal had earmarked him as one of the best three young keepers in Europe. I could not stress any clearer how good Joe was and how much potential, in my opinion, he had.

I told Joe about this and kept Steve updated when Chris Woods, the Everton goalkeeping coach at the time, came and worked with him at our training ground. When it became evident that Joe would be joining Manchester City, it turned out it was because apparently the powers that be at Arsenal decided Joe was not agile enough.

Whoops!

I was now regularly playing in the reserves as the season moved to its climax. Bearing in mind I had another year on my contract, I was not particularly fussed about missing out on so much playing time because I was more concerned about being fit and raring to go for my second season. However, I managed to force my way into the first-team squad and make a couple of cameo appearances during the last two games of the season away to Swansea City and at home to already promoted Scunthorpe United.

The Swansea game especially sticks in my mind for two reasons.

Firstly Mick Wadsworth was in charge of the team as GP was away on scouting duty. This was Swansea's last ever game at its Vetch Field ground and, with about twenty minutes to go, Mick told me I was going on. I wasn't ready, though, as I didn't have my shin pads on. He gave me a right earful and told me how unprofessional it was not to be ready. To be fair, he had a point, and from that day onwards, whenever I was on the bench, I would always be ready to go on at a moment's notice, wearing full kit.

During my brief spell on the pitch that day I also became another one of Swansea striker Lee Trundle's victims. During that season he was show-boater extraordinaire and regularly embarrassed many League Two players. It was strange as, during the early part of my career, I had played against Trundle many times in the Conference and thought he was pretty ineffective. Then suddenly he turned into a top player at our level and above by adding productivity and goals to the flashes of skill he used to show. Anyway, just after coming on, I sensed an opportunity to do what many League Two players had wanted to do all season: give him a friendly but fair dig. He was wide on our right, facing the crowd with the ball. I went flying in, but he impudently flicked it through my legs and ran round the other side to take the ball (and the cheers from the fans).

Apparently it was a tradition at Swansea's last home game of the season for the home fans to slowly approach the pitch until it looked like a Sunday League game – with them all on the touchline – before turning the approach into a full-on pitch invasion as the final whistle sounded. With this being the last ever game at the ground, the tradition was magnified.

The tunnel was located in a corner of the ground by the goal we were defending. I was playing right wing so was probably the player furthest away from it. Bearing in mind how lively the south Wales residents can be, and that I was arguably the slowest player in the Football League, this was not looking good!

Thankfully my trepidation was shared by the referee. He gave us a signal just before he was going to blow his whistle and, by the time he did, I was standing next to Trevor Challis – our left back – and made it back to the safety of our dressing room.

On this occasion we lost 1–0 so the locals were in a jovial mood as we had not ruined the leaving party.

Despite also making a brief cameo appearance in our last game at home to Scunthorpe United, the season had been an absolute disaster for both me and the club. We eventually finished the season in twenty-first place on forty-nine points and I personally made only twelve starts and two sub appearances, and scored only three goals.

It was not just me who thought the season was a disaster. GP obviously concurred because he released every player who was out of contract bar one

(Stuart Whitehead). I was under no illusion I wouldn't have suffered the same fate had I not had my second year looming.

Even though I hardly kicked a ball under the new management it was looking pretty obvious I would not fit into their plans, but I was confident in my ability and set out to try to prove them wrong.

I did receive a tentative enquiry over the summer from Richard O'Kelly, who was still at Bournemouth, regarding my availability. At that time, however, Bournemouth were going through one of their many crises and the club appeared very unstable, with regular reports of players not getting paid on time. That, and the fact I was settled in Shropshire, meant things never went any further than one brief chat. In hindsight, I feel not delving a bit further was another mistake.

.   .   .

20 APRIL 2013

I have been back at school a week since the Easter holidays and currently feel really low, bordering on depressed. I didn't want to go back after the holidays and I don't want to go in every day, full stop. I am getting into the building later and later and leaving as early as possible. It is a real struggle just to get out of bed in the morning.

I am now, in the main, teaching football, business and PE, but still not enjoying it and not feeling like it's getting any better. If anything, teaching PE is harder than teaching in the classroom. At least in the confines of a room I can keep the kids relatively under control and in their seats; out on the field they just run free. We are in the summer term and playing sports like cricket and athletics – both of which I only have a passing interest in and little knowledge of, other than the basics.

I cannot even moan at the school any more: they have given me pretty much everything I asked for. But I still hate it. I have spent the week being disrespected and mugged off by moody teenagers.

I asked one student to do something and finished off by calling him 'mate'. He turned round and said, 'I ain't your mate.' So I asked him to do it again and this time called him 'dickhead'. He looked at me and muttered, 'I'll get you sacked for that.' I simply responded with, 'Let's hope so. That will do us all a favour.'

The more I seem to treat the kids with respect, the less respect they seem to give me. The angry teachers who roam around the school, screaming and shouting at kids, get their respect, yet the teachers like me, who try to treat the kids like young adults, just get disrespected in return.

We have something called DEAR at the school, which stands for 'Drop Everything And Read'. For twenty minutes once a day, the students stop what they're doing and pick up a book. I think it is a great concept but it can be challenging to implement sometimes, especially in PE.

Once I had a very lively class of Year 7s who refused to be quiet as a DEAR session already doubled to forty minutes. Midway through the struggle one of the female PE teachers had to come into the changing room and she screamed at the kids. They shut up instantly but, as soon as she went out of the room, they started talking again. I asked them why they would be quiet for her? They said I had to shout at them as they were scared of her but not of me. I did not know whether to laugh or cry; in actual fact I just thought it was sad. I was sad for them and myself.

A couple of days later that same teacher who helped me came over and, as she could see in my eyes how much I was struggling, asked if there was anything she could do? I did not know where to start and felt like crying. I appreciated her concern but felt pathetic that I could not get a group of twelve-year-olds to be quiet.

The only time I feel comfortable is when working with the sixth-form players in the football academy. They are more mature and I can talk to them on an equal level – no surprise, as this is what I have been trained in. I do love coaching – it just needs to be on a subject I know.

To compound my misery, I can't even release my frustrations on the football pitch. I am still playing for Thurrock but we are struggling big time. Due to the terrible weather throughout winter and spring, I have just come off the back of nine games in nineteen days. My body is screaming for a rest but I need to keep going.

I have been playing really averagely too. I am working hard and doing my best but I feel like a shadow of the player I was even a couple of years ago. The fact I no longer train every day means I have lost all my sharpness. Mark Stimson, our manager, is great and shows me a lot of respect, but he must expect more from me. I definitely expect more from myself.

I'm really not sure whether to play next season, but the way things are going at the moment it might be out of my hands anyway. I am worried, though, as I can't seem to find another job. I have applied for many – and even been recommended for some – but I still can't get an interview. However, I do think being unemployed would be better than my current reality; I refuse to let the fear of having no wage allow me to waste my life doing something I hate.

I put the fact I feel so low down to my job and nothing else. I want to leave right now but the upbringing and principles my parents instilled in me will not allow me to let anyone down. I am definitely leaving at the end of my contract. The only way I will stay is if I can just coach the football academy, even on a part time basis – but nothing else.

What I will do alongside that, however, I don't know. I feel lost.

CHAPTER 13

A CLASH OF STYLES

SEASON: 2005/06
CLUB: SHREWSBURY TOWN
DIVISION: LEAGUE TWO
MANAGER: GARY PETERS (GP)

O VER THE SUMMER break I continued my shoulder recovery and worked really hard on my fitness. It was always going to be a real struggle to cement my place in the team but I wanted to give myself the best possible opportunity.

On our last day of training the previous season we had completed a set of fitness tests and knew we would be doing the same tests on our first day back. We did, and I flew through them. I have never had any pace but have always been near the front in any type of endurance activity. Gary's recruitment strategy, in the main, had been to bring in young, hungry players who had been released from higher-ranked clubs. This made it even more satisfying to beat the majority of them in testing.

Pre-season, in general, went well. The most important thing is to be in the team for the first game of the season and that only happens if you do well in the weeks leading up to it. I remember performing well against a strong

Stoke City team in our first friendly and scoring against Telford United in the Shropshire Senior Cup.

It became evident there was not much chance of getting a game in my favoured central midfield role but it looked as though I had nailed a position on the left wing. Not ideal for me but better than sitting on the bench. The style of football was direct and our job was to win the ball back, give it back to the opposition nearer their goal and repeat this cycle until we won a set piece or found a position to deliver the ball into the box.

In the first game of the season, we played Rochdale at home and I had secured a place in the starting line-up. I began on the right of midfield and, during the course of the game, also played down the left, off the striker and directly up front. Rochdale, however, led from the front by Grant Holt and Rickie Lambert, beat us 1–0 via a winner from the former. Both players went on to play in the Premier League and Lambert even went with England to the 2014 World Cup in Brazil.

Apart from missing a great chance to equalise in the second half, I was happy with my performance. Although they do not always correlate, I was awarded 'Man of the Match' – and rightly so, in my opinion.

One of the new initiatives GP had implemented was a lengthy debrief after every game at the start of the next training session. The management would go through the match DVD beforehand and then critique our performance. This was quite clever on their behalf as it gave them an opportunity to watch any incident numerous times and made it pretty futile for us to argue against what they said – although I did try to on more than one occasion.

Gary must have sensed my air of contentment as he went for me straight away. He first told me in front of everyone that there was no way I was 'Man of the Match'. I told him that, believe it or not, I did not select the award, even though I felt it was correct.

He then went on to blame me for Rochdale's goal. Remember, I'd not had the fortune of watching the game again on DVD but, off the top of my head, I couldn't think of a reason why it was my fault. When he explained his logic I knew it definitely wasn't my fault. We'd had a corner and it was my job to cover any deliveries that got flicked on or were over-hit to the back post – GP was unhappy I'd not done my job and the ball had gone out for a goal kick as Rochdale eventually went on to score from it. Now, I may have been in the wrong for not going round the back for the corner, but I thought it was ridiculous to blame me for a goal that had started from their goalkeeper.

I thought a manager's job was to support and build his players' self-esteem, not to knock it down. It got my back up and I just ignored everything else he said.

As part of these debriefs we were all given a copy of the match DVD with a form that had twenty questions for us to fill in – a sort of self-assessment. At the end of it was a box to write your own personal comments about your performance. According to GP, players could put anything in that box and it would not be held against them as it was a private document for his eyes only.

However, this was not necessarily the case.

We were all expected to watch the DVD and fill in the form before the next game. We were due to play Boston United away on the Wednesday. When I arrived for training on Tuesday, Mick Wadsworth, again in front of the group, came for me. He said, 'Have you watched the DVD yet?' I told him I had not had time and I would watch it that night. The manager chipped in and said, 'Make sure you do.' I said I would, but Mick would not let it go.

'Too busy were you? Didn't have time?' he accused, which wound me up as he was trying to embarrass me, so I replied: 'Sorry, Mick, I was too busy drinking my bottles of "Man of the Match" champagne from Saturday!'

Have that.

I knew it was a good retort as the reaction from the lads was a combination of laughter and sharp intakes of breath. It was a bit close to the bone but he'd started it and I'd shut him up. He gave me plenty back during the training session, however, especially when I gave the ball away.

The next day we played Boston away and drew 1–1. I started up front, scored, got criticised for not scoring a 35-yard chip, was blamed for their equaliser and eventually substituted. That pretty much encapsulates my time playing under GP. I suppose I should take it as a compliment that he expected me to score such a lob but, in reality, it was just another opportunity to dig me out. Again, I was not overly fussed as I was pretty happy with my performance, although he did have a point about me ball-watching for the equaliser.

As much as the manager was trying to undermine me, it was not working. Even though I had not played that many games for the club I was quite popular with the supporters. It seemed to me GP was trying to turn people against me.

We lost the next game away at Bury, but I kept my place for a hard-fought draw at home against Northampton and then scooped 'Man of the Match' again – less justifiably this time, really – in a League Cup victory at home against the higher-ranked Brighton & Hove Albion.

My prize was a crate of those small Stella Artois bottles you used to get on a booze cruise to Calais. After the presentation, I cracked them open in the dressing room with the lads. It was like something you'd see in a dressing room from the 1970s, all that was missing was the huge communal bath. I'm not sure that went down too well with the management and I can understand why, looking back. In the debrief that followed it was again made clear to me that I was not 'Man of the Match' in Mr Peters's opinion.

Everything seemed to be going well until we played Wycombe Wanderers at home in the next game. They were one of the best teams in the League and, even though we managed to escape with a draw, we got absolutely battered.

At half-time, GP went for me: 'Smithy, I want to fucking punch you!'

I had been below par but was giving it everything; his reasoning behind this outburst was that I had the audacity to track back, clear the ball for the umpteenth time in 25°C heat, but then not immediately sprint up the pitch after it.

He went on: 'You've got five minutes to liven up or you're off.' He should've just taken me off then and there, but he wanted to humiliate me a bit more. Within three minutes of the second half, the substitutes board went up. I didn't even look at it as I began trudging over to the dug-out.

That game was over a bank holiday so we were in for training on the Sunday before heading straight down to London to prepare for a game against Leyton Orient on Monday. Up until this point I had started in every game, but on Sunday I got the dreaded knock on the door of my hotel room. I was being dropped.

GP told me he thought I had been poor in the last game, which was fair enough, so he was leaving me out of the next one. I appreciated him coming to tell me but what he did next was another example of the way he was trying to chip away at me. After our chat, we all had a pretty light training session before GP got everyone together and said that two or three players were being rested. He then went out of his way to say that I'd been dropped, not rested. Thanks for that.

We went and won the game 1–0. We only kept a clean sheet because of our future England goalkeeper.

GP and Mick were having a discussion in the technical area regarding a substitution. GP looked back to the bench and said nothing. He didn't need to because his mannerisms said it all. If he'd been a cartoon character, a little thought cloud would've appeared above his head reading: 'Shit, I can't put any of them on – they are all useless!' I clocked it and thought it was hilarious and ridiculously disrespectful at the same time.

As those two games had come so quickly we'd not had time to do our 'homework' and fill out any self-assessment forms. I saw this as an opportunity to vent some frustration, putting in the 'any other comments' section the following: 'I am the scapegoat for this team, whenever anything goes wrong I get the blame or get replaced.'

Maybe not the greatest career move but GP did say you could write what you wanted and it would not be held against you.

Initially it was not as I started the next game against Oxford, which we won 2–0. I played central midfield and was solid rather than spectacular, but I was replaced midway through the second half, ruining the experience for me.

GP took me into his office on the Monday morning and simply told me my performance was really average. Now, I was aware of this but I really couldn't see the point in him reiterating it. He didn't go into any specifics about my performance, how I could improve or what he wanted me to do in the future – he just said my performance was average. That left me even more upset and frustrated than I had been after the game.

This started a strange spell where I was in and out of the team. For some reason GP felt I could only play in home games, so I would spend one game in the team followed by another on the bench. Torquay away I was sub; Notts County at home I started. GP wanted to do his customary substitution midway through the second half but, not only was I working hard, I was turning it on too, so he had to wait 'til the last ten minutes before taking me off. He even attempted to give me a 'well done' hug as I came off, like he did with his favourites, but it was awkward at best.

I was back on the wing for a midweek home game against Sheffield United in the League Cup and made it through to the seventy-second minute. After that I didn't start a game for a month. I had played OK when I'd been in the team – not brilliant, but as well as others who were playing regularly. When you bear in mind it was clear to everyone, not just me, that GP and I did not get on, then my performances were more than acceptable. Anyone who has played professional football will tell you that it is very hard to play with freedom and express yourself when you do not have your manager or coach's confidence.

My next start was during a home draw against Stockport County. I cannot remember a great deal about the game but I did play the whole ninety minutes. Even though I hadn't played for a month, I was 'rested' for the next game. It was the end of October by that point and my next start was two weeks later at home to Chester, which we won 3–1. Again I completed the full game. Moreover, in the second half I tucked in from my position on the left wing. A long ball had been hoisted into the air, which I took down with one touch, and then, with my second touch, I put our striker Kelvin Langmead clean through. It was a great bit of play, even if I do say so myself. But what was my manager's reaction? He turned to his bench and said: 'Flash cunt.'

What chance have you got as a player when your manager says that about you after some good play? I dread to think what he used to say when I made a mistake.

In our next game we were playing Braintree Town in the FA Cup. That week, GP and I had the sort of conversation that punctuated my time at the club. He told me in this particular lecture that I would never play central midfield for his team and that I was too slow to play on the wing. I told him that, with regard to playing on the wing, we could've saved a lot of time and effort with me telling him that at the start of the season. I'd always been one of the slowest players at all the clubs I played for and there was no great chance of that changing. We agreed to disagree on my qualities (or lack thereof) as a central midfield player, however.

So, after such a discussion you can imagine my amazement when I started against Braintree Town in central midfield! I believe there was a more sinister side to it all, though: as I mentioned earlier, I was respected by the supporters and I think this was part of GP's plan to undermine me.

Did it work? Well, it didn't break me, but it didn't help my mental state either. In the long term it did toughen me up, but I was losing the will to prove GP wrong. At that stage I just wanted to move on and play for someone who appreciated the talents I knew I had.

We won the cup game 4–1 but my performance, while not great by any stretch of the imagination, was acceptable, particularly considering the mind games I was embroiled in with the manager.

We were away for the next game so I was obviously dropped. I then managed another first in my career: I was dropped without playing. We were due to play Mansfield at home and I had been selected to play. Tragically, during the pre-match warm-up, the Mansfield goalkeeping coach collapsed and died on the pitch so the game was cancelled, and, since our next game was away to Rochdale, I was technically dropped without even kicking the ball.

That game at Rochdale produced an interesting incident in the dressing room afterwards. We had been 3–1 up at half-time but eventually lost 4–3 after that pair of Grant Holt and Rickie Lambert scored two goals apiece. No one in our camp was happy, as you can imagine. In fact, striker Colin McMenamin was foaming at the mouth and going mental, blaming Gavin Cowan for not clearing the ball for Rochdale's winning goal. Gavin let it slide initially, but Colin wouldn't let it go and continued to scream at him. Gavin finally reacted and all hell broke loose. I was in the corner, brave as ever, watching and wondering what everyone was getting so wound-up about. GP came flying in, well and truly nailing his colours to Colin's mast by pinning Gavin up against the wall and giving his opinion of the situation.

Being the Neanderthal-like figure that GP was he loved the raw emotion Colin was exhibiting but it has never done anything for me. Coming into the dressing room screaming and shouting at your teammates does not make you more passionate than someone who keeps himself to himself and gets on with their job.

I see this kind of reaction as being for 'show'. They are effectively saying: 'Look at me boss, I really want to win.' My answer to that would be how about you show how much you want to win on the pitch rather than smashing up the dressing room and team morale. There is nothing wrong with a heated, constructive discussion that gets issues and disagreements out in the open, but screaming and shouting obscenities is pointless.

The next week we were at home to Colchester United in the second round of the FA Cup and I was back in the team but, pre-game, I had yet another surreal GP experience.

The manager decided every player in the team had to wear studded boots. If you didn't have them you weren't allowed to play. GP then decided to go round and check what type of boots each player had on. It was ridiculous.

I had worn Adidas Copa Mundial boots for years and, for wetter conditions, I would get them modified – someone would shave down some of the moulded studs and put in longer screw-in ones. I liked this as I always found Copas to be the most comfortable pair of boots. Their studded alternatives, Adidas World Cups, were a lot narrower and not as comfortable.

GP rather awkwardly checked everyone's boots. When he came to me it was decided my modified boots were not up to his standards. He said if I did not find a pair of studs then I would not be playing – this was at 2 p.m. I had always been anal about my boots and did not feel comfortable wearing someone else's in training, let alone in a big game against higher-ranked opposition. I did what he wanted as I was not going to give up my place in the team, but I found this to be another example of his need for total control over everything we did.

We lost the game 2–1. It was played on 3 December and was the last time I was in the squad for Shrewsbury Town. The manager was pretty scathing regarding my performance and said he could not play me when I was performing like that – which was fine as I didn't want to play for him anyway.

He said I should look for another club and I said I would see what came up. He warned me that I would not get another club 'if I waited until the end of the season', which basically meant I should leave as soon as possible.

I'm sure getting me off the wage bill had absolutely nothing to do with that instruction…

I was more than happy to leave but it was going to be on my terms, not forced by a bully like him. I still had over seven months left on my contract so I was in a strong position. I'd gotten rid of my ineffective agent so it must've been GP who was putting my name about as I received a call from ex-Hornchurch manager Garry Hill, who was now at Weymouth.

Joining a club like Weymouth was initially of no interest to me: they were in the Conference South and I had no desire to drop down two leagues. But Garry was very persistent. They were a full-time club and he did not baulk at my £800-a-week wage – in fact, he said he could better it. My ears started to prick up.

He was also positive that if I were to leave Shrewsbury I would be due a settlement on the remaining time of my contract. I told him Shrewsbury were insisting I wouldn't get any type of pay-up, but he was convinced they were bluffing.

For those who are not aware of the protocol: if a club wants to end a player's contract early, both parties must come to an agreement on the remaining value of it. Often, at the lower levels of the game, a contract will just be terminated to let the player move to a new club for no fee, but in some situations, depending on how much you earn or how badly the club wants to get rid of you, the player will be paid to go. The beauty of this situation is that any pay-off under a certain amount – I believe £30,000 – is tax-free, as it is considered severance pay.

Suddenly Weymouth had become a viable proposition, but, after speaking to my former teammate Jamie Pitman, I also got a phone call from Graham Turner saying he would like to see me return to Hereford United.

In the middle of January I went to speak to both clubs on the same day. I ventured down to the West Country the day before and stayed at my old mucker Skivo's house.

I went to Weymouth first and Garry, plus his assistant Kevin Hales, showed me the training ground and stadium. It was refreshing to talk to someone who was really enthusiastic about my attributes and what I could potentially bring to the team. I had not had a manager speak that positively about me since I was at Hereford. It was just what my ego needed.

Garry is a very astute businessman. He does not initially come across that way but I think he does it to lull people into a false sense of security, getting them to drop their guard. He said I had to speak about the terms of my contract with chief executive Gary Calder, although we were both aware it was Garry who would make the ultimate decision.

I said that I wanted £1,000 per week, plus a few small bonuses on a two-and-a-half-year contract. He didn't agree to it but he didn't say no either. We left it at that and agreed to speak again in the next few days.

I left Weymouth to drive up the M5, happy with what I saw and had been told. I was now off to meet Graham Turner. He and I met at the services on the M5, just before the M50 turn off.

Graham asked me how it had gone at Weymouth and was a little taken aback by the figures I had been offered. He went on to say that he would match my Shrewsbury wage of £800 a week, and add in appearance money over eighteen months. That was a good offer and it meant I wouldn't have to move house because I could easily commute to and from Edgar Street. Hereford was also a league higher than Weymouth.

I had plenty to think about.

I was back in training at Shrewsbury on the Thursday and it was pay day, but I had only been paid half my wages. We normally got paid two weeks in arrears and two weeks in advance. GP was obviously so sure I was leaving that he'd had the second part of my wages stopped. I was not best pleased and asked him what was going on. He said I was leaving so I was only getting half pay.

This was where the bluffing had to start. I told him that both clubs I visited had offered me less money than I was currently earning so I would not be leaving unless Shrewsbury paid me to leave. He reiterated that I should leave immediately as there was no chance I would get another club in the summer. Like most things GP said, I ignored it; both Garry and Graham had said they would wait and take me in the summer if they had to.

The next day I was called into GP's office as soon as I got to training. He said, and I quote, 'The chairman says you were injured when you joined, you've done fuck all since you've been here, so won't get a penny from this club!' I calmly replied that this was fine and I would see out the rest of my contract.

As a result, Duane Darby and I were sent to train by ourselves. Duane, I imagine, was one of the biggest earners at the club and did not fit into GP's plans either. As a result, we spent an hour running – which didn't bother me in the slightest as I now enjoyed keeping fit. However, within an hour of getting home I had a call from GP asking if I would leave for £5,000? I said yes, I would, thank you very much. What a U-turn from the conversation we'd had three hours previously! I should have perhaps held out for a bit more but this was effectively free money I had not expected.

Garry Hill was on the phone straight away asking what it would take for me to join Weymouth. I told him what I'd told Gary Calder: I wanted £1,000 per week. He said they would give me £925 but I held firm. Garry said we wouldn't fall out over £75 so was willing to offer me the full amount on an eighteen-month contract. There was also a clause that if I started thirty games in the full season I would automatically get another one-year contract on the same money.

The owner of the club owned a chain of hotels so agreed to put Emma and I up in one of them until we found a house. Garry was in a rush to get the deal down and got all the forms faxed over to a local hotel.

I rang Graham over at Hereford and told him I had decided to join

Weymouth. He was surprised and disappointed but ultimately respected my decision.

It would have been easier for me to join Hereford as there would have been a lot less upheaval, but I was really disillusioned with everything and just wanted to get away. I would be lying if I said the money was not a factor but it was not the be all and end all.

Another reason I joined Weymouth was because of how desperate Garry was to sign me. I really needed a manager who thought a lot of me, who not only wanted me in his team but would build it around me. After a year of being told what I could not do it was nice to find someone who was waxing lyrical about my strengths.

I was pretty happy with myself and the way I had handled the negotiations. I had managed to get myself a 25 per cent pay rise and £5,000 to leave Shrewsbury. GP had given me a tough time over the last year but I felt I had won a small victory.

During that first part of the 2005/06 season I made sixteen appearances, via fourteen starts and two sub appearances. I scored one goal.

· · ·

1 MAY 2013

Another football season has come and gone with Thurrock. It has been pretty nondescript and summed up by mine and my team's performance in our last game of the season, which we lost 4–0. Rather surprisingly, manager Mark Stimson is very keen on me staying for next season.

We had a chat after the game but I was very non-committal. I didn't particularly enjoy much of the season, but every time I was ready to quit something happened to remind me how great football can feel and lure me back in. I have made many bad decisions during my career, never more so than over the last twelve months, but I do not want to make another one by stopping playing too early.

I know that once I stop that will be it for me. However, I am really keen to start working in a professional academy with young players. The money is low but it is where I want to be and I am pretty sure that, if I am happy and enjoying myself, everything else will fall into place. In an ideal world I would marry the two together – playing and coaching – but, as I have learnt, this definitely is not an ideal world.

Talking of being happy, I have told the school I no longer want to teach next year. I spoke to the headmaster and said all I'm willing to do is work with the football academy part time and find myself more work around that.

It seems ironic as one of my main motivations behind moving away from football was a desire to have a secure income after years of not knowing where I might be or what I might earn.

Unfortunately, I am now as unsure of what the future holds as I've ever been.

CHAPTER 14

RE-BUILDING ON THE SOUTH COAST

SEASON: 2005/06
CLUB: WEYMOUTH
DIVISION: CONFERENCE SOUTH
MANAGER: GARRY HILL

FOOTBALL MOVES SO quickly. I signed my release forms from Shrewsbury on a Friday, packed up the house on Saturday and travelled down to Weymouth on Sunday, ready for training on Monday. Emma and I arrived on Sunday, with me nursing a raging hangover after celebrating my parole from Shrewsbury the night before.

My new club put us directly on the seafront in the Prince Regent hotel and, as tends to be the case when you have played professionally for a few years, there were a few familiar faces upon my arrival in the dressing room.

Weymouth were flying high at the top of the League when I joined but I was thrown straight into the first team. Although we were the 'big spenders' of the League, a young, vibrant St Albans team was pushing Weymouth all the way.

My initial thoughts within a couple of weeks of moving, however, were along the lines of *what have I done?*

The hotel we were staying in was like a something out of the film *Cocoon*. Emma and I were the only people in residence under the age of sixty. The most excitement was when the weekly game of bingo was held or when one of the old dears fell down the stairs.

I quickly found out that some old people can be quite rude. I believe, due to their seniority, several of them felt they didn't have to queue up at meal times, but their pushing-in wound me up. It was also very challenging for Emma and I to share one little double room for three months; she was doing my head in and no doubt the feeling was mutual.

To add to all that, the weather was horrendous. I subsequently found out that when living on the coast you suffer the extremities of the conditions. When the weather's nice it's an amazing place to be, but when it's bad – like you'd expect it to be in January – it's terrible. It seemed to be raining and blowing a gale-force wind every day.

My performances were nothing more than average on the pitch. I arrogantly thought, after dropping down two leagues, that I would be the best player in every game – but that definitely was not the case.

We won three out of my first four games and I scored in two of them. I went on to also score against Weston-super-Mare to make it three goals in seven games, but we lost two of those overall. We then went unbeaten for a month until losing away at Welling at the end of March. I remember this game well as I over-indulged in the pre-match meal at the hotel on the Friday night and ended up ambling around the pitch in first gear – more so than normal.

My performances were still up and down – some games I would coast around thinking how easy it was and on other occasions I felt like everything was passing me by. It was at those times that I became acutely aware of how much money I was earning for this level of football and I expected a lot more from myself.

After that defeat, we kept winning – but so did St Albans. Everything came down to a 'winner takes all' game on Easter Monday when they came to our Wessex Stadium. All the pressure was on us: Weymouth were the hot favourites; St Albans were just the young up-and-comers playing with total freedom and surprising everybody.

A crowd of over 5,000 squeezed into our ground and the game lived up to its billing. We sneaked a 3–2 win, mainly due to a true captain's performance from skipper Matt Bound, although we lost Shaun Wilkinson to a red card midway through the second half and were holding on for dear life near the end. It was a brilliant game to play in but very nerve-racking.

I remember the game vividly for two reasons: firstly, because I won the penalty for our third goal; and secondly, because I nearly dislocated my left shoulder at the same time. As I hit the ground my arm was doing its best to come out of its socket, though this time the ligaments and muscles did their job and just about kept everything in place.

As I write this, I am reminded how quickly life moves on, let alone football. Two of the main protagonists in that game have sadly passed away now. Both Weymouth owner Martyn Harrison and St Albans manager (and my former Yeovil gaffer) Colin Lippiatt succumbed to cancer recently. It seems like only yesterday we were all battling it out and now they are no longer with us. Colin especially was someone I knew very well and had a lot of time for. He was a great, fun-loving guy and I often cringe when I think about some of the things I did under his management. He was very patient with me though. We always had great chats whenever we bumped into each other throughout my senior career and I will always be grateful to him.

Emma and I had finally bought a house in Weymouth just before the St Albans win too, so it was a successful couple of weeks. The weather was also improving and I was starting to realise why so many people migrate to the coast. We now needed just two points from the last two games, which seemed a pretty routine task.

Those last two weeks did not go without incident, however.

The next game was due to be played away at Bishops Stortford. In the hotel on the Friday night, however, our manager was in a foul mood. I'd come to realise his personality could swing occasionally, but it seemed a little strange for this to be the case when we were on the verge of achieving promotion.

He called a late evening meeting to tell us that the club had been charged with fielding an ineligible player called Solomon Taiwo and that Weymouth could lose the four points they gained while he was on the field. Garry was livid and poor old Gary Calder, who was ultimately responsible for registering players, was getting it in the neck big time.

If we now didn't win our last two games we might not go up.

Thankfully we did what we needed to do at Stortford and won 2–0, plus St Albans lost one of their final two anyway, so we won the League. I think the administrators of the competition were happy with that as well because they could be seen to be punishing us, knowing, in effect, it made no real difference at all.

We finished the season with a win at home against Lewes – a game in which the match ball was dropped in by a parachutist. Bit much for a Conference South title win, if you ask me, but the chairman was putting enough money into the club to do what he wanted.

We finished the season on ninety points (after the four-point deduction) and were clear of St Albans by four points. My gamble in dropping down two leagues had paid off as I was now back at the absolute minimum level I expected to be.

Since joining in January, I'd ended up making nineteen appearances and scoring three goals. Alongside the sixteen appearances and one goal I contributed to Shrewsbury, it meant my season was a combined total of thirty-five appearances and four goals.

Before we broke up for summer we all had one-to-one meetings with the manager to discuss the season. Garry said I had done OK but he expected more next season – a fair appraisal of my performance. It was the first time I had moved clubs during the season and, if I'm honest, I didn't realise how tricky it would be – especially considering all the personal upheaval that goes along with it too.

Emma was now working at Haven holiday park, so we stayed down there for the summer break. This was when I really started to fall in love with living on the south coast. The summer was beautiful and I spent my time going to the gym, jogging down the seafront or sunbathing on the beach while Emma was at work.

Places like Weymouth come to life in the summer as all the tourists invade the town. It went from being a sleepy retirement home to a vibrant, lively resort. Our house actually backed onto a nature reserve, which in turn led to the beach – I could have gladly stayed living there for ever.

CHAPTER 15

GETTING BACK TO MY BEST

SEASON: 2006/07
CLUB: WEYMOUTH
DIVISION: CONFERENCE PREMIER
MANAGER: GARRY HILL

AS IS ALWAYS the case when a club steps up a division, our manager was strengthening his squad and recruiting enthusiastically. Garry and his team brought in some real quality, including players who were established in the Nationwide Conference or above.

One of our boys left, however: captain Matty Bound. There was no real outstanding candidate for his replacement as skipper so I thought I would put my name forward. I had never been recognised as 'captain material' at any of my other clubs – although I had badgered Graham Turner mercilessly, and ultimately unsuccessfully, to be vice-captain at Hereford. Most of the lads thought I was joking – and I don't think the Garry took me too seriously either – but I thought I could do the job successfully, even if I wasn't your stereotypical captain.

During pre-season the gaffer gave a few players the opportunity to lead the team and I got my chance in a low-key friendly at home against MK Dons, which we lost 2–1. I'd never led by screaming and shouting at people, but I knew I was respected and could possibly lead by example, which I hoped would cajole my teammates into following suit.

I was starting to feel comfortable and happy within the team. Once that happened I knew good, consistent performances would follow and, during our preparation, I'd been one of the more influential players in the squad.

Garry pulled me aside before our final friendly match and revealed I was to be his captain for the season.

I was delighted. What had started as a joke to some had become a reality. I would've loved to have seen Gary Peters's face when he found out I was a captain!

I was really enjoying working under Garry Hill. Some regard him as a Del Boy-type figure, but he was – and is – a lot more than that. I think he played up to that persona so people underestimated him. I'd be amazed if he has any type of real coaching qualifications but he knew – and still knows – just how to manage people. Plus, like any good leader, he employs people who have the skills that he lacks himself. In this case he had Kevin Hales, the ex-Chelsea and Leyton Orient player, who provided coaching and looked after the tactical side of the game.

Garry definitely knew how to handle me. I liked to be left alone to get on with my game and he recognised this but, every now and then, he would set me a little challenge or throw a sarcastic comment about a bad performance to give me a kick up the rear.

In Weymouth's first game back at the top of the non-League pyramid we were playing away at Tamworth. This was a happy hunting ground for me as I had scored two goals there at the start of the season a couple of years ago. This game was no different as I managed to score our opening goal within six seconds of the game starting.

We employed the normal predictable English-style kick-off of playing the ball to a full back who then smashes it down the line. However, on this occasion, their defender was stretching and he headed the ball inside to me. I instantly saw the keeper off the line and side-footed the ball on the volley over his head. It turned out to be the second quickest goal in the history of the Conference and a great way for me to commence my tenure as team captain. We went on to win the game 3–1 and I was delighted with both the team's and my own performance.

Our next games saw us win against Aldershot, Cambridge and Kidderminster Harriers and draw with Oxford United.

We were quickly brought down to earth, though, after being comprehensively beaten away at Morecambe and held to a draw by Burton Albion. Despite winning two home games after that, my performances were pretty nondescript. Even though the results had been quite good, I wasn't happy with myself and was starting to think the captaincy was more of a hindrance than a help.

Being the captain of a team can often make or break a player. From the outside looking in the change from another part of the team to skipper is minimal. However, I have seen it affect, both positively and negatively, different players in a variety of ways. Some thrive on the responsibility, stick their chest out and revel in being the main man – John Terry springs to mind. Others visibly shrink as the extra expectations of them become too much – the feeling of having to constantly prove you are worthy of both your position in the team and the captaincy becomes a burden and an unwanted distraction.

I saw both sides of this argument. When things were going well I loved nothing more than parading round the midfield with the armband tight around my left bicep, acting like the master of everything I surveyed, and then telling the press in great detail what good players my contemporaries and I were. On the flip side, the feeling of embarrassment was always magnified when you were in a team that was struggling. Somehow you felt more accountable for not only your own performance but for the team's as a whole.

Anyway, I digress…

We then lost away to Stevenage but both mine and the team's performances were positive and from that point on my personal form really improved. Despite being beaten heavily away at Dagenham & Redbridge, I managed to score a header (while also getting part of my front tooth knocked out for my troubles). This pattern continued though: our home form was very strong but our away form left a lot to be desired.

We then won two home games in a row, including one against Gravesend where I scored a 30-yard volley live on Sky Sports. It was strange – when I messed up my live TV interview a couple of years previous I had about thirty missed calls from people taking the mickey, but not one person called after I had scored a wonder goal!

We picked up a point away at Altrincham and beat Crawley 3–0 at their Broadfield Stadium. I scored a cheeky back heel and Lee Elam added a great solo goal.

We were now finding our form as a team. An indication of how far Weymouth had progressed came when we played Rushden & Diamonds at home at the end of October. They had just been relegated from League Two and we had just been promoted from the Conference South, yet they came and parked the proverbial bus, resulting in a 1–1 draw.

More worrying, however, was the fact our manager had to be taken to hospital before the end of the game and was never quite himself for the rest of my time at the club.

In early November we played at home against Bury in an FA Cup game shown live on BBC One. We more than matched our higher-ranked opponents to secure a creditable draw and a replay at Gigg Lane. It was great for the club to get such exposure, although the game was not so great for me. Our centre half Ashley Vickers decided to use my head for leverage while winning a header in the first five minutes. As part of this process, he pushed my head into the back of my opponent's and broke my nose. I played on but looked uglier than usual in front of millions of people on a Sunday lunchtime. I apologise to anyone I put off their roast!

The broken nose did not stop me playing but I had to go to a private hospital in Bournemouth to have it re-set. My face is naturally not particularly symmetrical so the last thing it needed was any help looking less attractive. A doctor injected some local anaesthetic into the base of my forehead, warning me beforehand that it could be quite painful. I was very blasé and explained I had suffered multiple dislocations of the shoulder, so this would be fine. I was wrong but I don't think I was the only one who made a mistake.

The doctor administered the anaesthetic, then instantly started to move my nose. It was agony. I could feel every movement and I thought it was strange the pain relief was not easing anything. After ten minutes the anaesthetic finally took effect but I'm pretty sure my nose was already re-set before any numbness kicked in. On top of that, it still isn't straight.

Back on the pitch, we suffered a drop in form as we lost three games in a row, including a thrilling 4–3 defeat in our FA Cup replay – I had a stinker and was at fault for two of their goals. We also lost 4–0 away at Woking where, although it was not actually credited to me, I scored an own goal – a shambolic end to a horrific performance.

On Wednesdays, my day off, I used to go to college to study for an HNC in business. On one of these days I got a phone call from an agent called Dan Fletcher, who told me Macclesfield wanted to sign me up. Initially this news did nothing for me as I didn't see Macclesfield as being any bigger a club than Weymouth, even though they were a league higher at the time. But I did remember that Paul Ince, one of my boyhood heroes, was their then manager. I was flattered that such a great midfield player wanted to sign me and started thinking how much he would be able to improve me. Dan also said Macclesfield were willing to pay me £1,500 a week – a 50 per cent pay rise!

I was really happy at Weymouth, however – my girlfriend and I loved the area and I was content and comfortable at the club.

After thinking about it I went and spoke to Garry. I didn't make any demands to leave or anything like that, I just told him what had been happening. Unsurprisingly he had no desire to let me go – plus I was only four or five games away from triggering an automatic one-year extension to my contract, so the ball was very much in Weymouth's court.

I had no problem with another year there as both the boss and the club had been very good to me. The sheer fact that I had attention from higher-ranked teams illustrated what a positive effect the move to Weymouth had had on my faltering career. But I was not going to look a gift horse in the mouth and I knew this news put me in a strong position to negotiate a new contract with Weymouth. I was earning £1,000 per week so it was unlikely I would get a pay rise at that level, but any extra years I could secure would give me the stability every lower-league footballer craves.

The gaffer also knew that my signing a new long-term contract would be positive PR for the club. After a little bit of negotiation we agreed on a new two-and-a-half-year contract on the same basic wage of £1,000 per week, plus a signing-on fee of £4,000 to be paid in instalments over that time. I was delighted my short- to medium-term future had been secured.

Or so I thought…

Safe in the knowledge my immediate future was safe, I began playing some of my best football of the season. I scored the only goal in a 1–0 away win at Northwich Victoria, was credited with a dubious goal in a 2–1 win at home against Exeter City – I bundled into their keeper and, if I did touch the ball, it was with my hand – and got both goals in a 3–2 defeat away at Forest Green Rovers on New Year's Day. Those goals made it ten for the season for me, all from open play, and triggered a clause in my contract that meant I got a bonus of £1,000.

That trip to Forest Green also helped dispel the theory Emma had that us footballers have 'great fun' during overnight hotel stays before a match. As we were staying in a hotel on New Year's Eve, the club paid for us to bring our girlfriends along. These trips were pretty boring and, if I'm honest, I wasn't too keen on the idea of partners coming. This was work time and I wanted to concentrate on the game, not have to listen to Emma worrying about whether or not her nail varnish matched her top. But all the lads were bringing their girlfriends so I agreed.

The trips consisted of training before we left or stopping and training somewhere on the way or training at the hotel upon arrival. We then ate dinner at about 7 p.m., went back to our rooms and had an early night. The fact it was New Year's Eve didn't change our routine, other than the fact we all stayed up to see the New Year in before bed.

I think the girls had thought that we'd get to a hotel, have a few beers, go out all night and then play the next day. They got a rude awakening when they realised how dull the trips actually were, experiencing one of the tamest New Year's Eve celebrations ever.

I also picked up my fifth booking of the season during that game so I was suspended for the next one. Little did I know that those two Forest Green goals were to be my last contribution for the club.

Early in the New Year Garry informed us we were going on a short break to Spain for some warm weather training and team bonding. This news went down well with the lads, as you can imagine. A couple of days before the trip the gaffer called a meeting. We all assumed he was going to tell us the itinerary for the trip. Unfortunately that could not have been further from the truth.

He came in and very matter-of-factly told us that he, along with his entire coaching staff, had been sacked and all of us could leave with immediate effect. The club said it could guarantee to pay us up until the end of January but, after that, they could not promise anything. Initially I thought it was a joke and started laughing but I could tell from the manager's face that this was serious.

I found it strange that, a month after sanctioning a new long-term contract for me, Weymouth suddenly didn't have any money. It was clear that the club was not self-sufficient but there was no indication of any money problems. I always got paid in full, on time, every month.

This kind of thing always makes me wonder why successful businessmen from different industries want to invest money in football clubs. There must be some sort of ulterior motive: is it a way of offsetting profits from a successful business to a loss-making one or do they like the publicity that owning a football club brings? It seemed the motive for Martyn Harrison, the Weymouth owner, was land development. Weymouth's home ground was on a big plot that included the ground itself, a huge car park and a speedway track. The story goes that Harrison had been in long-term discussions with the local council and a supermarket chain to relocate the football club to a new ground and sell the existing site. If that happened, he would recoup all the money he had invested in the club and make a large profit. However, it became evident this was not going to come to fruition and, realistically, there was no chance of him recouping his investment, so Martyn, along with his business advisors, decided they would no longer fund the club.

This was all really disappointing as we were challenging for a play-off place. I'd have understood it better if we'd been struggling, or perhaps floundering in mid-table, but we'd actually had a realistic chance of being in the promotion shake-up come the end of the season.

The club, as a result of sacking the coaching staff, had to pay off their contracts. It wouldn't have cost any more money to keep them on and, if we hadn't achieved promotion at the end of the season, they surely could've reassessed the situation then?

Thankfully I was having a good season so knew I wouldn't have a problem getting a new club; others who had struggled with injury or form were not so lucky though. There was now a fire sale at the club and I was one of the main assets available for transfer.

CHAPTER 16

DECISIONS, DECISIONS...

IT'S AMAZING HOW quickly news travels. Within an hour of the Weymouth situation arising, before it had even become public, I was getting phone calls from other clubs and agents promising me the world.

Nigel Clough, the then manager of Burton Albion, was the first to call. I also had Stevenage Borough, Kidderminster Harriers, Grays Athletic, Rushden & Diamonds, Hereford United, Cheltenham Town, Macclesfield Town, Peterborough United and AFC Bournemouth all contact me within forty-eight hours.

In this instance I knew I was in a strong position and so I decided to do to the agents what they do to players all the time – I used them for my own gain. I told each one of them I would not be signing any contracts but I would pay them a one-off fee if anything they did secured me a transfer. They all seemed happy with this arrangement – I'm pretty sure any club would have paid them a fee anyway.

With this much interest it was not feasible for me to go and visit every club so I had to firstly rule out the ones I was not going to sign for. This time I was determined not to make a decision based purely on financial terms. I was at a stage in my career where I had to be playing week in, week out.

As there were five Football League clubs offering me contracts I decided to turn down all the ones at Conference level. I rang every manager personally to explain my decision as I knew we may cross paths in the future. Some took it better than others. Mark Yates, the then Kidderminster manager, offered to match the £1,000 a week I was on at Weymouth and the length of contract as long as I did not publicise what I was earning because it was head and shoulders above what anyone else was on. He also understood though that I wanted to play in the Football League.

Grays Athletic were willing to offer me silly money. The club talked about a £30,000 signing-on fee among other things but joining them would have been a backward step. Justin Edinburgh, the then Grays manager and former Spurs player, understood but I ended up working as an intermediary for some of the Weymouth lads, including Dean Howell and Abdul El Kholti, into securing contracts there.

Neither Burton, Stevenage or Rushden & Diamonds could get near the money I was earning so I politely declined their offers,

I know lots of players who would just ignore a manager if they didn't want to sign for him and wouldn't even have the decency to explain their decision. I was determined to conduct myself with a bit of class, though.

Then it was a case of arranging meetings with the five Football League clubs: Hereford United, AFC Bournemouth, Macclesfield Town, Cheltenham Town and Peterborough United. I wanted to have a chat with each club about how they saw me playing in their team, as well as discussing the financial side of things.

John Ward, the manager of Cheltenham Town, seemed very keen so I met him first. As the club was relatively local to Hereford I also arranged to meet Graham Turner on the same day.

I met John at the Thistle hotel in Cheltenham. He signalled how serious he was about signing me by bringing chairman Paul Baker along with him. We talked about football and John said he saw me as an attacking midfielder who would have licence to get in the box. This was great but he then admitted to not actually having seen me play. I knew Keith Downing, his assistant, had seen me play as he was a former Hereford player and attended many games at Edgar Street. John also said his secretary had been impressed with the two goals I grabbed against Forest Green.

I found that very disconcerting because, as I've mentioned, my style of play is not to every manager's taste and I was concerned I might not be John's type of player. We did have a good chat about football, however, and I liked him.

John and the chairman then asked the big question: what was I earning? I did what everyone does in this situation and told a little white lie. I said I was due a £5,000 signing-on fee and was on a basic of £1,100 a week.

They asked me if I could give them five minutes in private and, when I returned to the table, I got a lovely surprise. They said the club was willing to offer me a three-and-a-half-year contract with a £20,000 signing-on fee, plus £1,200 a week for the rest of the season (which would rise to £1,300 a week for the first full year, £1,400 a week in the second and £1,500 finally). There were also some bonuses included, such as goal bonuses and £5,000 for every year the club stayed in League One.

I managed to suppress a smile somehow and told them I would have to think about it. When I got back in the car I just laughed to myself. I was expecting Cheltenham to match my Weymouth contract at best, not blow it out of the water. Previously they had missed out on a lot of transfer targets and I think they saw me as a realistic signing who they wanted to grab.

I began driving up to see Graham Turner, convinced Hereford wouldn't be able to get anywhere near that offer. We sat down and, as usual, just talked about football. Graham explained how much he wanted me back in his team. I was comforted by the fact he knew my game well and was aware of exactly what I could and couldn't do.

Graham knew I had been talking to Cheltenham and when I told him what they were offering I think he thought I was being economical with the truth. I had to show him the paper the deal had been written on, which on the opposite side contained a Cheltenham reserve-team line-up. At that point he had to accept I was telling the truth!

Graham explained Hereford would not be able to equal that deal, but would offer a two-and-a-half-year contract on £1,100 a week, match the £20,000 signing-on fee, give me £5,000 if the club got promoted, raise my wages to £1,400 a week if we got into League One, and pay £100 per goal and £100 per appearance. He also told me that his current captain, Tamika Mkandawire, was leaving at the end of the season and I would have every chance of taking the armband. That appealed to me as I'd really enjoyed being skipper at Weymouth and, despite my early reservations, felt it had helped raise my game.

Clearly the offer was not as lucrative as Cheltenham but, in my opinion, it was close enough for money to not be an issue – I was going to get paid well wherever I went. Graham also explained that if I turned him down again there would not be another opportunity to re-join the Bulls while he was in charge.

I felt really happy driving back to Weymouth that night; I could have easily joined either club and was confident I would be happy at whichever destination I chose. It seemed funny to me that only two and a half years previously Hereford would not, or could not, offer me more than £550 a week but were now proposing a package of more than double that.

The next day one of the agents who was trying to get involved in my transfer said how happy he was that one of the clubs he had spoken to, namely Cheltenham, had offered me a contract. I asked him how he had worked that out because they had rung me directly and I had gone to the meeting alone. He reckoned his firm had sent the club an email alerting them to my availability. I told him there had been no mention of this at the meeting and he could forget any slice of that deal.

As happy as I was with these offers, I wasn't going to rush into anything as I still wanted to consider the three other clubs on my radar.

My next stop was Dean Court to speak to Kevin Bond at AFC Bournemouth. I went down there early on a Sunday morning to have a chat and look around the ground. We had a good conversation and I liked Kevin but, much like Weymouth, Bournemouth was lurching from one financial crisis to another. Kevin assured me they were getting new funding in the near future but these off-field developments never happen as quickly as the on-field football people hope.

Bournemouth would have been a great move geographically as Emma and I wouldn't have had to relocate but, with the options I had, I didn't think I would've been looking after my best interests by signing there. In the end, they were put under a transfer embargo and Kevin rang to say the prospective transfer could not go ahead anyway. I said all the right things about how disappointed I was that the deal could not go through but, in reality, I had already made my mind up to turn him down.

Next I spoke to Peterborough United. They had an FA Cup replay at Plymouth and chairman Barry Fry wanted to meet me on the way down to discuss a transfer. Garry Hill seemed especially keen on me speaking to both Bournemouth and Peterborough; I imagine he would've been 'thanked' if any deal went through.

At the time, Peterborough were buying up all the most talented players in non-League football. I was flattered that a club signing the likes of George Boyd and Craig Mackail-Smith was interested in me. However, I was also a bit concerned. Wherever I went I wanted to be playing regularly and I wasn't sure that would be the case at Peterborough. I had no doubt it would've made me the best overall financial package offer but I wasn't fussed about that. I was also troubled by the fact I hadn't spoken to then manager Keith Alexander. Dan Fletcher, one of my freelance agents, spoke to him on my behalf and reported that Keith knew me and liked me as a player, but didn't need me. That made my mind up about Peterborough instantly.

I called Barry Fry and told him that I was flattered by the club's interest but didn't think the deal was right for me. He promptly hung up on me...

At least one of us conducted ourselves with a bit of dignity.

That left Macclesfield Town. It's not every Sunday evening that an ex-England player rings you for a chat about signing for his team, but that is exactly what happened to me in mid-January. Cheshire was a long way from Dorset so Paul Ince and I had our first chat over the phone.

Paul explained he had seen me playing in our televised FA Cup game against Bury and was impressed by my performance. This surprised me as I thought my display that day was nothing more than 'acceptable'. He went on to say how much he would like to sign me and spoke enthusiastically about where I would fit into his team.

I liked him straight away but was conscious of how well he was doing and concerned he would soon move on, leaving me stuck in Macclesfield – no offence intended. Paul was really the only reason I was contemplating the move there.

I told him this and he stressed that if he moved on, he would take me with him. That is easily said but not quite so easily done. What if he moved to a Championship team? I doubted he would take me there. Or what if the club he joined had an abundance of midfielders? Moreover, even if he did want me to follow him, there was no guarantee Macclesfield would let me go.

Due to these concerns, I decided to turn the move down – but who knows if that was the right move. Paul, as I expected, did move on, but only to fellow League Two club MK Dons, so maybe he would have stuck to his word and taken me with him – or maybe not. To be fair, he looked after people like Keith Andrews – a central midfielder who played for him at MK Dons and then went to play in the Premiership at Blackburn (although Keith was a much better player than me!).

After much deliberation, I decided I would join either Cheltenham Town or Hereford United. If I were to join Hereford, however, they would have to improve their offer slightly.

As I had two acceptable offers, I went to Weymouth and asked them to release me from my contract. At the initial meeting, when Garry had explained the situation, we were told we could all leave for free. I made a mistake not getting this in writing as, when I spoke to chief executive Gary Calder on this occasion, he said the chairman expected a fee for me. I was really disappointed by the club's stance. I argued my contract was worth over £125,000 but I was willing to write this off. In theory, I could've either negotiated a settlement or insisted the club honoured my contract, which would've sent the club into administration or even put them out of business.

Obviously that was not something I wanted to do. Even though it was all turning sour, Weymouth had given me the opportunity to re-launch my career and I appreciated that. Unfortunately the club was refusing to budge and I was not sure where this left me. I was not willing to sacrifice anything from my future earnings but these new deals were agreed on the understanding that I would be available on a free transfer.

I spoke to both John Ward and Graham Turner and explained the situation to them. Thankfully neither of them seemed particularly fazed by the introduction of a fee and said they would be in touch if, or when, a fee was agreed. So now it was just a case of sitting and waiting. I didn't say anything to Macclesfield as I wanted to keep them on the back burner in case either of my preferred destinations could not agree a transfer fee.

On Tuesday 23 January, Weymouth were due to play Exeter City away. I was still suspended after accumulating my five bookings but travelled with the squad. Jason Tindall, one of our more senior players, had taken over the role of manager and this was his first game. We had already lost some important members of our squad and were fielding a much weakened team than the one that had beat Exeter on Boxing Day. We lost 4–0 and, to rub salt into the wound, Lee Elam, one of our former players, scored a hat-trick.

Before the game, Gary Calder pulled me to one side and said that both Cheltenham and Hereford had agreed a transfer fee of £20,000, so now it was down to me to decide who I wanted to join.

I woke up early Wednesday and rang Graham Turner. I told him if he could raise my wages to £1,200, honour the £20,000 signing-on fee, pay me £5,000 in the event of promotion, raise my wages to £1,400 in League One and give me a £100 goal bonus on a two-and-a-half-year contract then I would sign.

Hereford's contract offer was a year less than Cheltenham's so I was effectively sacrificing a guaranteed £75,000 to join them. As a result of this, I told Graham I also wanted a one-year extension written into the contract, which would be triggered if I started thirty League games in the last year of my contract. He agreed, but that was a big mistake on my part.

It was not just me holding the club to ransom, however. As part of the deal I had to agree to my wages dropping to £750 a week if we got relegated to the Conference. This deal was a lot riskier than the Cheltenham deal, which guaranteed me more money and had no such clauses regarding relegation written in.

Money was not my main motivation on this occasion, though. I had moved clubs previously and things had turned sour for different reasons. This time I wanted to make sure I moved to a club that gave me the best chance possible to play every week. I believed that the fact I had played for Graham before – and he knew my strengths and weaknesses better than anyone – gave me that opportunity. I drove up to Hereford and signed my contract that same day.

Once the deal was complete I rang John Ward and explained my decision. He seemed to take it quite well but I am led to believe he had a little whinge in their local paper. I also spoke to Dan Fletcher, who relayed my decision to Paul Ince.

Football moves so quickly that I was due to start training at Hereford the following day. My adventure at Weymouth was over after one year, fifty-two appearances and thirteen goals. I was moving back to Herefordshire after two and a half years away.

. . .

31 MAY 2013

I left full-time football a year ago to avoid the uncertainty 90 per cent of footballers feel at this time of year:

Who am I going to play for next season?

Where will I be living?

How much will I be earning?

It has not worked out that way, however. I have told the school I will only stay next year if I can just work with the football academy. Unfortunately, this will only be a part-time role so I will have to find other work too. This is a positive, though: at least I can see the light at the end of this tunnel and will not be stuck painfully struggling through maths lessons for much longer.

Thurrock, who I played for part time last season, want me to come back and play again, but I'm not sure I want to continue at that level. To make matters worse, the club has been charged with fielding an ineligible player at the start of last season and is facing a possible three-point deduction. As we only finished one point above the relegation zone, it could mean, pending an appeal, Thurrock will be in the Ryman Division One North next season. I started last season at that level with Sudbury and definitely do not feel like dropping down to that league again.

So, as of today, the only guaranteed income I have is a part-time job at the local comprehensive school – not exactly part of the script, but then what from the past year has been?

It is not all doom and gloom: I have an interview next week at Braintree Town to work at their football academy. The role is tutoring in the morning and coaching in the afternoon. I have got to deliver both a lesson and a coaching session as part of the interview process. I'm hopeful I'll get offered the job as it would mean career progression and the opportunity to coach players every day.

I also got a text from Dean Holdsworth yesterday asking if I would be interested in joining him at Chelmsford City, so I'm due to meet him in the next couple of weeks. I played under him briefly at the end of my career with little success, but I've learnt that a lot of these options quite often don't come to fruition anyway, so it's a case of watch this space...

CHAPTER 17

UNFINISHED BUSINESS

SEASON: 2006/07
CLUB: HEREFORD UNITED
DIVISION: LEAGUE TWO
MANAGER: GRAHAM TURNER (GT)

HAD TO pop back to Weymouth after signing my new contract to pick up some clothes. To make it a double celebration, Emma had passed her driving test so we went out for a meal and celebrated our good news – hers was arguably the best as I had been ferrying her around for two and a half years like an unpaid taxi service!

I left Weymouth early Thursday morning ready for my return to Hereford. Even though I had played for the club before, and knew a few of the lads, I still had that 'first day of school' feeling. I was a little apprehensive – nervous but excited – and looking forward to settling in.

As I'd had to relocate, Hereford would've put me up in a hotel, but since the cost would've come out of my financial package I decided to stay with Jamie Pitman and his family instead. We'd played together at Yeovil and during my first spell at Hereford and he was kind enough to offer me his spare room.

This meant that Emma and our new addition, a Dalmatian called Oakley, were temporarily left in Dorset while I sorted us out somewhere to live. We could have gone back to the house I still owned in Shrewsbury but I didn't particularly want to commute from Shropshire every day.

On the same day I re-signed, my old partner in crime from our first spell, Steve Guinan, also re-joined on loan from Cheltenham for the rest of the season.

I had not played since New Year's Day due to my suspension and some postponed games, but I was thrown straight into the team against Notts County at home. Except for not scoring, my second debut couldn't have gone much better, as I assisted two goals in a 3–2 win. I was given an attacking midfield role and was unlucky not to score within ten minutes after I slammed a shot against a post. I tired near the end, as expected, but thoroughly enjoyed myself and received a great reception from our supporters.

We followed this up with a creditable 2–2 draw at Bury but Stockport County came to Edgar Street for our next game and brought us down to earth with a thud, comprehensively beating us and having the game wrapped up by half-time.

After this we were at home against a strong Barnet team, but we won 2–0. They had the likes of Jason Puncheon, Nicky Bailey and Dean Sinclair in their side, all of whom went on to bigger and better things. I scored our opening goal via a fortuitous deflection and went on to win the 'Man of the Match' award.

We consolidated with a great win away at Lincoln where Steve Guinan, who got a hat-trick, Alan Connell, who scored the other, and Andy Williams absolutely ran riot in a 4–1 victory. Steve even managed to score a header from the edge of the 18-yard box but when you have a head as big as his, that is not as much of an achievement as it sounds! We then remained unbeaten with two solid draws – one at home to Rochdale and the other away against Chester.

I had been captain since the Barnet game because Tamika Mkandawire, our skipper and best player, had become injured, but I retained the captaincy after he returned. When I was in talks to sign and GT had mentioned me taking on the captaincy since it looked like Tamika was going to leave, I'd assumed that would all have transpired over the summer. I didn't feel particularly comfortable with the current situation, though. Tam was a highly respected member of the squad and I was still settling in and trying to prove myself. However, I wasn't going to turn the opportunity down so I just tried to lead the team in my own understated way.

The point earned at Chester pretty much meant we were safe from relegation and, whether consciously or not, we seemed to knock off early for the season – winning once in our last eleven games and scoring only five goals. That meant we unfortunately set an unwanted club record for the amount of games played without scoring.

There were a few incidents that stuck in my mind through this spell. One was away to Peterborough United where I was determined to put in a good performance after their interest in me in January. I should've known it was going to be a bad day when they scored after ten seconds. They went on to win 3–0. So much for me showing Barry Fry and Peterborough how good I was! We got totally overrun in midfield and I did not get near anyone. My opposite number Micah Hyde was replaced with five minutes to go and I think it must have been because he got sunstroke as I definitely did not get anywhere near kicking him.

Peterborough played with a central midfield three against our two. Their attacking pair flew forward with such vigour, pushing us back, giving neither me nor Steve Jennings any chance of getting near Hyde who was playing in the deeper role and absolutely running the game.

I bet the Peterborough hierarchy were devastated they did not secure my signature!

Our gaffer was getting more and more agitated and angry as the bad run of games continued – everything we tried failed to get us out of the slump – and, one morning before training, we were called into the home dressing room for a meeting. GT came into the room absolutely fuming. The only other time I had see him go off on one was after that humiliating away defeat at Shrewsbury, but this time the catalyst was an off-the-field matter.

Most days there would be footballs for us to sign in the dressing room that then went off to local schools and charities. On this occasion, some of the lads had, rather than sign their own name, put aliases such as 'Bobby Robson' and 'Posh Spice', and the manager had received a phone call from one of the recipients saying how disappointed they were – although I'd argue that if Posh Spice *had* signed the ball it would've been worth a lot more than one signed by us gaggle of goal-shy lower-league footballers.

GT went mental and smashed one of the aforementioned balls against the dressing room wall, saying: 'You cunts are taking the piss out of me and this club.' He added that unless we got our act together and the culprits came forward, we would only get the bare minimum of one month off over the summer. Wayne Brown and Andy Ferrell, being the people they are, stepped forward straight away and admitted their guilt for causing 'ball-gate' and that was the end of it. While the actual incident itself was quite amusing, it was clearly not the main issue. GT was displeased and frustrated with our overall situation and this just gave him the opportunity to tell us what he really thought.

The penultimate game of the season was against Shrewsbury at home. My old nemesis Gary Peters was still in charge at my former team and they needed a victory to secure a play-off place. We had nothing to play for but pride, but I was determined to scupper Shrewsbury's chances.

Like the majority of our back end of the season, things did not go to plan. We, unsurprisingly, did not score and Shrewsbury ground out a 1–0 win. Gary Peters ran on the pitch celebrating like a demented David Pleat and bounded over to me to compliment my performance. I felt like telling him where to go but instead settled on wishing him luck with about as much sincerity as he had displayed in his comment about my performance.

The only good thing to come out of this period was finding a lovely house for Emma, Oakley and I in Worcester – only thirty minutes away from Hereford. This made it close enough for me to travel in every day but far enough for me to get away from football when I wanted to.

GT was still in a bad mood leading up to the last game of the season (away at Torquay) and reiterated his threat about us training over the summer. He moved the goalposts slightly and said that if we didn't get any kind of positive result at Plainmoor then we would be training throughout May. I was pretty sure this was a bluff as I didn't think he wanted to be in over the summer either, but I wasn't willing to put my theory to the test. I reckon neutral fans were a little surprised to see the whole Hereford team celebrating like a bunch of lunatics when our keeper pulled off a great save in the last five minutes to secure a draw in a seemingly meaningless end-of-season affair, though!

My own form had been up and down during our poor spell and culminated in me being hauled off with about fifteen minutes to go at Torquay. My standards had dropped over those few weeks. Nothing was said, but I wondered if, at that time, GT was starting to regret the big outlay he had made on me.

Much like when I'd joined Weymouth from Shrewsbury, I struggled to adapt to a mid-season move. I'd been absolutely flying at Weymouth but hadn't transferred that form to Hereford – although, in my defence, there was a lot of stuff going on. Not only was I trying to adapt to a new team and style of play on the pitch, I was also commuting regularly from Weymouth and trying to sort out a new home.

I finished the season with eighteen appearances and one goal for Hereford meaning, when combined with my Weymouth spell, I'd played in forty-eight games and hit eleven goals. I did wonder to myself how many goals I would have got at Weymouth if I'd stayed for the season. I'm confident it would have been at least fifteen.

My first pen picture at Yeovil Town. And yes, I was a big fan of Jason Donovan…

Playing against a young Man United team in 1999. I even had the David Beckham highlights as well.

Had an absolute stinker in this game against Gravesend & Northfleet until this shot sneaked in.

© Steve Niblett

A comfortable victory for me in the 'who can pull the ugliest face' competition in March 2007.

Being as slow as I was, there was no chance I was going to catch anyone in a race, so I usually went for the lazy lunge – as demonstrated here.

Looking fresh-faced, but struggling as usual through another pre-season friendly in July 2007.

© Steve Niblett

The permanent players of the HUFC squad for the promotion-winning 2007/08 season. However, this group of players was supplemented by more than a sprinkling of very talented loanees.

© James Maggs/*Hereford Times*

Celebrating my second goal (and my team's third) in a comfortable home victory against Morecambe.

© Steve Niblett

A sudden burst of energy after scoring against Tamworth in 38-degree heat. Before that, I'd been overheating like a clapped-out old Mondeo.

© Steve Niblett

Clearing the
ball in a narrow
defeat against
Birmingham City
in August 2007.

© James Maggs/*Hereford Times*

Bradford at home.

© Steve Niblett

Another tackle, another
ugly face pulled.

Bursting through against Leeds in the FA Cup, but couldn't quite find the finish.

© James Maggs/*Hereford Times*

The favourite game of my career – a 1–0 win against Leeds United at Elland Road in an FA Cup replay.

© James Maggs/*Hereford Times*

© Steve Niblett

Photoshoot dressed up as an early 1920s Hereford United player.

© Steve Niblett

An enjoyable game to play in, even though we lost away to Leicester City in League One.

© Steve Niblett

One of my trademark outside-of-the-left-foot passes. Not sure how I developed that skill but it was something I used a lot over the years.

Celebrating a Simon Johnson goal with Richard Rose against my old team Shrewsbury (and a certain manager).

© Steve Niblett

© James Maggs/*Hereford Times*

The customary lap of honour after the final game of the season against Grimsby in the promotion-winning 2007/08 season.

The look on my face probably tells you how surprised I was when my volley flew into the top corner of the net.

© James Maggs/*Hereford Times*

Pretty sure I am giving the ball away here – as I did for the majority of this game against Southampton in pre-season 2008.

A rare touch of the ball in a 6–1 spanking by Bristol Rovers at the Memorial Ground.

Showing my explosive jumping skills by getting a good 3 cm off the ground…

CHAPTER 18

FINALLY GETTING SOMEWHERE

SEASON: 2007/08
CLUB: HEREFORD UNITED
DIVISION: LEAGUE TWO
MANAGER: GRAHAM TURNER (GT)

EMMA AND I spent the summer making our new house a home and, before I knew it, the next season was upon us. There had been a high turnover of players and, through a combination of letting players go and others rejecting new contracts, Hereford had only seven senior contracted players and three youngsters.

This was not seen as too much of a problem by the management. GT knew the club couldn't match the bigger teams in the League financially – and, geographically, the club wasn't ideally placed – but he also knew that if he sat tight he could attract players of the requisite quality within the club's wage structure.

My pre-season was terrible personally. I'd worked hard physically during the summer break so was at the front of any running, especially long distance, but my touch and timing seemed to desert me and I was all over the place technically.

A lot of our friendlies were against higher-ranked opposition so you can imagine how much fun it was scratching around for form against Championship and Premier League players. The more frustrated I got with my performances, the harder I tried – and, in turn, the worse I played.

The squad itself was starting to take shape, though. GT and his assistant John Trewick, whether by default or design, came up with a genius and unique recruitment strategy imitated by many clubs in subsequent years: they started signing highly promising young players from top Premiership and Championship clubs on six-month or season-long loans. There was no chance of Hereford obtaining players of that quality permanently but, as our management team was so well respected, clubs were willing to entrust their youngsters with Hereford because they would get the opportunity to play and develop in the right manner.

Over the course of this season we signed Robbie Threlfall (Liverpool), Toumani Diagouraga and Theo Robinson (both Watford), Lee Collins and Stephen Gleeson (both Wolverhampton Wanderers), Sherjill MacDonald (West Bromwich Albion), Gary Hooper (Southend United) and Chris Weale (Bristol City).

I was getting asked by the local press if I was captain of the team for the coming season. I told them I wasn't sure as nothing had been said directly to me – which was true, although I must admit I was expecting to get the role. Karl Broadhurst aside, who had been brought into the club and seemed to be 'classic' captain material, there were no other stand-out candidates.

We were fine-tuning our preparations in the week leading up to our first game against Rotherham when I was called into the manager's office and told I wouldn't be captain that season. Karl was given the role and I was to be vice-captain.

I was pissed off; not so much for losing the captaincy – although I was gutted about that – but because I felt I'd been led on all pre-season by being named captain in every game. If I wasn't going to be captain, why hadn't I been told sooner? In hindsight, my poor performances probably contributed to the decision and perhaps GT had been trying to give me a chance to recapture my form. That was never mentioned, though.

During the conversation there was also never any inkling that I wouldn't be starting in the season opener. You don't need to be a fan of *A Question of Sport* to guess what happened next!

We trained as usual on Friday but the manager gave no indication of who his team was going to be. During both this spell and my first at the club, I'd never been dropped and had always started every game I'd been available for, so I arrived at Edgar Street on the Saturday convinced I would be playing. As I went into the dressing room, John Trewick said the gaffer wanted to see me. I knew instantly what this meant. GT said he'd been wrestling with the decision for a couple of days but had ultimately decided to place Kris Taylor alongside Toumani Diagouraga in central midfield.

I felt severely pissed off for the second time that week.

We put in a creditable performance to secure a 0–0 draw against a strong Rotherham team while I sat on the bench and sulked for the first seventy minutes, before replacing Kris for the last part of the game. I then went home and sulked for the rest of the weekend. My dad and his girlfriend had come up to see Emma and me, but, with the mood I was in, I imagine they were happy when the weekend was over and they got to go home!

Games come thick and fast at the start of a season so I was forced to snap out of my bad mood and challenge for my place as we prepared for a League Cup game against Yeovil that coming Tuesday night. Surprisingly, bearing in mind the previous Saturday's good team performance, I was selected to play this time. The team as a whole played well and we blew Yeovil away 4–1.

But, while the team in general was brimming with confidence, I was struggling. If you hadn't been watching me specifically you probably would've said I played OK; however, if you knew me better, you would've been aware I was devoid of confidence and just playing from memory. As an experienced player, you learn to get through these games by doing things really simply until something happens to allow the confidence to flood back.

Even now, a great indication of how I'm playing is to watch what I do with the ball. If my confidence is high, I like to hold onto it and attract opposition players before releasing it to my teammates into the space created. When this isn't the case, I just move the ball really quickly, one- and two-touch only.

I kept my place in the team for the next few games – away to Barnet, Rochdale at home and Birmingham City away in the second round of the League Cup – but I was still desperately scratching around for form and got substituted all the time. If you're playing central midfield in an orthodox 4–4–2 formation, getting constantly replaced is a sure-fire indication you're not performing.

Both Trevor Benjamin and I were really disappointed as we both got dragged off after an hour against Birmingham. GT sensed this and tried to placate us by saying we were being rested for the next game. This was a little white lie on his part because I was actually dropped for the next game!

In a game against Macclesfield we reached the seventy-minute mark and the usual substitution loomed. Rather than wait for my number to come up I just started jogging off the pitch. I did not have to be Nostradamus to work out who was to come off. I wanted to make a point that I thought these substitutions were pre-planned and not always related to my performance.

Luckily for me Trent McClenahan, our right back, would be on international duty for Australia when our next match against Morecambe arrived and this meant a tactical re-shuffle. Richard Rose switched from left back to cover Trent, Kris Taylor moved to left back and I retained my position in central midfield. I am certain that if Trent had been available I would have dropped to the bench.

These small details can change a season or even a career. It was the eighth game of the season and nothing seemed to be changing for me. My confidence was low and all sorts of things were going through my mind. *Was I good enough for this level?* I was, but it didn't seem that way then. *Had my legs gone?* No, but when you're playing poorly you don't feel that fit.

The first thirty minutes against Morecambe followed the usual pattern but then, out of nowhere, confidence started flowing through my veins. I couldn't put my finger on the source but I suddenly felt relaxed and began enjoying myself. I influenced the game more and more as it went on, created a goal for Trevor Benjamin and was widely accepted to be 'Man of the Match' in a excellent 3–0 away win.

I felt like a new player and now looked forward to going to training and games. My body language transformed: I was looking the management in the eye and went from having slumped shoulders to walking with my chest out. My normal chirpy persona returned too. Our next game was a strong 4–2 victory at home against Bradford City. They were the big-hitters in our league and, not that long ago, were part of the Premier League, but we tore them apart. It felt great.We then suffered a slight blip as we lost away to Grimsby but quickly bounced back with a 3–2 win at Notts County, where I scored my first goal of the season, before comfortably dispatching Brentford.

That last game was one of those rare occasions where I knew we were going to win even the day before. On the Friday we went through our normal routine of a warm up and some small-sided games. Every player looked totally focused and on top form, even those who knew they were not going to play.

This was brilliant because those players were pushing the boys in the team and I commented to John Trewick that everyone was flying. That must have been a great feeling for the management, seeing their team looking so highly motivated. We beat Brentford 2–0 but it was as comfortable a victory you were likely to see.

My fortunes had changed so much that I was genuinely rested for a Johnstone's Paint Trophy game against Yeovil before coming straight back in for the next League game. It was early October by that point and we were second in the table. We were flying high and playing well, although the general consensus was we were not any threat to those considered the main title challengers.

We built on our success with two wins against Mansfield Town and Stockport County, which sandwiched an excellent goalless draw at home to Leeds United in the FA Cup first round. I'm not sure what that draw illustrated best: how far we had come as a club or how far Leeds had fallen. Only a few years before, I'd been playing for Hereford in the Conference while a young, vibrant Leeds team had been competing against – and beating – some of the best teams in both the Premiership and Champions League.

We were in good form leading up to the replay at Elland Road and, because Karl Broadhurst was out injured, I led the team. We scored early on and we were expecting a bombardment thereon, but we went toe to toe with them throughout. It was not your average 'David v. Goliath' clash – Leeds had chances to score but so did we.

In the end, we – and, I can say, relatively comfortably – saw the game out to add another victorious chapter to Hereford United's glorious giant-killing history.

Afterwards I had that lovely post-game sense of satisfaction both with my own and the team's performance. The following day I found out none other than Chris Waddle had named me 'Man of the Match' on BBC Radio 5 live. That gave me a real buzz as I had grown up watching and admiring Chris and his style of play.

The mood in the camp was great when we returned to work on the Thursday. After training, John Trewick asked me to come into his office. That wasn't always something to be celebrated as John's meetings had become legendary: he would just talk and talk while whoever was listening would simply nod their head in agreement as it was the only sure way of getting out within half an hour! However, on this occasion, it was short and sweet.

John said he had watched the Leeds game on DVD and thought my performance had been brilliant. That was pretty much all he said, but it made me feel a million dollars. I floated out of his office feeling like the best player in the world.

The only downside was the fact we lost Lionel to Watford; the transfer window was closed for permanent moves but the Hornets used a loophole that allowed them to sign him on a temporary loan, which turned permanent on 1 January. It was a blow but we had a readymade replacement who had been waiting patiently in the shadows – Simon Johnson. He was a child protégé at Leeds and was chomping at the bit to play.

We had Accrington Stanley at home for our next match and, before the game, GT reiterated in front of all the lads what John had said to me privately. GT, as a rule, gave out very little praise and definitely not much individually; I normally knew I had played well when he said nothing to me. So I liken that moment to what I call the 'Simon Cowell effect'. Every competitor on *The X Factor* or *Britain's Got Talent* is looking for a compliment from Cowell; when they get one, it means ten times more than one from any other judge.

The match, like so many that follow a big game, was a bit of a let down. We disappointingly drew 0–0 with Accrington, but I played really well and felt great. The Leeds game had begun the most consistent and productive run of form I ever experienced in my career – across ten games I was either 'Man of the Match' or close to it in six or seven cases.

We were now fourth and sustaining a challenge most expected to have faded away by now.

The loanees at the club were making a big impact – Toumani Diagouraga and I built up a great relationship in central midfield in particular. I had never been the most disciplined player and, when playing well, I liked to drift around the pitch. Toumani recognised this and was intelligent enough to let me do it while covering around me. He was also technically good and this allowed us to combine together effectively when we had possession. I might be biased but I would say our partnership was comparable to any other central midfield pairing in the League at that time.

Another loanee who was doing well was Theo Robinson, who had that wonderful arrogance of youth about him. No doubt in his head he was by far the best player in our team and the job of the rest of us was to get the ball to him at all times. He was, in reality, athletic, quick and very direct but he was still raw and a bit erratic on the ball. Some games his hold-up play was OK and other games it was non-existent, but a couple of the games around this time really highlighted his value to the team.

Theo, when we played away at both Wycombe and Bury, was having the type of days where he could not hold up a little kids party let alone the ball. He did however score in both games; at Bury he even turned and hit a shot with his weaker left from 18 yards which flew into the top corner. If I was playing as poorly as him I would not have dreamt of having a shot from there but Theo did and it won us the game.

The look on Steve Guinan's face when that goal went in was priceless – he had done all the donkey work throughout the ninety minutes and Theo would be getting all the plaudits.

This was in mid-December and, straight after the game, we went to Manchester airport for a two-day trip to Dublin. While having a couple of drinks at the airport Wayne Brown, our rather outspoken goalkeeper, complimented Theo on his goal but added that apart from that he had been poor, which was true. The look on Theo's face was priceless and he was amazed Wayne thought that; he was adamant he had performed exceptionally.

Everyone thought it was hilarious and gave him plenty of stick but I weirdly admired him. I often thought I was too honest with myself and wished I could have this unshakeable self-belief Theo exhibited. He was not one of those people that said stuff but did not really mean it, he genuinely believed he was brilliant. Theo could be very frustrating to play with at times but, being fair, he worked so hard for the team and was a big part of this current success.

After that trip to Dublin, which I will dub 'lively', we suffered an extended hangover as we got demolished 3–0 by Morecambe in a game which was by far my worst performance in a while. So far we had not lost two games on the trot and happily this was no exception as we ground out a workman-like victory at Macclesfield on Boxing Day. Over the hectic Christmas and New Year period we followed up that visit with a trip to play Bradford City at Valley Parade. In the pre-game warm-up a few of us were discussing how playing at such venues would become a regular occurrence the following season if we were to sustain our form. It clearly inspired us as we comfortably won the game 3–1 in front of over 13,500 fans.

That performance was a wonderful advert for the counter-attacking football that had become our trademark. We lined up with two banks of four without the ball and then utilised the pace of Simon Johnson and Theo when we regained possession. Those two, alongside Trevor Benjamin, destroyed Bradford while ably assisted by the rest of us.

I was back on top form after a couple of average outings and Toumani, Clint and I were dominating midfield.

Our away form was superb because the onus was always on our hosts to come out and attack, which played perfectly into our counter-attacking style although we found it a little trickier at home when we were expected to break the opposition down.

GT liked to break the League down into chunks – say six games – and set us both team and individual targets. He would normally expect around ten or twelve points and we were regularly hitting his targets – which also meant a few hundred quid went into the players' kitty to be spent on an end-of-season party.

People often say Cup competitions can be a distraction when you are challenging for promotion, but I think they provide a chance to forget about League pressures for a week and play a game against higher-ranked opposition with no real expectations. We had already beaten bigger and better teams though so we were really confident we could get a positive result against Tranmere Rovers.

The game was a pulsating Cup tie and a great advert for the FA Cup, finishing in a 2–2 draw. Tranmere, as you would expect being the home side, put us under real pressure in the first half. The second half was totally different, however, as we came out, went toe to toe with them and I opened the scoring with one of the best goals of my career.

We broke forward and I miss-hit a shot into a Tranmere defender just outside the box, but it bounced back to me and I hit the sort of volley you dream about. As soon as I connected I knew it was destined for the top corner. Such was the velocity of the shot, it was a good job the net was there otherwise it might have seriously hurt someone in the crowd.

In fact – and I do not use these words lightly – it was arguably my best ever performance. Aside from one sloppy pass, my display was pretty much faultless. When you are in a good run of form it can get tricky because you can be so excited for the next game that you struggle to sleep and become restless. This was the case for me, particularly as I knew the Shrewsbury game was coming up. All I could think about in the week leading up to the game was how I was going to prove Gary Peters wrong.

The game eventually rolled around and it was a horrible wet and windy Sunday in early January. A crowd of just under 5,000 crammed into Edgar Street. I loved playing in front of a big crowd at our rickety old ground. The fans were so close to the pitch that you could smell what they had been drinking (normally cider) and the atmosphere was especially rocking as the Shrews brought a good following too.

As you would expect from a local derby, the game started off competitively but it was clear to see we were the more confident of the two teams. I had so much energy that day I felt I could've run everywhere and was really relaxed in possession of the ball – always a great sign. Just so you don't think I'm simply blowing my own trumpet here, below is an excerpt taken from the *Daily Telegraph* on the Monday morning:

> The admiration was mutual as Ben Smith came off the Edgar Street pitch clapping Hereford's supporters who responded, in turn, by applauding their captain all the way down the tunnel.
>
> Deserved too, for Smith had played no small part in the victory that took the hosts back into second place. His contribution included an assist, a shot that rebounded from an upright, and a neat pass that deserved better than a wayward finish from Simon Johnson. 'He teed us up nicely,' Johnson said, 'but I wouldn't expect anything less from the lad.'
>
> Shrewsbury's fourth successive defeat led to a 'Peters Out' banner being displayed by the visiting fans, but it will take more than that for Gary Peters to resign. 'If you walk away, you are a quitter,' he said.

I was really proud to receive such words from a well-respected national paper, and just as satisfying was the mention of the chance of Gary Peters resigning.

Although a great victory for us, I did feel for some of my old colleagues at Shrewsbury. I looked at their faces and could see the pain in their eyes. Peters had done to some of them what he had done to me: if you continually tell someone they are rubbish at something they are going to believe it in the end, no matter how strong a character they are.

He had a player of the quality of Marc Pugh on the bench whom he should have been building his team around, not marginalising on the sidelines.

Still, I was happy with my own renaissance. If the season had ended then I am convinced I would have romped away with any 'Player of the Year' award.

Next up was the FA Cup replay against Tranmere. We got battered and played terribly – especially me. After a virtuoso performance in the first game, I was the opposite this time.

It was a warning and one we did not heed. We went to Saltergate for our next game against Chesterfield live in front of the Sky cameras, but were promptly torn apart. The 4–0 scoreline flattered us.

I was captain and embarrassed by both my own and the team's play. After about sixty minutes it became clear there was only going to be one winner and I was just desperate to get off the pitch and erase the debacle from my memory.

It wasn't great preparation for our fourth-round FA Cup match at home to Cardiff City. The game was scheduled to kick off early on a Sunday due to police advice. To ensure we were fully prepared, we stayed in a hotel the night before, but that didn't quite go according to plan since the hotel dished up our pre-match meal of beans on toast and cereal as our evening meal.

The match itself was a bit of a damp squib. We didn't play anywhere close to the high level we were capable of and Cardiff had a pretty comfortable afternoon, leading 2–0 until the last fifteen minutes when Theo Robinson scored for us and we pressed for an equaliser. I was relatively happy with my own performance and enjoyed pitting my wits against Stephen McPhail, who I thought was a very elegant, thoughtful midfield player.

We were in a mini-slump and, for the first time that season, we lost three games in a row. The small squad that GT and John put together was starting to feel the effects of a challenging season, especially the younger players who were not used to working towards playing fifty games. We needed a boost and the management did this by signing two strikers on loan: firstly Gary Hooper from Southend United and then Sherjill MacDonald from West Bromwich Albion.

Hoops joined us just before the Barnet game and initially I wondered why we had signed him. Southend were after all only one league above us and if he could not get in their team would he be good enough to get in ours? I could not have been more wrong.

After feeling his way in during the Barnet game, he was absolutely brilliant and in my opinion the difference between us getting promoted or not. He was ice cold in front of goal – it got to the point where he would get clean through and I would start preparing for kick-off because there was no chance he was going to miss.

As our home form hadn't been great but away we were excellent, GT, being the superstitious manager he was, decided we should prepare for our next home game against Dagenham & Redbridge by having a pre-match meal together like we did for away fixtures. So we met at the Three Counties Hotel on the Saturday morning of the Daggers game. The news that we had signed another new player, Sherjill, had broken the night before, but I knew very little about him.

It was very rare for a new player to go straight into playing for the team without having at least one training session with his new teammates but that is what was happening with Sherjill. Once we started to warm up we realised why, though.

We were going through our normal pre-game regime when Simon Johnson and I noticed Sherjill playing around with the ball. The Dutchman was doing stepovers at the speed of Ronaldo and we looked on in amazement. We didn't say anything but you could tell we were both thinking *you do not see ability like that at our level*. As I've said before, you can tell how good someone is just by watching them warm up – it definitely rang true on this occasion.

Sherjill and Hoops, even though they had never met before, absolutely destroyed Dagenham & Redbridge. The rest of us simply had to get the ball up to them as quickly and frequently as possible. Those two proved the old adage 'good players can play together' by clicking instantly. As a contest the game was over by half-time and we showed mercy by declaring at four goals, eventually winning 4–1. Sherjill scored two on his debut, Hoops got one and Johnno slotted away a coolly taken penalty.

So, after a slight lull, we were flying again. My performances had slipped a little but I was still contributing to the team. My body was screaming at me to rest, though: I was picking up little niggly injuries – nothing that stopped me playing but a warning I needed to take it easy … a warning I ignored until we played away against Rochdale.

My groin was still stiff and aching from the game on Saturday but I was not going to give up my place in the team on the off-chance I might get injured. I was named in the team and started to warm up as usual, but the stiffness in my groin was not easing. Once my body warmed up, any aches and pains normally disappeared – but they didn't on this occasion. In actual fact, the ache was getting worse; I was getting a shooting pain every time I kicked the ball. So now it was serious and there were two things I had to take into account: I didn't want to make the injury worse and, more importantly, I didn't want to let the team down. As much as I didn't want to pull out, I knew I had to.

I shouldn't have worried: Kris Taylor (or Gonzo, as he was known – and if you've met him you'll know why) took my place and played excellently as Sherjill and Hoops ripped the opposition apart. We comfortably won 4–2.

I definitely made the right decision as my groin was much sorer after the game then it was during the quite sedate warm-up (I dread to think what it would've been like if I'd attempted to play). The injury caused two problems, though. Firstly, I was out of action for ten days so it was touch-and-go for the return match at Shrewsbury, which I was desperate to play in. Secondly, as a result of my fitness issues, the club signed Stephen Glee-son on loan from Wolverhampton Wanderers and I was determined not to be sacrificed to allow him to play.

So I only missed one other game and was back training on the Thurs-day – two days before our big game against Shrewsbury. I was all over the place and looked very rusty; I nearly played myself out of the team in that session. However, as Toumani was out injured, the gaffer showed great faith by putting me straight back into the team at the expense of the unfortunate Gonzo.

I remember going into the referee's room with GT to have the usual pre-game chat with the officials and our opposite numbers. I exchanged pleasantries with Gary Peters and remember him making some sort of comment that wound me up.

We won a hard-fought game 2–1. I hadn't played as well as I had in our first meeting but I was satisfied with my performance as I'd done all the unspectacular parts of the game that Peters had always insisted I couldn't do: I broke up play and did a good job for the team.

It was a great feeling to go there and captain the team to victory. Peters was very bitter after the game and came out with a lot of comments regarding us being an amalgamation of Premiership and Championship players. He had a point, to be honest, but it all smacked of sour grapes. I'm sure if our management had the budget he had then the recruitment strategy would've been different.

A few days after the game, John Trewick spoke to GP. John told me my old manager was surprised Hereford had got me playing the way I was. We had a laugh about it and I commented it was amazing what players can produce if they're not continually being told what they can't do.

We followed this victory up with a shock defeat at Dagenham & Redbridge and a narrow loss to a fast-improving Stockport County, who were quickly coming from nowhere to become rivals for an automatic promotion spot.

Whenever we looked like we were feeling the pressure, we managed to go on a run of victories – and this was no different. We beat Accrington, followed that with an away win at Mansfield and then won a hard-fought home game against Wycombe Wanderers.

We were now in the third automatic promotion place. At the start of the season, just reaching the play-offs would've been a great achievement, but, at this point, anything less than automatic promotion would be a disappointment. Easter was coming up and we knew a good points haul would put us in a commanding position, although we suffered a blow as we were unable to extend Sherjill's loan.

We suffered a wobble when we sacrificed a two-goal lead at home to Chester City to draw 2–2, which left GT fuming. As with any poor result, we had a post-match debrief that involved going into the board room and watching all our mistakes in super-slow motion. This was especially painful for someone like me, who was slow in real time let alone in any other. GT was especially scathing about our lack of professionalism in the second goal we conceded. He felt we should've been smarter in closing the game out. The ball had gone out for a goal kick to Chester with one minute left and Toumani threw the ball back to their keeper, who duly launched it up the pitch. The gaffer told us in slightly more industrial language that the ball should have been in the Meadow End.

The gaffer did make us all laugh as well, however, when he told us that Simon Johnson had been overtaken by the referee when attempting to track back. In Simon's defence he was running up the Edgar Street hill!

We now entered a ridiculously hard run of fixtures: Darlington away, MK Dons away and Peterborough at home. The latter two were above us at that point and Darlington were hot on our heels.

We arrived at Darlington's impressive new ground and I commented that the huge TV screen in the corner – much like the ones you see at Premier League stadiums – probably cost more to maintain than the whole of Edgar Street. The ground was worthy of the top leagues in Europe so it seemed a strange decision for a club marooned in the basement of English football. Clearly the club had not learnt from its previous overindulgences and periods of financial turmoil.

The game itself had a strange atmosphere. It was a big game for both teams but, even though 4,331 fans were watching (a good crowd by Darlington's standards), they did not have much of an impact when spread across a 25,000-seater stadium. The game was, as I'd expected, a tense affair. The team that scored first was probably going to win and that turned out to be the case.

Midway through the second half Simon Johnson fed to Gary Hooper, who, after having his first shot blocked, coolly rounded the keeper, put a defender on his backside and then just rolled the ball into the net...

What a cool bastard!

We were all buzzing after that win but knew we had two massive games to come. I'd never been so desperate to get promoted. We'd pretty much taken Darlington out of the equation but Stockport had beaten Peterborough away to become our main rival.

We went to Stadium mk full of confidence and promptly got absolutely battered, although we somehow managed to hold out for a 0–0 draw. It was not a good performance, especially from an attacking perspective, but we earned a valuable point.

The final game of the trilogy was at home to Peterborough United but we got well beaten. It hurt to see them celebrating their own promotion on our pitch but the gaffer and John used it as motivation, saying we could be doing it ourselves in a couple of weeks.

We had three very winnable games lined up to clinch promotion; three victories would guarantee it.

The first game was a derby of sorts against Wrexham – a club on the verge of relegation. After a couple of early scares, we took charge of the match and eased to a comfortable victory.

Two wins to go, then – but we were also aware we could clinch promotion in our next game away to Brentford if other results also went our way.

Normally when travelling the day before an away game, we'd stop off en route and use another club's training ground or find somewhere suitable at the hotel or nearby. This was because most of the players didn't live in

Hereford so it wasn't feasible for everyone to travel to Hereford on a Friday morning before heading to the game.

There was usually a park near our hotel where we conducted a light training session, however, on this occasion, our hotel was right in the middle of west London so there wasn't any green space available. This led to a surreal experience of preparing for the biggest game of our season by training in a car park. The 'session' was regularly interrupted by office staff, from the company whose car park we had commandeered, knocking off for the weekend.

It is quite a funny memory in hindsight, but I remember a few of us not being particularly impressed at the time. The management had emphasised all week the need for us to be professional when preparing for the game and then that happened.

While Hereford didn't have a huge home support, fans always travelled in big numbers for away games and were typically vociferous – never more so than on this occasion. They filled up a stand behind one of the goals, and in the dressing room there was a great vibe between the players as we knew we were on the verge of getting the rewards for all our hard work.

Hoops, as usual, delivered the goods and got us an early goal. Theo missed a penalty but immediately redeemed himself by adding a second goal. Simon Johnson added a tap-in.

Our supporters started celebrating as if we had scored midway through the second half as it was also becoming apparent that Stockport were losing at Barnet. If the results stayed that way then we were promoted.

And they did.

What a feeling! Hereford, a club that had only a handful of players at the start of pre-season and had been tipped for relegation, had upset all the odds and won automatic promotion from League Two. When I joined the club the first time, they had nearly got relegated from the Conference, but now we were in League One, competing against the likes of Leicester City and Leeds United.

The combination of results had caught us out because we had all genuinely expected the promotion race to boil down to the last game of the season. A lot of the boys were from the south and had arranged to stay in the area after the final game so, instead of celebrating after the game we'd just played, we all went our separate ways. We still had time for the customary 'sneak up and soak the manager with a bucket of water' moment, though – the look on GT's face was priceless.

Even though it was job done, we still had one more game to play. We beat Grimsby Town at Edgar Street so made up for the muted celebrations of the previous week by partying after the game and enjoying an open-top bus ride and civic reception on the Sunday. I was a bit wary of the bus ride as I didn't believe many people would show, but there was an excellent turnout, particularly outside the town hall.

Surprisingly, considering our success, not one of our players made it into the annual PFA 'Team of the Year' even though we had some really consistent performers; Wayne Brown was as good a keeper as any in the League and I thought centre back Dean Beckwith had been superb. He defended brilliantly and was very good with the ball at his feet, something that was important considering the way we played. I also felt my midfield partnership with Toumani was comparable to any other combination in the League, although individually we may not have been as good as some of our peers.

Clint Easton had given us great balance on the left of midfield with his game intelligence and clever use of the ball. He was a man after my own heart, making up for what he lacked in physical qualities by being a couple of seconds ahead of everyone else in his head. Nobody could get near him in the small sided games in training other than on Monday mornings when he was the stiffest man in the world – he was typically still recovering from Saturday's game and any post-match exertions!

At different stages during the season I believe we had the best player in the League as well. Lionel was superb before he was sold to Watford and Gary Hooper was the main reason we got over the line during the run-in.

Hoops' goals were important but the thing that differentiated him from other centre forwards was his movement, defenders at our level could not cope with it. Gary was definitely the best outfield player I ever played with and his career trajectory has not surprised me in the slightest. He fully deserves it as well – Gary was very humble, never got carried away with his success and worked very hard.

As frustrating as he could be to play with at times Theo Robinson had also had an excellent season. For a young man to make the kind of impact he did in his first proper season of senior football was impressive. His direct running and hard work without the ball caused teams a lot of problems. I have seen him play a few times in the ensuing years and he looks to have improved both his general hold-up play and finishing too.

I think the fact none of us made it into the PFA selection was down to the fact Hereford was such an unfashionable club and so probably did not get the recognition it deserved.

I did well out of the season financially. Winning promotion triggered a clause in my contract that entitled me to a payment of £5,000 and my basic wage was set to increase from £1,200 to £1,400 a week. We picked up additional win bonuses throughout the season and, on top of that, players shared a pot of £60,000 between us, which was divided pro rata based on how many games we'd played. I ended up getting around £5,000 from that pot.

As an extra reward, the club also paid for the whole squad to go to Ayia Napa, Cyprus for a week. All accommodation was paid for and we were given some spending money.

The trip didn't quite go according to plan, however. We were booked into a nice all-inclusive hotel but I knew, almost as soon as we arrived, that it was unlikely we would make it through the whole week.

Our group of twenty excited young men checked in at around 11 p.m.

and quickly got ready to hit the town. We were buzzing around, borrowing each other's hair straighteners and gel – you know, all the usual things a group of young men do (OK, maybe that was just me then!).

Straight away a lady came out of her room complaining in some foreign language about the noise. I remember thinking *blimey, she is not happy – and she hasn't seen anything yet.*

During the first couple of days, we got up to the normal shenanigans: coming in at all hours of the morning, slamming doors and generally being a bit boisterous. Then goalkeeper Ryan Esson managed to be sick in the hotel reception. All the lads began panicking after hotel management informed them they were being ejected, but since my name and room number weren't linked to any complaints I felt secure I wouldn't be thrown out of the hotel.

I discovered my confidence was slightly misplaced when I, along with the rest of the team, was wheeling my suitcase around Ayia Napa an hour later looking for new accommodation!

Luckily Simon Johnson had frequented a local establishment during a previous visit to Cyprus that was more suited to our basic needs of a toilet, bed and bar. Unfortunately it was not all-inclusive, but my rather large bonuses cushioned any financial blow.

Writing this now I realise how lucky we were to receive fully paid club holidays, but at the time those sorts of trips seemed to be the norm – something we deserved.

I'd always been told to strike when the iron was hot so, upon my return from Cyprus, I thought I would ask for an extension on my contract. I still had a year left but it didn't feel unreasonable to ask for an extra year.

I rang up Joan Fennessy, who was club secretary and part owner, to ask for a meeting with GT. She told him while I was on the phone and I heard him shouting in the background 'if it's about a new contract he shouldn't bother'.

I can only guess I wasn't the only person who'd had that idea. However, for me, that summer was the first time in my career I felt like I was getting somewhere – like I was on the cusp of actually being a 'proper' footballer.

I certainly holidayed like one! As well as the Cyprus trip, Emma and I had a week in Zante and two weeks across Orlando and New York. I worked really hard to maintain my fitness too, knowing a huge challenge awaited me when I returned.

. . .

8 JULY 2013

I'm not sure how, but I'm close to completing a whole year at the school. There have been plenty of disastrous lessons but I finally feel like I'm getting the hang of it all – ironic really, because I've managed to secure myself a new job.

Remember the job I mentioned at Braintree Town? Well, I got it and I start in September. I will be tutoring sport every morning for two hours and then coaching football every afternoon.

I am delighted as it means I can continue my obsession with football. I want to make sure I never get myself in a position where I'm standing in front of a class attempting to teach ICT again.

I've also decided to play for Thurrock for another season. None of the jobs coaching in professional academies came to fruition so I'm going to continue playing with a view to working in an academy next season.

Things are never simple at Thurrock, however. After struggling all season and only securing our place in the Ryman Premier League three days before the end of the season, we have been retrospectively relegated. A guy called Joel Barnett played four games for us in August, one of which we won. It subsequently turned out he was banned from football, but that didn't show up when the club and local FA registered him – indeed it didn't come to light until well into the season.

So the club had three points deducted – enough to see us swap places with Carshalton Athletic and end up in the relegation zone. Thurrock appealed but the appeal was thrown out, so they have now begun the process of appealing to the European Court of Arbitration for Sport. This could have huge ramifications as none of the Ryman Premier or Division One North/South leagues will be allowed to start until the appeal has been heard. It could take up to 102 days.

This may seem an extreme course of action but for Tommy South, Thurrock's owner, it is a matter of principle. From what he's told me, the FA have a very flimsy case. It's been alleged someone at the FA made a mistake and Thurrock have been made the scapegoat for it.

I've had some really sad personal news, as well: my friend Alan Bailey passed away this weekend from cancer. I'm devastated and quite angry. Alan had been complaining for some time about problems with his breathing but his hospital continued to misdiagnose him. I keep thinking that if they'd got to the cancer earlier they may have been able to treat it. Instead, it has beaten him in four months.

He taught me when I was a student and was instrumental in getting me my job at the school. Obviously that didn't quite turn out as hoped, but it was through no fault of his. Alan was a great man who only wanted the best for his pupils.

Often I hear people saying nice things about someone when they pass away and think: 'You're only saying that because they've died. In reality, they weren't that nice a person.' On this occasion, however, I know every tribute is totally sincere as he was a wonderful man.

When I first did voluntary work at the school I used to come home to Emma and say teaching was easy. I thought that because Alan made it look easy. When I started teaching by myself though, I soon realised that wasn't the case. He was especially skilled at dealing with the more awkward characters; I've tried to use some of his techniques myself but with limited success.

Although I'm not continuing my secondary school teaching career, Alan has inspired me to become the best football coach I can be. His influence will play a big part in any future success I may achieve.

Alan – thanks for your help and support. Without it, I would never have made it through the year. I will miss you greatly and hopefully I will see you on the other side one day.

CHAPTER 19

A FALSE DAWN

SEASON: 2008/09
CLUB: HEREFORD UNITED
DIVISION: LEAGUE ONE
MANAGER: GRAHAM TURNER (GT)

AFTER THE EUPHORIA of the previous season, I was excited. This was going to be the highest level I had played at as a key member of a squad.

I was also aware that we were in big trouble. Last season, GT and John Trewick had come up with the strategy of supplementing a reliable core of permanent players with talented loanees. Some of those lads were clearly too talented for our level but needed to gain experience playing 'proper games', where points and livelihoods were at stake, rather than the tamer stuff they were accustomed to in the reserves and youth teams.

The problem was retaining the loanees. They would go back to their parent club to compete for a place in the first team or get loaned out to (or bought by) a higher-ranking club that Hereford had absolutely no chance of competing with financially.

When the fact we also lost some permanent players the club would've liked to have kept was factored in, we had a much weakened squad for our assault on League One. Goalkeeper Wayne Brown departed when the club offered him a small pay rise after his great season. He was, to put it mildly, very disappointed and there was not much chance of him re-signing after that. Trevor Benjamin, who played brilliantly in the first-half of last season before he got an eye injury, was also released alongside John McCombe, who had been solid in defence.

I was suddenly the top goalscorer left from the promotion season squad with a less than impressive six goals to my name.

In hindsight, the management should have pushed the boat out and signed some experienced players. They instead persevered with the same strategy, but the temporary players coming in had nowhere near the same kind of impact.

What that showed was that, while the plan to get us into League One was genius, it was all in vain if there was not an effective strategy for making sure we stayed there.

Pre-season began well and I scored twice in a comprehensive victory against local team Ledbury Town. We then drew 2–2 against a strong Birmingham City team at their training ground. After that it was an unmitigated personal disaster as I began scratching around for form. John Trewick noticed it straight away and thought I was trying too hard. He was probably right as I ended up getting frustrated with myself and, in turn, became less effective. I toiled through but was still not happy with my performances as we reached the week before our first competitive game. There was one friendly left (away to Wrexham); I was not due to play but asked to anyway.

We lost 2–1 but I felt a little bit better about myself afterwards. Incidentally, our goal was scored by a young Ashley Barnes, who went on to play for Brighton and Hove Albion and Burnley. He looked raw and was a real handful but GT decided against taking him on loan.

The management decided we should play a 4–5–1 or 4–3–3 for our first game against Leyton Orient, depending on how much of the ball we had.

We had experimented with this formation during the friendlies but the lads were not really buying into it. At the time, that style of play was quite a new concept. We had enjoyed the vast majority of our success playing a tried and tested 4–4–2 but we were pretty much forced into this new style of play through our lack of strikers.

Dean Beckwith, one of our stand-out performers from the previous season, gave us an early lead, but it didn't give us the boost we'd hoped for and we deservedly lost 2–1. Orient were no great shakes but we looked like a team that didn't believe it was good enough to be at that level.

My performance mirrored my team's and I was dragged off before the end. My former teammate Tamika Mkandawire marshalled me with ease and barely broke sweat. I was still desperately searching for some sort of form.

The gaffer was not happy and we had an inquest on the Monday morning – something that became a pretty regular occurrence that season. However, he persevered with the same style of play for our League Cup game against Crystal Palace at Selhurst Park.

We lost 2–1 to a Victor Moses-inspired Palace, but during the game I had that sudden feeling you get when you start to regain some form. Palace won pretty comfortably but I felt good and thought I had turned a corner. I wanted to be influencing games like I had during the vast majority of my two spells at Hereford, but I had to bear in mind the fact that the quality of players and teams we were up against was of a different level.

Just three games into the season and it was already getting to the stage at which I was struggling to see where our first win was going to come from.

Next up was a trip to the Memorial Ground to play Bristol Rovers. I had always loved playing there as they had a really vociferous crowd who created a great atmosphere. I also knew their passionate fans would turn against them if we could keep the score level for the first thirty minutes.

Craig Sansom, one of our new goalkeepers, had joined us from Scotland. Before the game I warned him about Rovers' centre forward, Rickie

Lambert, whom I likened to Matt Le Tissier. I told Craig that he loved to hit shots from distance.

The advice worked really well as we managed to keep Lambert quiet for a total of seven minutes before he smashed in a great strike from about 30 yards…

To make it worse, this was not even the first goal – we had already gone a goal behind after three minutes. Their strike force of Lambert and Daryl Duffy was cutting through us like a hot knife through butter. The game was effectively over after twenty-two minutes as we went 3–0 down.

Ironically we were playing quite well on the ball and enjoyed a lot of possession. The problem came when we didn't have the ball. By the seventy-eighth minute, Lambert had curled their fifth goal into the top corner via a 25-yard free kick. I was still captain and had never felt so embarrassed on a football pitch.

All I wanted was for the final whistle to go so I could get changed, go home and lock myself in the house for the rest of the weekend. Unfortunately Rovers had not finished handing out the punishment and still had time for a sixth goal. Steve Guinan did manage to nick a goal for us but we still lost 6–1. As I'm sure you can imagine, almost 7,000 enthusiastic Bristolians thoroughly enjoyed it.

Now, you are probably assuming that after a result like that us players faced some severe repercussions – GT giving the hairdryer treatment, players arguing with each other etc. Sorry to disappoint, but that wasn't the case. Maybe that was our problem though – we were all just too nice. The gaffer and John just said the usual lines about the result being unacceptable (as if we needed to be told – although, saying that, we did have a few players who were a little deluded, so maybe we did).

The results were confirming what many of us senior players had suspected from the off: our squad was not good enough. We would probably have been struggling in League Two, let alone League One, and I believe we would've been battered by our team from the previous season.

That week officially saw the club hit the panic button. The management was keen to make changes after our heavy loss so a midweek reserve-team match was arranged against a young Aston Villa side to give other players some game time. This plan massively backfired though as Hereford got spanked 7–1. I wonder if a club has ever had a worse week!?

We had dabbled with 4–4–2 but, after Bristol, we reverted back to 4–5–1 with a tweak to the midfield. It worked particularly well for this game as Crewe played a 4–4–2, allowing us to put pressure on their central midfield players. We went on to win the game 2–0, which was a great relief and meant we were picking up our first points of the season. You could almost feel the pressure being lifted from our shoulders; after the game, we all took a deep breath and relaxed. What that led to is something I witnessed throughout my career and is what I think separates top players from us also-rans. Everyone instantly became visibly relaxed and the whole place became a happier environment but I think, instead of taking our foot off the pedal, we should've been channelling the hurt we'd felt after the Bristol Rovers game and the intensity we'd trained with leading up to the Crewe game. We had only won one game, after all. That isn't necessarily a criticism of the management as this pattern happened at every club I had ever played at; it is just more of an observation.

We consolidated our win with a home draw to Swindon, but our mini-revival came to a swift end when we lost our next game away to Southend United – one of my former clubs.

Our results clearly showed we were not good enough so, as you would expect, the gaffer continued trying to strengthen our squad and he did so by adding former Everton and Plymouth Argyle striker Nick Chadwick. Nick made a great early impression by putting us 1–0 up on his debut at home against Scunthorpe United. That game also marked the return of Gary Hooper to Edgar Street.

We were still ahead at half-time and GT praised me for conscientiously tracking back during the break, which was unusual as he very rarely gave out praise and I very rarely tracked back.

Ten minutes into the second half, though, Scunthorpe equalised. The ball was played into Gary Hooper's feet and, being the clever midfielder I thought I was, I tried to nick the ball from the front. I should have known better because Gary's touch was as immaculate as usual and the midfielder I was supposed to be marking ran off the back of me. Before I knew it, Hoops had flicked the ball into him and the midfielder had smashed it into the back of the net.

I instantly knew I was at fault. If I hadn't tried to be so clever and had just stayed with my man, the goal would not have happened. Within five minutes, the inevitable had happened: Hoops had got his customary goal and we'd lost the game 2–1.

My lapse in concentration had shifted the whole momentum of the game. I was really frustrated with myself. Ironically I had played quite well but, at that higher level, any little mistake I made was punished. So far in the season, I had already been directly at fault for two goals that had cost us points.

GT was fuming and made a specific point about how he had praised me for my diligent defensive work and I had then switched off. I might be paraphrasing him slightly, but I'm pretty sure he said: 'I don't know why I fucking bother!'

Even more concerning for me was the fact I'd made a high-profile error in the weekend preceding one of the biggest games of our season. We were due at Elland Road to play Leeds United and, after winning and performing so well there the season before, I was desperate to play.

A couple of days before the game, the gaffer added to the squad again with the temporary signing of Bruno N'Gotty, who had played for the likes of Lyon, PSG, Marseille and AC Milan. It was an amazing coup for our club but what I admired most was the fact he was willing to come and play for a team of our stature when he was no doubt financially set up for life. He was coming to the end of his career and sitting on a nice, chunky contract at Leicester City, but he wanted to play first-team football rather than just sit in the reserves.

His class was immediately evident. One thing I hated as a midfield player was having my passes read by the opposition. I prided myself on being able to punch them through at such a pace that my opposite number couldn't intercept them or to put enough disguise on them that I fooled my opponent. However, during his first couple of training sessions, Bruno read my passes so comfortably that it felt like he knew where they were going before I did!

In the week leading up to the Leeds game we did a lot of work on the shape of our team. It was clear we were going to change our formation and revert back to five in midfield. What was also clear was that it was between Simon Johnson and I for the position just off the striker. John Trewick, who led the vast majority of training sessions, kept interchanging us for that role.

I was wary because I knew GT had a knack for playing people against their former clubs, thinking they would feel as though they had something to prove. Simon had spent many years at Leeds, both as a schoolboy and a professional, so, adding that to my lapse in concentration the previous week, it was not looking good for me.

We travelled up to Yorkshire on the Friday and stopped off to train at what is now the St George's Park training complex (back then it was just a collection of nicely manicured football pitches). The team was not confirmed that day but it seemed clear that I was going to be left out.

It was confirmed the following day and a very disgruntled midfielder took his place on the bench. The game itself was a non-event – we lost 1–0 but it was as one-sided a 1–0 as you will ever see. I managed a ten-minute cameo on the wing.

As I'd got older, though, I'd realised I couldn't let managers get away with leaving me out without getting an explanation. After all, if it wasn't clear what I'd done wrong then how could I rectify it?

The process of seeking out an explanation was a little different at Hereford United. Normally I'd have a chat with the manager, but because Graham was both the manager and the chairman he was always very busy. So how it worked was you spoke to John Trewick, unless it was something really important.

I had been stewing all weekend about not playing and went straight in to see John on Monday morning. Meetings with him could often be long, drawn-out affairs and normally took the following format: ask a question; John rocks back in his chair and brushes his hands through his very-impressive-for-a-man-of-his-age hair; question is answered with a question.

On this occasion, I asked him why I had been left out of the team and it went something like this:

JT: Why do you think you have been left out of the team?

Me: Well, if I have been left out for my performance last week then that is unfair, but if I was dropped because of my mistake then I can understand that.

JT: No, you have not been left out because of the mistake; we just wanted to freshen things up.

Me: Well, I'm not happy then as I thought my overall performance last week was good.

JT: It was.

Me: So I was dropped because of the goal?

JT: No, but you were at fault for the first goal, which changed the whole game.

Me: OK, we are going round in circles here but it seems pretty clear why I was left out.

John just gave me a knowing look. I knew I had to take responsibility for my mistakes and I had no problem with that, but what frustrated me was not getting a straight answer.

Whether my little whinge worked or not I don't know, but I was named in the team during training the day before a home game against Walsall. Unfortunately I fell ill on the Friday night and missed out. I was back available for the next game away at Oldham and it looked likely I would play until, I think, I managed to take myself out of contention with a very sloppy and lethargic performance in training on the Thursday.

Missing the Oldham game turned out to be a blessing in disguise as we put in an abject performance and got absolutely battered 4–0. I spent the majority of the second half drinking as much water as possible as it was made known that I had been selected for a random drugs test.

I personally had to wait a full five weeks and six games before I got another start – at the New Den against Millwall. In the past, I might've gone off the rails after not being involved for so long but I had matured and knuckled down by this point and ensured I was ready to play when selected. There was not much chance of us putting a ten-game unbeaten run together so I knew I wouldn't have to wait too long.

We got beaten 1–0 but put up a really good fight, only losing to a goal in the last ten minutes. I started the match like someone who had not played for a month, but soon warmed to the task and put in a strong performance. Playing at the New Den was a real eye-opener. It's not often you get shown the middle finger and called every name under the sun by both dads and their eight-year-old sons! In a perverse way, I really enjoyed it.

The Millwall game was in late October and from then until Christmas I managed to stay in the team and be captain whenever Karl Broadhurst wasn't available. Our results were still poor, illustrated by a disappointing defeat to Dagenham & Redbridge in the first round of the FA Cup, but we were picking up the odd result and just about hanging in there.

During this period I was starting to find some decent form. I felt I was finally competing at League One level and had eradicated the silly mistakes I'd been making – at least until we played Tranmere Rovers at home on Boxing Day.

It was a tight game and, by the start of the second half, finely poised at 1–1. At around the hour mark, Kris Taylor – my good friend and gym buddy – won the ball and gave me a horrible pass on the edge of our box with me facing our goal. Looking back, I take it as a compliment that he thought a man of my ability would be able to deal with it.

But, if that *was* the case, he was wrong…

I should have just smashed the ball into row Z but as that goes against all my principles I tried to wriggle my way out of trouble with my trademark Cruyff turn (OK, technically it is Johan's, but you know what I mean). Unfortunately, the opposition either knew I would do this or I executed it very poorly. Either way, I got dispossessed and the ball was in the back of our goal before I knew it. Thankfully Steve Guinan rescued a point with a great finish to ensure the game finished at 2–2. I had recovered enough from my mistake to create a goal but, even with nearly half the season still remaining, it had become pretty clear home draws would not be good enough to keep us in the League.

Even more worrying was the fact we had Leicester City away in the next game. I had already missed the Leeds game due to an error and I was concerned my very recent history was going to repeat itself.

Fortunately I kept my place for our visit to the Walkers Stadium, where just under 23,000 people were packed in. We went 2–0 down, fought back to 2–1, but couldn't salvage anything from the game.

Once again the plucky underdog came up short but this now seemed to be a regular occurrence. We were competitive throughout against Leicester and put in a decent performance. I was happy with the way I had personally played but still got a footballing lesson from the opposition.

You've probably deduced that the season had, up to that point, been pretty depressing, but one incident helped lift the mood. The FA and UK Sport had brought in a new rule during the season regarding drug testing whereby you had to text or call UK Sport on your day off and give them an hour slot where someone could pop round and test you if they so desired.

Not an overly testing task, you'd imagine. What most people did was text them a time they would be in bed – between, say, 5.30 and 6.30 a.m. – so it didn't disrupt their day. If memory serves me correct, you had to text your name, location, the hour slot and your club.

Unfortunately a lot of players were struggling with this and kept forgetting to text. Every time you forgot and UK Sport picked up on it you would get a strike, and three strikes meant you were liable for punishment. Many players across the Football League were on the cusp of being reprimanded.

One morning Graham called a meeting to tell us the club had been warned by the FA and UK Sport that its players were either forgetting to text in their details or doing so incorrectly. The example he gave us was Kris Taylor. Kris had not forgotten to text, but he'd only sent his name and the time he was available, meaning the testers had no idea where he was…

Everyone was having a chuckle and I asked Kris if he thought UK Sport was like Father Christmas and just knew where he lived. Believe it or not, Kris was one of the more intelligent members of our group.

In actual fact, I think this situation illustrates how players can be overly mollycoddled and how, as a result, some struggle when asked to think for themselves.

It was the start of January and, after Leicester, we hadn't had a game for two weeks through a combination of our home League fixture against Leeds being cancelled and us already having been knocked out of the FA Cup.

The transfer window had opened, however. Given we were struggling so much, it was obvious there would be additions to the squad. There were plenty of positions in the team the management wanted to strengthen; unfortunately for me, they secured someone in mine.

The club made a double loan signing from Manchester United – Febian Brandy, a centre forward, and Sam Hewson, a central midfielder, both arrived. I knew straight away I was in trouble – you never got bad players from Manchester United and Sir Alex Ferguson didn't let them out on loan unless they were guaranteed to play.

I wasn't going to give up my place without a fight, however, so I made sure I worked even harder and was even bubblier than usual that week in training as it was clear my position was under the most threat.

My strategy made absolutely no difference as I was left out of the next game against Oldham Athletic at home. We won 5–0 mainly down to virtuoso performances from Steve Guinan, who scored a hat-trick, and Lionel Ainsworth, who scored a brace and generally tore them to shreds. Lionel had returned to us on loan from Watford less than a year after going in the opposite direction.

What a player Lionel had the potential to be! He had lightening pace, great technique and a wonderful footballing brain. The only thing holding him back was himself and his lack of mental strength. If he had managed to develop that he could have gone on to be whatever he wanted.

After such an amazing result I decided to make myself as comfortable as possible on the bench as it seemed I would be there for a while…

Luckily for me, though admittedly not so much for him, Sam Hewson picked up an injury and I was back in the team for a 1–1 draw at Walsall. Both the team and I played well and probably deserved to win the game. I retained my place for the midweek game at home to Millwall too, but we lost 2–0.

Next up was Stockport away. Sam's fitness was touch-and-go as he only played a very small part in Friday's training session. We did some work on our set plays and I was involved in all of them – another strong indicator that I would be playing the following day. I went home that night as certain as I could be that I would be in the team.

After the pre-match meal we had a meeting at the hotel and the gaffer named the team; I was on the bench and very annoyed. I had no problem with being left out when there was a level playing field, but I knew at that moment in time that I had no chance of playing, irrespective of my performance.

Obviously this was no criticism of Sam, who just wanted to play first-team football and gain some experience, but it was no good to me.

That was the first time I smelt a rat. As I mentioned earlier, I had a clause in my contract that meant I got another year's contract on the same wages after thirty starts. I knew the club was aware of this because Jamie Pitman had told me they were keeping an eye on it.

We lost the Stockport game 4–1, but Sam did get our only goal so maybe starting him was the right decision. When I turned up at Edgeley Park I wasn't quite as devastated to be left out since the pitch looked as though a herd of cows had just been taken off it. You wouldn't have wanted to have a kickabout on it, let alone a professional football match.

The defeat seemed to galvanise us, though, as we went on to beat both Cheltenham away (in a game where my replacement scored twice) and Leeds United at home. We followed that up with a defeat against Peterborough and a home win versus Leyton Orient. We'd been looking dead and buried, but those three positive results had given us an outside chance of salvaging something from the season. Our next game away to Crewe Alexandra brought us back down to earth though – we lost again.

We were due to play Bristol Rovers at home next and I really wanted to put in a good performance as we were still smarting from the annihilation we suffered in the reverse fixture. The gaffer named the team and I was in it. On this occasion, John gave me one of the most underwhelming pep talks I ever had the pleasure of receiving. It went like this:

> JT: You're playing against Craig Disley today; he likes to make a lot of forward runs and you aren't very good at tracking them.
> Me: OK.
> JT: We need to try to exploit them with longer passes, but you haven't got a very good range of passing.
> Me: OK.

JT: However, you are good at twisting and turning with the ball so stay
on it and don't panic when we have good possession.
Me: OK. (*Read: Thank God for that – at least I'm good at something!*)

I may have paraphrased John a little, but that was the general gist of the conversation.

All that advice was immaterial anyway as we got torn to shreds by Rickie Lambert again – he scored a hat-trick within an hour, decided that was enough pain for one game and Rovers comfortably saw out a 3–0 win.

John was right about Craig Disley and me, though – Craig did like to make forward runs and I wasn't very good at tracking them. I know this because I remember quite vividly one occasion when he ran off me and nearly scored. It sticks in my mind because I was near the dugout and I can still hear the expletives GT shouted at me now.

It felt obvious I would be left out of the next match and when you've just been part of a heavy defeat, irrespective of your own thoughts on your performance, you don't really have a leg to stand on.

I sat in the dressing room before the Southend United game, waiting for the inevitable, and, sure enough, I wasn't named in the team. I waited for confirmation that I was on the bench, but that didn't come either – I was left out of the squad entirely.

As a group of players we were doing terribly so I had just as much right to be left out of the squad as anyone else. What made me so angry was the fact I was club vice-captain and had had nearly four and a half years of success under the manager. I thought the least I deserved was an explanation. After all, how was I expected to know what they wanted me to work on without one? Mind you, after John's 'pep' talk before the Bristol Rovers game, it didn't take Einstein to work the answer out.

We lost the Southend game narrowly 1–0, but my punishment was prolonged as I travelled all the way up to Scunthorpe too just to sit in the stand and watch us get beaten 3–0.

The gaffer was fuming after that game and scheduled a meeting the following Thursday to discuss what was going wrong. 'If anyone has anything to say they should say it on Thursday,' he announced. That was like a red rag to a bull: I was wound up and had plenty to say.

Thursday came and GT called the aforementioned meeting. We were all sat in the gym and he opened discussion up to the floor. As usual, everyone had been moaning in private but nobody wanted to be the first to speak.

'Who has got something to say?' he asked.

No one spoke so he repeated the question.

'I've got something to say,' I said. 'Why do we not work on the shape of the team any more? Why don't you warn people who haven't played for a while that they are going to start before naming the team an hour and a half before the game? Why don't you explain to people why they have been left out?'

Well, this clearly hit a nerve and GT went for me. 'Would working on the team shape make you track your runners? Would letting someone know they are playing make you track your runners?'

Ouch.

'I appreciate that is something I have to work on, but it's not relevant to what I've just asked,' I replied.

GT was clearly not happy and it was becoming a personal slanging match. I found his reaction quite strange as he'd asked for people's opinions but become very defensive upon receiving them. My speaking up worked, though, as it led to other players putting their thoughts across and getting some of our other issues out in the open.

I was really disappointed though and I lost a bit of respect for GT that day. I knew he had a tough job being both the manager and the chairman of the club – and he no doubt had an abundance of issues to deal with – but if he'd had a problem with me we should've talked about it in private. That meeting was not meant to be about my deficiencies but about the team's, so I don't think he should've been taking out his frustrations on someone who, on the whole, had done well for him.

I was still unhappy the next day and went in early to speak to John. I asked him if the gaffer had a problem with me. He gave me that incredulous look he had mastered and rocked back in his chair.

'What makes you say that, Smudger?' he said. I, rather flippantly, referred him back to the previous day's 'discussion', but John assured me there was no problem and I'd only got the thick end of the stick because I was the first one to pipe up. I wasn't totally convinced by his explanation but decided to let sleeping dogs lie and get on with it.

By the way, if you're wondering who 'Smudger' is, that would be me. As I'm sure you're aware, footballers are not known for giving their teammates imaginative nicknames. Having a surname like Smith meant Smudger was the most obvious option; however, bearing in mind some of the other deficiencies I had, I wasn't going to disagree with the moniker.

Next up was Swindon Town at their County Ground. I had somehow managed to get myself back in the match-day squad and watched from the bench as we were comfortably beaten 3–0 again. I came on for the last twenty minutes, replacing Sam – who had picked up an injury that actually finished his time at Hereford. Obviously it was a disappointing way for him to end his spell, but it meant I had an opportunity to get that thirty-game mark required to trigger my new deal – although it was by no means a foregone conclusion that I would be back in the team.

Next up was the trip everyone looked forward to – Carlisle away!

I got the nod and not only did we win 2–1 but I scored as well, my first of the season (an embarrassing stat for an attacking midfielder like me, but an indication of how poor the season had been personally). It was also one of my best performances of the season, although my frailties nearly came to the fore again.

I was having a great midfield battle with Carlisle's old warhorse Graham Kavanagh but, early in the second-half, he exposed my Achilles heel by making a run off the back of me. I held my breath as he ran through but, luckily, he hit a post and we scrambled it away. If that had gone in I very much doubt I would have had much involvement in the rest of the season.

The result was a false dawn as we didn't win a single game in our remaining nine fixtures. I managed to stay in the team for the majority of those and put in a couple of good displays against Hartlepool United and Leicester City, plus a terrible one against Tranmere Rovers. We lost the Tranmere game 2–1, but it was especially poor as it confirmed the inevitable: our relegation back to League Two.

According to my calculations, I'd made twenty-nine starts by then and there were four games remaining. I was left out of our next game versus Colchester United and was pretty sure it was due to the contract clause. In fairness though, after my abject performance in the previous game I did deserve to be dropped.

I was now in a quandary because it seemed clear I wouldn't play another game thanks to the clause in my contract: should I go to see GT and tell him I would waive the clause to at least play some more and put myself in the shop window; or should I play dumb, sit tight and hope I'd just been dropped because of my poor performance?

After the defeat to Colchester I decided to give the situation more time to develop and, to my surprise, I was named in the team away to my former club Yeovil Town. This guaranteed me another year's contract – or so I believed. I wasn't expecting it but I also wasn't going to look a gift horse in the mouth.

Even though I was recalled to the team, I'd seemingly lost my role as vice-captain. Nothing was said directly; the gaffer just named the team and announced Steve Guinan was captain. He'd easily been our best player all season and deserved it, but, then again, I would've appreciated a subtle word explaining the situation beforehand – even if it was just: 'You've been rubbish and don't deserve to lead the team.'

The Yeovil game encapsulated the embarrassment our season had inflicted on the club and its supporters. We started the game well and went 2–0 up before an inevitable collapse. Huish Park erupted and their players went off celebrating like they'd just won the FA Cup, which was understandable as it confirmed Yeovil's safety in League One for another season. I, on the other hand, just wanted the ground to open up and swallow me. It felt like everyone was laughing at us. In the grand scheme of things, the result meant very little – but it dented my professional pride.

There was a huge change at the club before our next game away at North-ampton. GT decided to step down as manager and John took over the reins.

Obviously it was a shame GT stood down in such disappointing circum-stances. After saving Hereford United from the brink of bankruptcy and turning the club into a profit-making organisation, he deserved to go out in a blaze of glory – but he was doing what he thought was best for the club.

From a personal perspective, I didn't think the change of management would have much of an effect on my future, whatever that may be.

We lost 2–1 in Northampton but put in what was a decent performance for us. A few things John did then made me question his managerial cre-dentials. During his first team talk he gave an aggressive speech making it clear that if you 'didn't do what he wanted' you'd be removed from the pitch 'irrespective of the time in the game'.

I never liked such threats as I felt they put players on edge before a game had even started. We were unfortunate not to get a result at Northampton but, in Monday's debrief, John again blamed me for us conceding a decisive goal.

The ball had gone in to their striker Akinfenwa on the edge of our box so, as one of our defenders marshalled him tightly from behind, I tried to nick the ball from the front. I was unsuccessful and he laid it back to my former Arsenal youth-team colleague Jason Crowe who smashed it in from 25 yards.

I was definitely partially at fault for the goal of course but to lay all the blame at my feet seemed harsh. However, this season had highlighted the fact I did have a problem with following the ball rather than staying with my man.

That was always a weakness of mine, even as I remember all the way back to my days as a schoolboy at Arsenal. Fred, my then coach and whose surname eludes me, would say after almost every game that I was great going forward but not as good defensively.

Unfortunately, we were getting battered most weeks. Defending was all I was doing – and I clearly wasn't doing it very well. I remember once reading a quote from Johan Cruyff: 'If a defender has to sprint, it's too late.' I think that summed up my defensive skills. I'd regularly think *oh shit* when someone ran off me, but by then it would usually be too late.

We finished our season at home to MK Dons. We lost and my performance was pathetic; I was anonymous until I managed to be at fault for their winning goal. I looked over to the bench and John was going ballistic. Before the ball had been returned to the centre spot, my number was up and I'd scuttled off the pitch without making eye contact with him.

I was embarrassed. I didn't recognise this player who, just a year earlier, had been dominating games from midfield. GT came in after and thanked us for our efforts, but I wasn't really listening as we all knew he was just going through the motions.

John added that he would be contacting everyone by phone regarding the club's plans for next season. There was no last debrief or meeting – that probably told a story itself.

It was fine by me though – I just wanted to go home and forget about the whole season. I thought I'd triggered the clause in my contract entitling me to another year but I was sceptical because nobody at Hereford had confirmed anything.

Within a week of the season finishing, while I was in my office working on my degree, John rang to inform me that every player would be getting a letter from the club saying they had been released. Some, however, would be getting contract offers.

That was a naughty move and an unethical way of doing things. How it normally works is if a Football League club offers you a contract, they have to confirm it in writing. Once you get the confirmation, you have twenty-eight days to accept or reject the offer. It is a legally binding document.

If, after twenty-seven days, the club decides to retract the offer but the player wants to accept, they then have to stand by the offer or agree a settlement with the player. So, by telling us all we had been released, Hereford could then give verbal offers that it could withdraw whenever it liked.

John went on to say my £1,400 per week contract was massive – which I took as a compliment to my negotiating skills – and that if I were to stay he would be looking at me taking a pay cut of 50 per cent. I took the opportunity to tell John I was entitled to another year on the same money and I heard the deep gulp he took before saying he would call me back.

Within ten minutes, Joan Fennessy, the club secretary, called to inform me that I was not entitled to another year as, even though I had made thirty-two starts, only twenty-nine of them were in the League. What a coincidence…

She also added that, because we'd been relegated, I was only entitled to £750 per week. I explained the £750 per week deal was only if we got relegated to the Conference and, as far as I was aware, we'd only been demoted to League Two. I told her I would have to look at my contract to confirm this.

There was one small problem with me looking at my copy of the contract: I couldn't find it! In the end, I had to ring the FA and get a copy faxed over. Unfortunately, it confirmed what Joan had said about the thirty League starts.

John rang back and said he knew I wouldn't be in a rush to accept a 50 per cent pay cut but that he would give me a call in June to discuss the situation.

I was really disappointed – not so much with the contract offer but with the way the management had blatantly stopped me reaching the thirty-game mark. I understood the financial landscape had changed since I'd signed the contract, but what I didn't understand was why GT hadn't just pulled me to one side and discussed the situation. If we'd had a meeting then I'm sure we could've come to an agreement. Instead, management had pretended to know nothing about the situation and basically insulted my intelligence.

If I was someone who'd done nothing at all for the club then I might've had some sympathy for the management. However, bearing in mind the overall contribution I had made, I felt I deserved at least an admission as to why they did what they did.

I also learnt a lesson – the only mistake I made in my negotiations with Hereford was I should have insisted on an extra year's contract in the event of promotion, rather than based on the number of games played in my last season.

The clause I had was worthless – detrimental, in actual fact. If a player has such a clause, not only do they not get their new contract if the club wishes them not to, but they also don't get the opportunity to play and impress another prospective employer.

Don't get me wrong – I personally had a poor season. But, the year before, I (along with a lot of my teammates) made big contributions in getting the club promoted. In my opinion, there was no reason why we couldn't, with some decent additions, do it again. To get rid of players, or make very little attempt to keep them, seemed a short-sighted approach to me.

The more I thought about it, the more I was determined not to take the mooted offer. The reason I say mooted is because John never formally offered me the revised contract. Out of principle, I decided I would find a new club. It was a big decision as both my girlfriend and I were again settled and happy, but she understood the life of a footballer.

It was a really disappointing way for everything to end and I didn't want my legacy at Hereford to be that last season. I'd thoroughly enjoyed my two spells at the club on the whole, having built up a great rapport with the supporters and enjoyed working for GT. I'd lost a little bit of respect for him with the way my exit was handled, but I'd learnt a lot and he'd really helped my career. When I'd re-joined the club, I'd wanted to stay for a long time and really make myself a home in Herefordshire.

I wasn't going to kid myself into thinking any League One clubs would want me, but, after the season before last, I was confident there would be some interest from within League Two.

Even though it had been a terrible season, I'd still made forty appearances, including thirty-two starts, although I'd hit just one goal.

. . .

26 JULY 2013

Somehow I've managed it – I have completed a school year and discovered a newfound respect for teachers. Before I started I thought I'd be waltzing into school at about 8 a.m. and be home by 4 p.m. – how wrong was I?!

I was in school, more often than not, by 7.30 a.m. and often didn't leave until 5 p.m., doing between forty-five and fifty hours a week, split between the school and work I did at home. When you think I was earning £410 a week, that works out at a pretty poor hourly wage.

What about all the holidays you got, I hear you say? Correct – there were a lot of holidays, but if you think teachers just sit at home and relax then you are sorely mistaken. Those breaks were a godsend as they either allowed me to get ahead of the game and do some planning or marking, or they enabled me to catch up and keep my head above water – more often than not I was doing the latter.

It's strange: I've been looking forward to leaving for so long but now it's finally happened the buzz isn't the same. On the last day I even started thinking that maybe I'd done the wrong thing – but that thought only lasted about a minute before I started thinking about all the hours struggling in front of those ICT classes.

The day I left was strange. As a footballer you're normally ushered quietly out of the back door, but at school I was given gifts by the business, ICT and PE departments – and also some of the kids.

The gifts included a manual called PCs for Dummies (I could've done with that a year ago!), a book about publishing your own book (hopefully reading that has paid off!), a football from the Year 10 team I very unsuccessfully tried to coach all season, and a picture of the Year 7 PE class from hell (by the end of the year, I was actually starting to make progress with those nutters).

That represented what I've enjoyed most about the job: building relationships with the kids. There were many facets I was poor at, but this was something I definitely had an aptitude for. I talked to the kids on their level and, in actual fact, felt more comfortable talking to them than I did to many of the staff.

What I like is that kids don't have any airs and graces: they tell you what they think and don't care about the effect it has on your ego. Over the course of my year, I've been told I have grey hair, a wonky jaw, a bent nose and a lazy eye. All deficiencies I'm well aware of – mainly due to my mates who I grew up with – but I don't think you can ever be told these sorts of things too often!

CHAPTER 20

ON THE MOVE AGAIN

PRE-SEASON 2009/10 - bearing in mind the way it had ended with Hereford, it was unlikely I would be returning, so it looked like Emma and I were on the move again. We made a conscious decision to either try to find a club around the Midlands, so we could stay in Worcester, or one in the south east, so we could move back to Essex. I was thirty now and not sure I wanted to keep traipsing around the country on one-year deals.

I still had no agent so I did my usual trick and sent my CV to every club in those two regions. I was experienced enough to know that if anything were to come from this exercise it would normally happen within the first week of sending them out.

Sure enough, within that time frame, I had three phone calls – one each from Crawley Town, Macclesfield Town and Mansfield Town. None of them really got me excited, to be honest, but I thought it only right I spoke to them.

First to call was Gee Evans from Crawley – chief scout and brother of their infamous manager Steve. He made all the right noises, telling me if I dropped into the Conference I would be the best midfielder in the League. His words lacked a bit of sincerity but were nice to hear nonetheless. Steve Evans wanted to have a face-to-face chat so we agreed to meet a week later at the Holiday Inn in High Wycombe – another famous haunt for lower-league football deals.

Next on the phone was, the now sadly late, Keith Alexander, then manager of Macclesfield Town – which was, at the time, in League Two. He was straight to the point and quite abrupt on the phone. I reckon he didn't have many 'free minutes' available because he definitely wasted no time on small talk!

He asked what I'd been earning the year before and then instantly explained that the club couldn't get anywhere near it. I politely informed him I wasn't expecting similar terms and was open to discussions. He said he would have to speak to his board and, before I could say that was fine, he'd put the phone down.

To be perfectly honest, I had no real interest in going to Maccesfield. Keith had a reputation for employing a direct style of play that didn't appeal to me and the club seemed to never really go anywhere either.

The last call came from David Holdsworth at Mansfield Town (also in the Conference). I'd played briefly with his brother Dean at Weymouth, but didn't know David. He made it clear he would love to sign me, though, and asked if I'd pop over to Field Mill for a chat and a cup of tea.

I said I'd get back to him and checked the distance once off the phone – it was over 90 miles, going from the West Midlands to the East Midlands. Neither that daily commute nor the club itself appealed to me – and I don't like tea – so I gave it a miss. It was only mid-May and I was confident something better would come along.

The following week I went to meet Steve Evans and his assistant Paul Raynor from Crawley. I'd witnessed Steve's actions on the touchline – and heard plenty of colourful stories about him – but I was determined to go to the meeting with an open mind. I've always tried to live my life by making up my own mind about people.

It went well: Steve knew a lot about me and the way I played; I liked the idea he had regarding where I would fit in his team. He wanted me to play in an attacking midfield role that would release me from any defensive duties. He also re-iterated his brother's words about me being the best mid-fielder in the League.

Finally the talk got round to money and Steve's reaction was the same as everyone else's when I said what I'd been earning. However, he could offer a two-year contract on £800 a week in the first year, rising to £850 in the second. As I would have to move house, the club would also give me a re-location fee of £8,000 to be paid over the course of the contract and would be exempt from tax.

It was a decent offer but still £600 a week less than I'd been on before – therefore not something I was going to take at this early stage of the close season. Steve told me to have a think about it and call him in a couple of days.

When I got home I did a bit more research on Crawley Town. It only averaged around 700 fans during the last campaign and I was wary, after my experience at Weymouth, of joining a club whose income clearly did not get close to its expenditure. The club was located near Gatwick and it would be a long commute from Essex if I moved back home.

Sure enough, two days later, Steve phoned for my thoughts. He used a tactic (which I subsequently found out he used a lot) to try to force my hand, explaining that an alternative midfielder, who was due to go on holi-day, would be signed if I didn't agree to the proposed deal. He needed my answer immediately. I was in no rush and not particularly excited about the move so didn't take the bait.

I told him: 'I'm in no rush to drop into the Conference and want to try to stay in the Football League, although this may change as the summer wears on.' He was very understanding and said to keep in touch.

A couple of days later, he rang again telling me he was going to the races with the then club owner Bruce Winfield and asking what money it would take for me to join the club. I told him it was not about money – I simply wanted to play at as high a level as possible. Again he seemed to respect my stance and we amicably parted ways.

I was sure something better would come up, so I waited and waited for the phone to ring…

I went on holiday to Mexico early in June and was starting to get concerned. Though I was loath to do it, I got in touch with a couple of agents and asked them to put my name about. To be fair, there are some good agents out there and I think the one time you need one is when you've had a poor time on the pitch.

I was never going to pay 5 per cent of my wages to an agent again though, so I agreed one-off fees. While I was in Mexico, Dan Fletcher, one of the agents, let me know that he'd spoken to Aldershot Town but that they weren't interested. I appreciated his help but really didn't need him to tell me every time someone said no – I had a feeling that could become a little soul-destroying!

I returned from holiday and the phone was still silent. It was the end of June; I had nothing and had never been in such a position before. Pre-season was due to start and all I had planned was training down the gym with Gonzo. But, on the last day of the month, I got a phone call from Martin Allen at Cheltenham Town asking me to come train and have a chat.

Cheltenham was only about twenty minutes from my base in Worcester so geographically it was perfect. The club often got mentioned in the local press and I'd seen it linked to quite a few midfield players over the summer. It was clear I was not their first choice, but beggars definitely can't be choosers.

To be honest, the club was not on my initial radar because I knew a few lads who'd played under Martin and they all said he was a bit eccentric. I hadn't even bothered sending my CV to the club as a result. Martin mentioned he had gotten my name from the Professional Footballers Association list – a register that goes out at the end of the season and outlines which players are out of contract and which ones are available for transfer.

My first impressions were quite good. I got to the training ground early on 1 July and we had a positive chat. Martin insinuated he wanted to sign me but said it would take a few days to sort everything out. I took all of this with a pinch of salt but, worst-case scenario, I was still getting an opportunity to stay fit somewhere close to home.

Martin had an assistant working in his office – I think his name was Alistair – who was introduced as a sort of 'life coach' (Martin said he liked to have this guy around to bounce ideas off him). Martin wanted to get a bit of background on me so I told him about my studying for a degree for the last four years. He seemed genuinely impressed I was preparing for the future, but I found it a little disconcerting that he would not look me in the eye when he spoke.

John Schofield was his first-team coach and someone I took an instant liking to. He was really enthusiastic, had a bubbly personality and showed an obvious love for the game. These qualities reminded me very much of Richard O'Kelly, my old coach from my first spell at Hereford, and I cannot pay John a bigger compliment than that.

Just as I was leaving training, Martin called me over to say he was having an early morning meeting with the club chairman. I told him I already knew the chairman as he had previously tried to sign me. Martin said he was aware of that fact and, tomorrow morning, he wanted us to go through a role-play in front of the chairman – although the chairman was not to know it was pre-planned.

I thought this was a little strange but who was I to argue?

We were due to train early the next day as it was going to be very hot, so I was instructed to knock on the office door at 8.30 a.m., despite knowing full well he was in a meeting with the chairman. Our conversation was going to go like this:

Me: Gaffer, can I have a quick word?

Martin: Sorry, Ben – I'm in a meeting with the chairman. (*Points at chairman.*) Have you met him?

Me: Yes, we met a few years ago.

Martin: Mr Chairman, Ben is a very intelligent boy who is studying
for a degree, plus he lives very locally in Worcester. I would love him
to come and play for us.

That was the level of dress rehearsal Martin and I went through!

Martin thought this would be enough to get me sat down with the chairman so we could all talk about my potential future at Cheltenham. As I drove home that afternoon I had a little chuckle to myself about the plan.

The next day I went through the rigmarole of the 'role-play' and, to be fair, it went exactly as Martin had predicted. We did our pre-planned routine and had a short chat. I played my role of 'Ben Smith' brilliantly, although I was conscious of becoming typecast!

The first thing chairman Paul Baker asked me was why I'd turned him down to join Hereford. I was honest and told him I knew Graham Turner well and wanted to play for someone who knew my strengths and weaknesses. He went on to re-iterate that Martin was keen to sign me and wanted to know what sort of money I was looking for. I proposed £1,000 a week, with a view – a view I didn't reveal – of taking no less than £900. Paul didn't agree to it then and there, but he didn't baulk at the figure either, which I took as a good sign.

On the Friday morning we trained at Gloucester University, doing some fitness testing before a friendly in the evening against local side Bishop's Cleeve. Games like that can be a problem when you go somewhere on trial: the management are busy planning for the first proper match of the season so aren't particularly bothered about the warm-up friendlies. However, when you are unsigned, you really need to impress. It isn't good enough to be 'OK' – you need to stand out and be better than what they've already got.

I was back training on the Monday and, as I'd suspected, the promised offer hadn't materialised. To make matters worse, Michael Pook, a central midfielder from Swindon Town, had also arrived on trial. The club wouldn't sign both of us, I was certain of that.

The week dragged on and still nothing was mentioned regarding a contract. I persevered, but at the end of the week we had another friendly away to Weston-super-Mare that confirmed the inevitable. Martin played what was clearly his main team in the first half and I was not in it. To top it off, I came on in the second half with all the young professionals plus a lad who had won a competition! The lad tried his best but how was I supposed to impress when trying to anticipate Joe Bloggs's runs? I'd had enough and went to see Martin straight after the game. He gave me the stock answer of money being tight and said he wouldn't be able to offer me anything. If I'm being really honest, I didn't do enough to impress him – but it would've been nice to get an opportunity to play with the senior players.

I'd known it was going to be tricky as I'd never produced my best form in the first month of pre-season, but, as my short spell at the club had progressed, I'd realised their style of play wasn't right for me anyway. I would only have signed because of the location – although, having said all that, if an offer had materialised I would've taken it regardless.

So I was back to square one. The next day, with my tail very much between my legs, I texted Steve Evans at Crawley to see if the deal we'd previously discussed was still on the table. He replied that his budget had been spent but that he had money available for two more players if his chairman liked the look of them during a game.

What great negotiating on my part: I'd managed to turn a two-year deal into a trial!

Could things get any worse?

Yes they could…

I decided to send out my CV again. A couple of days later, Steve Guinan – who had just signed for Northampton Town – rang me to say his manager,

Stuart Gray, had received my letter and was asking about me. He didn't know his manager's intentions but said to expect a call.

Sure enough, Stuart called the next day and informed me that Northampton didn't want to sign me. I tried my best to stay professional but what I was really thinking was *why have you rung me then?* I can only imagine he thought that if he didn't let me know I was definitely surplus to his requirements, I would've turned up at Sixfields on Monday morning, pen in hand, expecting to sign a lucrative contract.

Talk about kicking a man when he's down…

Things were getting so bad I was seriously considering a weekend of shopping in Birmingham with Emma. However, late on a Friday night in the middle of July, Steve Evans texted to see if I'd be interested in playing against a Chelsea XI the following day. I had nothing to lose, so I agreed.

I arrived and knew one familiar face: former Yeovil Town colleague Chris Giles (always nice when entering a new environment). I was named as a substitute but came on at half-time in a game we lost 2–1.

I managed to make an instant impact, however, and scored within ten minutes, via a rare header. I later read on the Crawley Town website that it came from a choreographed set-piece routine – I found this quite amusing because I had no idea where their training ground even was, let alone participated in any choreographed sessions. This was my first experience of Steve using creative licence.

I enjoyed the position I played in – just off the striker – and I was happy with my performance, even picking up the sponsor's 'Man of the Match'.

Even though we had competed admirably against a strong side, Steve was not happy. After the game he had a moan at left back Sam Rents about something I remember thinking at the time was really unjustified. He also said he needed more from me. I thought if he wasn't impressed with that then he hadn't seen anything yet – I could get a lot worse!

I spoke to his assistant Paul Raynor as I left and he said they would be in touch – nothing more than that.

On my way home, I rang Emma to tell her how the game went. Normally she couldn't care less about football, but she knew the situation we were in and humoured me this time. I told her that, although I had done well, I didn't think the manager was my cup of tea.

We were coming to the end of July and there was still nothing on the horizon. I spoke to Steve Evans a couple of times but he was just dragging his feet and it looked like nothing was going to transpire.

My mate Bease had been on the phone saying that, although Cambridge still didn't have a new manager after sacking Gary Brabin, Paul Carden (formerly the assistant manager and now caretaker) had the authority to sign players and wanted me to come down for a couple of days. I was a bit sceptical but really appreciated Bease's assistance – he was going well beyond the call of duty for me.

I travelled down to Cambridge on the Monday morning as the squad wasn't due to start training until the afternoon. On the way, I got a call from Steve Perryman (the director of football at Exeter City), who informed me that although the manager Paul Tisdale liked me, there was no more space in the squad. That was a bit of a blow as I had played with Paul many years before at Yeovil Town, and he had also contacted me at the end of the 2007/08 season, after Hereford had won promotion to League One, asking if I'd be interested in playing for him at Exeter.

I got down to Cambridge and had a chat with Paul Carden before he introduced me to chairman George Rolls. His first words to me were: 'How much money do you want? We don't pay any more than £700 per week.' I said that as we were close to the start of the season, I was open to offers. George went on to say that even though Paul was not the permanent manager, there were no plans to name a new one for at least a couple of weeks. As we left, Paul told me to ignore him as 'he speaks a load of bollocks'.

The plan was to train on the Monday and then be involved in a game against a young Liverpool team the following day. Training went well and I stayed at the house Bease shared with some of the other players.

Late that evening, news filtered through that the club had named a new manager. It was the former Leyton Orient boss Martin Ling. I found this strange as it directly contradicted what the chairman had told me that afternoon. He'd obviously known he was going to appoint a new boss so why had he lied to someone he'd only just met? I understood what Paul had meant!

It subsequently transpired that Mr Rolls had used an interesting strategy to appoint his new manager: he'd basically given three different people the job but whoever got to the ground first became the manager. The story goes that Alan Lewer, Liam Daish and Martin Ling had all been told they were successful applicants. Liam Daish was apparently especially annoyed with George's unique style of decision-making and tried to force his way into the Abbey Stadium to vent his anger.

As soon as I heard this I knew things were not going to work out how I'd hoped. When a new manager comes to a club, one of the first things he normally does is assess the players he's got – not the trialists. I was going to ring Paul but then I thought someone from the club would contact me if they didn't want me to play.

I waited around all day on Tuesday before eventually going to the game in the evening. Martin said his little introductory speech and then named the team and subs. As suspected, I was not named in either. I looked up, caught Paul's eye and he said the gaffer wanted a word.

Martin gave me the same generic statement he probably gave all wannabes about how he'd already inherited four central midfielders and had to look at them first. That was fair enough, but I didn't understand why he hadn't given me a call in the morning to save everyone the embarrassment.

Martin continued to dig a bigger hole for himself, saying that there was no chance of a contract but I was welcome to train. In my head I was thinking *you are not really selling this to me* so I just told him I lived 120 miles away and would not be making that journey every day, which only increased Martin's embarrassment as he hadn't realised I lived so far away. I decided to put everyone out of their misery and left.

I explained to Bease what had happened, thanked him for his help, said goodbye to everyone in the changing room and was in the car on the way home a good hour before the game had even started.

As I drove back I was at my lowest ebb. I was slowly coming to the realisation that this could well be the end of my footballing career. To be honest, I was sick of being treated like shit and I felt I deserved a lot more respect than I was getting.

The season was due to start in ten days and I was still no nearer securing myself a club. Forest Green Rovers were in the Conference and pretty local to me so I rang Garry Hill, who I knew was good friends with the chairman – I wanted to see if I could arrange to maybe play for them on a non-contract basis.

Gary spoke to chairman Trevor Horsley and I was subsequently passed the number of Jim Harvey, the Rovers manager. I was just about to call him when news broke that he'd been sacked!

I could not fucking believe it: I must have been cursed.

A week before the season was about to start, I received a text from Steve Evans. He offered me £700 per week and £4,000 to relocate on a one-year deal. This was a lot less than the offer he'd made in May but the landscape had changed and I no longer held all the cards.

But I wasn't stupid, so I said I'd accept the offer. In my desperation to get it sorted though, I nearly scuppered the whole thing. I rang Steve the following day to finalise the contract but he didn't answer. He'd obviously sensed my desperation because, a couple of hours later, he sent me a text saying the owners wouldn't sanction the wages and he could only offer me £600 a week. Knowing him as I do now, there was only one person holding up the deal – Steve himself.

I told him I was going to have to leave the offer as £700 a week was the absolute least I could afford to take (plus he was trying to take the piss and I wasn't going to allow that). I tried to ring him again but he didn't answer. Instead he swiftly texted back saying he was in a meeting with the owners, fighting my corner. My interpretation of what he was doing was slightly different. I imagined him sitting on his sofa at home in a dirty white vest and Y-fronts Rab C. Nesbitt-style, drinking an Irn-Bru and enjoying the fact he had me by the bollocks.

I'm pretty sure my version of events was a lot closer to the truth than his but, in any case, he messaged me and said the club would go to £650 a week. I said no again – there was no chance I would take anything less than the deal we'd agreed the night before. Hey presto, another text arrived about ten minutes later saying he had managed to secure me the original deal.

What a hero!

I felt like texting him back saying it was still nowhere near what I really wanted, but I played the game and thanked him for his help.

The only real positive I took from the deal was the fact my contract would run until 30 June 2010. Unlike the Football League, there was no standard contract at Conference level and often players' contracts ended immediately after the last game of the season. It was small consolation, though, as there was really only one person who had won the negotiations…

The irony was not lost on me that I had ended up signing a deal for the same sort of money I could have secured at Hereford. However, after all the water that had passed under that particular bridge, I didn't feel I could accept such an offer from them.

Emma and I had to move immediately as I agreed the contract on a

Saturday and needed to be in Crawley for training the next day. I moved back to my dad's house in Essex temporarily while Emma began renting our house out.

· · ·

1 AUGUST 2013

I am writing this sitting on the balcony of my friend's apartment in Spain, bottle of San Miguel in hand, thinking about the past year.

Yes, I realise the new football season is only two weeks away and being on holiday during pre-season is not the most professional thing to do, but this has without doubt been the hardest year of my life.

It hasn't been totally wasted, however, as it's confirmed what I want to do. Before I stopped playing professionally, I wasn't too bothered about whether I stayed in football or not, but now I know that's exactly where I want to be.

I'll be working really hard over the next few years to make that happen. In the upcoming season I'll be a coach and a sports lecturer, training an U15 team and playing for Thurrock.

I won't have many days off but I realise, just like I did when I was a professional player, that I need to do my apprenticeship before I can get to where I want to be.

CHAPTER 21

WHAT HAVE I DONE?

SEASON: 2009/10
CLUB: CRAWLEY TOWN
DIVISION: CONFERENCE PREMIER
MANAGER: STEVE EVANS (EVO)

STEVE EVANS AND his shenanigans are notorious within the lower leagues of English football and he revels in this notoriety. You will now get an insight into how he works and I will try my best to be objective – some of the things he got up to I would never have believed had I not witnessed them myself. He has faults but also plenty of strengths, which have allowed him to experience a lot of success over the last few years.

I arrived at Crawley's ground for my first training session and was struck by how professional everything looked. Each player had their kit laid out below a designated peg, plus food was provided afterwards. However, what Steve didn't say was how much we all paid for this privilege – namely £75 a month.

There was only a week of pre-season left and I was a fair bit behind everyone else in terms of sharpness. Luckily there were two games left and I played forty-five minutes in each. I was still quite a way from the level I should have been at, though. In the lead-up to the first game I had a chat with Steve and explained I was not yet match-fit – I said he could either play me and accept it would take time for me to get up to speed, or allow me to get fully fit first. He seemed to take on board what I said.

The key word in that last sentence is 'seemed'.

Everything was going swimmingly until the Friday before the opening game of the season (away at Mansfield Town), when Steve exhibited his bizarre tendencies for the first time.

I arrived for training as usual and was greeted by the sight of defender Glenn Wilson storming out of the car park. He was out of contract and under twenty-four so the club had re-engaged him in a new deal without finalising anything, which meant he couldn't leave the club on a free transfer and was instead on a week-to-week contract. The club had eventually offered Glenn something, but he was far from happy with it and was adamant about leaving.

I was taken aback by this and by another incident after training. The squad list of players travelling to Mansfield was put up in the changing room while goalkeeper Simon Raynor was moaning about how he was owed bonuses from last season. The gaffer overheard and went off on one, saying Simon was corrupting the newer players and could 'fuck off' because he would 'not be playing for the club again'.

I thought it was a massive over-reaction but the other lads seemed to find it quite amusing and explained to me that those types of outbursts were a regular occurrence.

The next day, sure enough, both Glenn and Simon had sorted out their differences with the big fella and were on the coach bound for the game. We travelled up on the day of play, which was different from what I was used to but not something I disliked.

The manager named a 4–4–2 and I was selected to play in central midfield. The game itself was a disaster: we got spanked 4–0 and were 3–0 down at half-time. We played more like a 4–2–4 and were way too offensive; Mansfield looked like they were going to score every time they broke forward.

I thought I performed fine in the first half: I was our most creative player going forward and also came closest to scoring, despite not being at my fittest. Unfortunately, this was not a sentiment shared by Evo and he made that very clear.

He came striding straight over to me in the dressing room at the break, his sweaty face bright red and contorted with rage. He got within 2 inches of me and went ballistic. I was trying to work out, in between the shower of saliva and gesturing, what he was saying in his broad Glaswegian accent.

'He fucking told me, didn't he, Rayns? He fucking told us!'

He paused for breath as his assistant Paul Raynor did his best impression of a nodding dog while saying: 'He did, gaffer. He did.'

Evo caught his breath and was off again: 'Turner said you are a fucking liability in a 4–4–2. Why don't you just fuck off? Go on, fuck off.'

I sat there saying nothing and trying to ignore as much of it as possible. I have no problem with criticism but it has to be constructive. If it isn't, I just switch off. He then went after centre half Chris Giles, who was sitting next to me, so I was still in full view of his gaze (and the recipient of the odd bit of misdirected spittle).

I survived the onslaught and played ten minutes of the second half before being dragged off. In hindsight, I think it was the gaffer's way of laying a marker down for new players. It was a tactic I subsequently saw him do many times – he'd wait for a small mistake by a new recruit and then jump on it to show them they wouldn't be treated differently to anyone else.

He was still fuming after the game and called us in for training at 9 a.m. on Sunday. We had a 'clear the air' meeting where he and Paul put their points across and we made ours. I had plenty to say and came out of the meeting feeling a lot clearer about what was expected of me.

I still wasn't happy about the 'liability' accusation though so I had a private meeting with Steve about it. He explained he had spoken to Graham Turner about me but that he'd also exaggerated the liability part in the heat of the moment. Steve had a very good skill whereby he could be mad at you one minute then treat you like it never happened the next day. It took a little bit of getting used to.

Our next game was at home against Forest Green Rovers. I vividly remembered Rayn's team talk, when we were told: 'If you can't get up for the first home game of the season, then you can't get up for anything.'

There were 693 people in the crowd…

We reverted to a 4–3–3 and won the game 3–1. Everyone who had been a 'useless cunt' on Saturday was now 'the best thing since sliced bread' – not one to overreact, our boss!

We followed that win with two more, at home versus Wrexham and away at Cambridge United – a game I was desperate to do well in after the pre-season debacle.

That desperation paid off at the Abbey Stadium as I set up our goal with a sumptuous through ball, which Jamie Cook finished with aplomb – cheekily dinking it over the keeper. There was a funny incident after the game too, as Paul Carden (the Cambridge assistant manager) had the ball in front of our dugout when the final whistle went and smashed it away in frustration – accidentally striking it into our gaffer's midriff! This led to all hell breaking loose and was Evo's cue to scream expletives down the tunnel and outside the Cambridge dressing room, mainly based around the fact Cambridge wanted to offer him the manager job but couldn't pay him enough money. Not a classy exchange but very amusing!

After that rather inauspicious start, we had nine points from twelve and were looking good. Next up was Gateshead at home and we seemed to have found a winning formula. However, I always felt at Crawley that no matter how well we were doing, we were usually one game away from a crisis – and we were about to encounter our latest one. Like the Mansfield game, we were 3–0 down at half-time against Gateshead and, as you can imagine, Steve was not impressed. He started dishing out a general dressing-down, telling us we were getting destroyed because he wanted our wide players playing high up the pitch. As a result he decided to switch to a 4–4–2, which meant I was sacrificed.

I was annoyed as I thought I'd been fine when I had possession – I'd just been starved of any good service. We played a very direct, no-risk style of football, meaning the ball went from back to front as quickly as possible. The gaffer was not particularly bothered about the quality of the ball being hit forward, just as long as we got it away from our goal.

This tactic worked OK if our opponents played a high line and left space behind. However, if the opposition had seen us play before, they would sit deep and we would either put everything on their defenders' heads or send it through to the goalkeeper. It was a very predictable way of playing and also meant that when playing 'in the hole' – as I did – you often got bypassed.

I sat in the dressing room as the lads were getting changed after full time feeling like I was back to square one. We'd improved marginally in the second half but still lost 4–1. Steve marched into the dressing room and started going mental at anyone and everyone who caught his eye: 'You cunts who started the game are all fined a week's wages.'

I wasn't sure how he was going to make that stick with the PFA – fining players for attempting to do their job?!

He then went straight for me: 'What the fuck are you smirking at? You can fuck off. Come into my office, sign your release forms and fuck off. You will never play in my team again. Come into my fucking office now.'

Sam Rents, our left back, then got similar treatment.

Before I went into his office we were informed that we all had to stay at the club to watch the DVD of the game at 7 p.m.

As I entered the room, Evo was still fuming and re-iterated what he had been screaming in the dressing room, telling me I would definitely never play for him again and had to sign my release forms. I asked what pay-off I would be getting and he replied I wouldn't get one.

'In that case,' I said, 'I will not be signing anything.'

I had ten months left on my contract and was not about to give that up, whatever the manager said.

We waited around in the hospitality suite until 7 p.m. for the video nasty, but it never materialised. We just got another bollocking and were told the whole result was down to us not working hard enough. (So nothing to do with us giving two penalties away, being tactically outsmarted by the opposition or regularly squandering possession – we just needed to run around more!)

Football is a simple game but theirs was an overly simplistic approach that absolved the coaching staff of any blame. They were acting like big babies and that was further illustrated by the fact they said we would no longer be getting our kit cleaned or any food provided after training – a rather petty type of punishment, if you ask me. It was like they thought we enjoyed being outplayed and then verbally assaulted in the dressing room.

Steve then surpassed himself by saying we were all in for training on Sunday at 7 a.m.

Unsurprisingly, everyone was in on time the next day and we commenced the second post-mortem of the Gateshead game. Right back Simon Rusk was the first to suffer Steve's wrath. Evo blamed Simon's positioning for one of Gateshead's goals and then called him a cunt. Simon is an intelligent and opinionated person who played for the gaffer for many years at Boston United so he was used to these frequent outbursts and took the majority of them with a pinch of salt. However, on this occasion, he was not willing to take it.

Rusky: You are just a fucking bully, but you're not going to bully me.
SE (*in a thick Scottish accent*): What did you say?

Rusky: You are a bully but you ain't going to bully me.

SE: You fucking what? Me? A bully? (*Incredulous expression; looks at Paul in amazement.*) Get out of the fucking room, fuck off! You are finished at this club.

Rusky: You can stick your club up your fucking arse! (*Storms out.*)

SE: Did you hear that, Rayns? He's fucking finished.

The manager went on to say, with a totally straight face, that Rusky had shown him a lack of respect, even though Evo had started off by calling him a cunt. His lack of self-awareness was brilliant.

I was totally ignored in the meeting, received no criticism and was not asked for my opinion – maybe he'd really meant it when he said I wasn't going to play for Crawley again.

After the meeting we went to the training ground, which was closed, and eventually ended up at an adjacent park, where we were made to just run and run – the sort of prehistoric punishment I'd been expecting.

On Monday we had a third post-mortem – sitting down to finally watch the DVD. It confirmed what I thought: I was not brilliant but I didn't give the ball away when I had it. I was not at fault for any of the goals either, but my set-piece deliveries were crap.

As everyone suspected, by the end of Monday, Steve had made up with Rusky and put his toys back in the pram. We were all getting our kit cleaned and food provided after training again too.

It was the first week we didn't have a midweek game so Emma and I went to Worcester to move out of our house. While carrying some stuff down the stairs I managed to misjudge a step and got one of my toes stuck under my foot. Within a couple of minutes it had turned black and was killing me.

I was in agony the next day. I knew I couldn't tell Evo the truth so I hatched a plan with Jamie Cook during a practice match I was attempting to hobble through. We were doing some work on the shape of the team and it was pretty evident I wouldn't be playing, so I marked Jamie from a corner and we pretended he'd stood on my foot.

After training I went to the physio to tell her what had happened and both she and the gaffer took the bait. At the time I don't think he was too bothered as he wanted me out of the picture anyway.

During my spell out injured, Steve was handed a thirteen-match touch-line ban for an incident that had occurred the previous season. He was not allowed into any stadium for the first three games and, for the remainder, he was not allowed into our dressing room before or after the matches. This meant that Paul Raynor took the team on match days – the main implication of which was the absence of a rather rotund Scottish man shouting expletives at us from the sideline.

I never actually got to the bottom of whether my toe was broken or not. The club didn't have a private healthcare policy for its players – well, not one they were going to use on me, anyway. I'm pretty sure I broke it in some way because I wasn't fit to start another game until the end of October.

What I always used to find funny were the gaffer's comments to the press: he always said the right things but did the exact opposite in the dressing room. One of his favourite mantras was: 'We never get too high when we win or too low when we lose.'

I can think of countless occasions when this did not ring true but one of the best was when we were playing away at Kidderminster Harriers upon my return from my toe injury. In the hotel before the game, Evo told us there would be no harsh words or recriminations after the game as long as we all worked hard. The lads did just that and we almost earned a draw until we succumbed to a last-minute winner. To be honest, Kidderminster deserved the win and it was only hard work and determination that kept us in the game.

Steve seemed to have no recollection of his previous promise and went off on a post-match rant. He and Paul had meetings with certain players at the front of the coach, which resulted in six of them being put on the transfer list. We were also summoned for Sunday training at 9 a.m.

We didn't get too high when we won or too low when we lost though, did we, Steve…?

On that occasion, however, he came into the dressing room on Sunday, saw how severely pissed off we all were and promptly gave us Monday off.

I got back in the team for a home FA Cup match against AFC Wimbledon. They brought a large number of supporters, which made for a really lively atmosphere inside our ground, and I was playing 'in the hole', which I did quite well, before tiring near the end and being replaced with fifteen minutes to go. I always enjoyed playing against AFC Wimbledon as they played expansively and gave you time when in possession of the ball. The game finished as a 1–1 draw and meant we had a Tuesday night replay at Kingsmeadow.

Our line-up for the replay was the same, other than one change due to an injury, so I retained my attacking role. We dominated the first half but, against the run of play, they took the lead. We equalised when I put a measured pass through to Jefferson Louis to score.

I played seventy minutes but was annoyed at being subbed because we were chasing a goal and I was one of our most creative players. Wimbledon continued their patient approach even after having a player sent off and ended up winning 3–1. As you can probably imagine, Steve was not happy and we were called in for training the following day. I knew the script by now. We got in at the allotted time and waited until the gaffer and Rayns were ready to grace us with their presence.

However, on this occasion, things went a little differently. Yes, we had a meeting, but it was not to sort out the previous day's deficiencies. We were instead told we were no longer getting our kit cleaned as people were not paying for it on time. We were also no longer getting food after training.

You may remember I mentioned this kind of tactic being pretty common, but the only people who seemed particularly bothered about it were the management staff. We all had washing machines at home and food in our cupboards so it really only meant we were £75 a month better off.

What about the game, Steve? I was thinking. *When are we going to address that?!*

Evo went on to talk about what was really annoying him. Apparently there were two 'snakes in the camp' who had been going to directors and telling them about some of his more left-field methods. He said he would announce who they were the next morning unless they confessed.

It was pretty obvious he had no idea who the 'snakes' were and was just trying to scare them into revealing themselves, although, to be fair to him, it nearly worked until us players had a chat and the more switched-on members of the group explained what he was doing.

Before dispersing the meeting, Steve told us we were no longer allowed to use club kit and had to supply our own. Oh, and we were training two hours later so needed kit for then.

Barry Cogan (my normal travelling partner) and I were going to the gym later that day so had some training gear with us, but the rest of the lads had to go down to a local shop. They came back with lots of Slazenger and Donnay gear before we all got our own lunches and had a picnic in the dressing room.

I often look back on that day and still can't decide if it was lunacy or a brilliant piece of management. The reason I say this is because it brought us all together with one common objective: resentment of the gaffer.

We went out to train looking like Rag Arse Rovers. I had my gym vest on and the rest of the lads looked like poorly dressed 1980s tennis players – all that was missing were wooden rackets and headbands. Training consisted of a very tedious run around the pitch.

The next day we bounced into training, waiting with baited breath for the public unveiling of the 'snakes'. Guess what – it never happened. In fact, those mythical creatures were never mentioned again. Were they a figment of Steve's fertile imagination or did they actually exist? We'll never know – unless he decides to release his own memoir someday.

We'd all turned up with our own kit and packed lunches but, before we went out to train, the gaffer made another demand: every player was required to buy their own private medical insurance and show evidence to prove it had been done. Those who didn't do it would not be selected to play.

Surely it's a club's responsibility to insure professional footballers? What was he going to do if nobody bought insurance? It was another idle threat and we knew it. There was no chance of me paying out of my own pocket and, being honest, I couldn't afford to.

Training once again consisted of a plod around the pitch and a picnic in the dressing room. Balls must also have come under the category of 'kit' as we hadn't seen one since Tuesday!

Training on the Friday was a jog around the pitch and some half laps at three-quarter pace. At the end of the session, the gaffer announced we would get our kit and food back on Monday (surprise, surprise) under the caveat that he and Paul wouldn't drop their professional standards for any-one! He then went on to say that if we won the next game against York we would either get the week off, as it was the FA Cup the following week and we had no fixtures, or we would be going on a club trip to Egypt.

Where had that come from?!

As I have alluded to, if you scraped away all the bullshit, Steve was no idiot. I think he realised that his behaviour had meant he was losing us lads and he couldn't afford for that to happen.

I was pretty sure the Egypt trip was not going to materialise and, to be honest, I wasn't particularly bothered. I was desperate for a few days off, however, so that tactic definitely helped focus my mind.

Sometimes things happen to contradict all conventional thinking. We hadn't had a day off for seventeen days and hadn't been near a ball since the previous Tuesday, yet we were playing a York City side that was on a long unbeaten run and near the top of the League. We started the game well but still went a goal down before half-time. Evo made an astute substitution at the break though – and I managed to get my first goal for the club – and we went on to win 3–1.

The gaffer stuck to his word and we got the next week off. It was now early November and I was starting to feel settled both on and off the pitch. For the preceding three months, Emma and I had been staying with her mum, but that week we moved into our new house.

Mansfield were our next opponents and, after a two-week break without a match, we lost 2–0 in a pretty unremarkable game. Steve typically went off on one afterwards.

Looking back, I had some of my funniest moments at the club during those tirades – and that time was no exception. Chris Giles and Evo had a mutual contempt for each other, which they both struggled to hide. Their dislike normally reared its head during heated discussions. On this occasion, the manager wasn't happy with Gilesy for taking a corner late in the game, even though we were losing.

> SE: I told you to stay back.
>
> Gilesy: But we were losing, I was just trying to get us a goal.
>
> SE: I don't care what you thought – I wanted you to stay back. Are you fucking illiterate?
>
> Gilesy: I think you'll find 'illiterate' is when you can't read or write.

I struggled to stifle my laughter when Gilesy came out with that and it totally knocked Steve out of his stride. Evo then went on to have a moan at Thomas Pinault and me for 'playing too much football'. *Thank you very much!* I thought – although it wasn't meant to be a compliment.

The answer to our latest defeat was, as always, to bring us in on a Sunday.

I wouldn't have minded if we'd used the time to address the issues in the game but, more often than not, it was just a punishment.

Next up was Hayes & Yeading away, where I managed to score again despite the fact we lost 2–1. Even though we were losing games, I was happy with my own performances and was starting to reach the level I expected of myself.

I reaffirmed this feeling when I scored again in a home win against Salisbury City – a match we actually struggled to put out a team and a full complement of substitutes for due to mounting injury problems. That result was quickly followed by a defeat at Gateshead. Steve went mental and told us we were all shit, which was lovely to hear as next up was top-of-the-League Oxford United. The gaffer clearly had a very short memory as, after that scattergun appraisal of our performance against Gateshead, he told us how good we all were before the Oxford game.

I went on to have my best game for the club, causing Oxford all sorts of trouble playing just behind striker Charlie Ademeno. We went 1–0 up, but sadly wilted in the last ten minutes and lost 2–1.

On Thursday's training session, the boss gave everyone marks out of ten on the white board and it was all very positive. He gave me a nine, adding I was brilliant going forward but could've done better defensively – where had I heard that before?!

Our form started to pick up as we won at Tamworth and then made heavy work of beating Bashley in the FA Trophy – a game in which I gave my first rubbish performance since coming back from injury.

As alluded to before, when any team I was playing for was performing well, the intensity of training would often drop as players relaxed – this was no different at Crawley. In the management's defence, we had such a small squad at the time that I think they were more concerned about injuries than our training programme. We ended up doing a lot of non-contact stuff, such as using the spinning bikes or working in the gym.

I could see the thinking behind it, but I thought it actually had a detrimental effect – the only way you get really sharp and confident as a footballer is to play football.

Due to a cold snap in the weather we didn't play again until Boxing Day when we drew 2–2 against Eastbourne Borough. We gave away two crap goals and should have scored about five. I could've scored a hat-trick myself. We had two more games over the Christmas period: a 3–2 win away to Grays Athletic and another victory, 2–0, against Eastbourne Borough on New Year's Day.

The poor weather returned and we didn't play again for nearly three weeks until another FA Trophy tie against Chelmsford City – my local club. I was desperate to perform well and for us to win. Unfortunately, neither happened! I was deployed on the left of midfield where my painful lack of pace was highlighted by our direct style of play.

As usual, we were in the day after and the gaffer criticised our performance – though on this occasion it was fully justified. Steve then asked us why we didn't create any chances. I commented that we were playing too directly; he took great offence to that and started attacking me for totally unrelated events.

It always made me laugh when managers asked for opinions but then went on the defensive if they didn't like the responses. In Evo's defence, while he never acknowledged anything we said at the time, I think when he went home and calmed down he did take some of our comments on board.

My form had dipped since Christmas but the gaffer kept faith in me and I started the next game at home versus Kidderminster Harriers. It was a mixed affair as I performed really well but was partly at fault for both their goals in the 2–2 draw. I got a right bollocking after the game from the boss but kept my mouth shut as he was making a valid point. I've always been willing to argue my side, but I also know when I'm in the wrong.

Our good League form continued with a hard-fought but ugly 1–0 victory against Cambridge United. I was pretty anonymous and my substitution with ten minutes to go was met with a clear 'about time' from the main stand – I'm still not sure whether it was aimed at me or the substitution in general, but either way it was not a glowing endorsement of my performance.

That win was followed by an almost identical one against Altrincham the week after. Steve was not happy at half-time and tried to lift us with a Churchillian speech (which wasn't particularly motivational). No doubt he sat at home that evening, cradling a picture of Sir Alex Ferguson to his ample chest, with a Mars bar and Irn-Bru in hand, telling his idol how his powers of motivation had made the difference once again.

Our run of form came to a resounding halt, however, as we were comfortably beaten at Wrexham. Next up was Luton Town at home, who had suffered a massive fall from grace.

These were the sort of games I loved: big matches against big teams who brought a large away support with them. It led to a great atmosphere and some banter between the two sets of fans. That game also saw a sudden improvement in my form, although not until the second half. In the opening forty-five minutes I was well and truly cancelled out by Luton's Keith Keane who, incidentally, I thought was the best midfielder in the League. He was playing in a deep midfield role so the majority of the time we found ourselves in direct competition – a battle he won hands down. At half-time I got a fully justified kick up the backside from the gaffer and responded by scoring both our goals in the 2–1 win.

I was looking forward to building on such a great performance, but I fell ill shortly afterwards and eventually lost almost four kilos, which meant I missed the next game and only made a cameo appearance in the one after that at Stevenage. I did recover enough to take my place against AFC Wimbledon, though, and played well in a hard-fought win.

We were now in a position where we weren't realistically going to reach a play-off situation – although there was still a small outside chance it could happen and the gaffer wasn't going to let us take our foot off the pedal while the opportunity existed. The intensity tailed off at times during training, but Evo had an absolutely insatiable appetite for winning and never let us tail off on a match day.

I quite admired that side of his personality, even though I didn't always like the way he went about it. At times the work rate was misguided and a bit wasteful, but it was a good base to build from. Having said that, as much as the gaffer tried to spin the situation, we knew the season was petering out. It was the first time in a few years I wasn't involved in a promotion race or relegation scrap. The idea of a 'pressure-free' run-in seemed like a good one but the reality was pretty boring.

We prolonged our outside chance by beating Ebbsfleet United in another nondescript performance, which included a hard-working but anonymous display from me. The gaffer loved those types of displays but I didn't. I'd always judged how well I was doing by my contribution on the ball but, due to a variety of reasons, I wasn't seeing enough of it.

Our play-off hopes were finally extinguished with a heavy 3–0 defeat at home to Stevenage. They weren't anything special but their discipline and organisation was more than enough to beat us. I was left out of the next game at Rushden & Diamonds. The gaffer mixed it up to give other players an opportunity, as it was coming up to that time when – with the club not fighting for anything – he wanted to make decisions on contracts for the following season. It seemed like, either way, a decision had already been made about me.

Next up was Hayes & Yeading. I was initially left out but then reinstated as someone cried off before the game. I know this because on the handwritten instruction sheets pinned to the wall – outlining each player's job in set pieces – someone's name had been scribbled out and mine had been added. I was given the graveyard shift on the left wing in a 4–4–2.

Steve had his own pecking order within the League. We were allowed to draw or lose without him going ballistic to those he placed higher than us; however, if he deemed us to be better than our opposition, we were not allowed to do anything but win.

Hayes & Yeading was one of the so-called 'lower' teams, so a 0–0 scoreline at half-time was accompanied by a tirade of abuse – nothing constructive, just the gaffer comparing us to female genitalia.

I'm not sure what the recognised name for a group of these are – I know you get a 'pride' of lions and a 'school' of fish so, if Steve was right, and I have no reason to doubt him, then it is a bunch of cunts!

I told him we had no divine right to beat any team and he eloquently told me to fuck off. He then added that I was crap in left midfield but effective in the hole – I couldn't argue with that.

It was now mid-April and the season was coming to an end. I wasn't sure what to do next – nothing had been said about a new contract but I didn't know if I wanted one anyway. I'd expected to drop into the Conference and be one of the best players in the League but I hadn't been. Yes, our style of play may not have been conducive to getting the best out of me, but I knew I'd been average.

I sent my CV out early to see if there would be any takers for my services. I wasn't keen on moving so my options were seriously limited. I sent my CV to Braintree Town and Chelmsford City too – both part-time clubs – as I was contemplating going part time and starting a new career for myself alongside playing.

Braintree Town took the bait straight away and I went to have a meeting with the manager Robbie Garvey. He was keen to take me and even mentioned a job working within a football academy they were about to set up – but I didn't really fancy it. Ironic really…

I told Robbie I would get back in touch once I knew Crawley's intentions.

Before the season was over, we still had the journey everyone looked for at the start of the season – and then timed their five-match suspension for accordingly: Barrow away (I'm joking … partly!).

Due to the recent bad weather and their run in the FA Trophy, we were playing them on a Thursday night. I left home at 8.30 a.m. for a 7.45 p.m. kick-off in Cumbria. We lost 4–1 but the game sticks in my mind as I completed a career first in it: I scored for both teams.

The own goal came first. I was tracking back when a Barrow player's shot hit a post and rebounded. Before I could react, the ball hit my knee and flew in from 6 yards. It was a reminder why I rarely tracked back – I wouldn't make that mistake again!

What pleased me most, though, was that I didn't let it affect me. I erased it from my mind and equalised with a header early in the second half. Unfortunately, we then got dominated by Barrow's forwards and gave away some terrible goals before eventually losing.

Even though there were only a few games left in the season and we had nothing to play for, Steve was not taking that as an excuse. After the usual volley of expletives and character assassinations – which now had little effect on me – we were informed we'd be training the following day.

I got home at 4.30 a.m. and was back into training for 12.30 p.m. I wouldn't have minded if we'd done something productive in training, but we just had a light jog and a stretch. I know sports scientists say that this is a worthwhile exercise, but surely any good effects are negated by being cramped up in your car for the three-hour round trip?

Fewer than forty-eight hours after, we were playing against Tamworth in a typical end-of-season affair. My body was screaming for a rest but to no avail. We won 2–0 and I scored one of the best goals of my career, curling a right-footed shot into the top corner from just outside the box – the keeper had no chance. Even the gaffer gave me some praise – that's how good a goal it was! I came off near the end as my hamstring was tightening up. It was my last contribution of the season.

We had two games left. The first against Kettering I declared myself unfit for as there was no way I would risk tearing my hamstring in a meaningless game with no promise of a contract. The last game was postponed as Chester City had gone into liquidation and folded.

I finished the season with thirty-four appearances and seven goals. In my opinion, that was a pretty average return for a player of my quality, but overall it was viewed as a pretty successful season for the club. We finished in a very creditable seventh place on sixty-six points.

All that was left now was to find out if I had any future at Crawley Town. We all had individual meetings with the management and the early vibes from other players wasn't great. Most were offered new deals but on reduced terms.

The gaffer, Rayns and I agreed during my meeting that my season had been OK, but that I could perform better. Evo then asked what my plans were and gave me the usual spiel about money being tight etc.

Steve said they would be willing to offer me a new contract but, like everyone else, it would be on less money. He proposed £650 a week and no relocation money, meaning I would be taking a £50-a-week pay cut plus as well as losing the £4,000 I effectively used to buy my petrol. I was also told the offer was non-negotiable.

The club knew they were in a strong position. I was pragmatic about the financial situation in football at the time and aware a lot of better players than me were pricing themselves out of a job. After moving back to Essex, I was also loath to move away again unless it was financially worth my while.

I said I would think about it and get back to them in a couple of days. My initial thoughts were that I could afford to swallow the £50-a-week cut but could not afford to lose out on the £4,000.

Rayns rang me the next day to ask for my thoughts. I told him I couldn't do it and, as the offer was non-negotiable, I'd have to move on. He asked what I would sign for – which I instantly realised meant we could agree a deal – and I told him I had to have the relocation money.

The day after, the gaffer rang (he always made the calls when the news was good) and said he could do my requested deal but I was not to tell anyone else. I imagine he said that to everyone. So I'd secured my future as a professional footballer for one more season. I knew that I could earn at least, if not more, money than I was earning at Crawley with a combination of playing part time and working another job, but I also knew that instead of fifteen hours a week I'd be doing about fifty. So I made a lifestyle choice: I'd have plenty of time to do long hours in the future.

I had my reservations about re-signing for Steve – after all, I had no leeway to moan any more as I knew exactly what I was letting myself in for. But, conversely, re-signing turned out to be one of the best decisions I ever made.

Once I got used to his unique and very aggressive style of management, I didn't find it too much of a problem. I didn't always like it, but I could handle it. Like anyone who was successful working under the gaffer, I learnt to take on board all the constructive stuff – which, contrary to popular belief, was there – and I let all the bullshit and insults go straight over my head. Easier said than done, but possible.

Yes, training was often boring and monotonous – and, for me, it didn't have enough relation to what we did on a Saturday – but I did play regularly when fit and that was all I really wanted.

It did stick in my throat that Evo's behaviour both on and off the pitch lacked so much class – I felt it reflected on me. However, I had to be selfish and do what was right for me. I was being offered a decent wage to do a job I loved.

I went away for the summer safe in the knowledge I would not be getting called every name under the sun for a couple of months and that I had at least one more year as a professional footballer to look forward to.

I also made the conscious decision to start gaining my coaching qualifications. I took my Level Two badge with the Kent County FA and soon realised how tough coaching actually was. I'd lost count of the number of sessions I'd been involved in as a player and had thought were rubbish. I always used to think I could do so much better, but it turned out – at that moment, at least – that I couldn't. I formed a newfound respect for many of the coaches I'd worked with.

I remembered on numerous occasions during my career when, mid-session, I had said to a coach 'this isn't working' or 'this is shit' – as if he didn't already know!

Well, karma came and bit me on the backside as I struggled through my own sessions as a coach. I knew exactly what I wanted to do, but breaking it down and explaining it simply to my peers proved trickier than I had envisaged.

CHAPTER 22

'PROJECT PROMOTION' (PART I)

SEASON: 2010/11
CLUB: CRAWLEY TOWN
DIVISION: CONFERENCE PREMIER
MANAGER: STEVE EVANS (EVO)

'D ALWAYS BEEN paid properly in my first season at Crawley – some months, a day or two after the agreed date, but that wasn't a problem. Over the summer, though, I didn't get the last two instalments of my relocation money – a total of £800. The gaffer was proving elusive to get hold of but I eventually spoke to him a couple of days before pre-season training was due to start.

I said I knew money was tight for football clubs during the close season but I needed what was owed to me. Steve said there were 'no cash-flow problems at our club' and then went on to say how he had just signed Matt Tubbs from Salisbury City for £70,000 and there was 'plenty more where that came from'. He added that we were going to be challenging for the title and that I would play a big part in it.

I took that last part with a pinch of salt, but definitely liked the idea of being part of a team challenging at the top of the League. He also promised me that I would get my £800 on the first day of training, which I did.

During the first couple of weeks of pre-season, the gaffer was as good as his word and the club went on an unprecedented spending spree for its level. On top of signing Matt Tubbs we added Craig McCallister, Dean Howell, Pablo Mills, Chris Flood, Liam Enver Marum and Sergio Torres. These players were not household names but very well-known at our level of football. Pablo even came down to the training ground to check Crawley were up to his standards – we must have been as I cannot think of any other reason why he would have signed!

The reason behind this show of power, according to Steve, was the fact that two Hong Kong-based English businessman had decided to invest in the club. It seemed a strange decision to me as, with the best will in the world, Crawley was hardly a 'sleeping giant', plus it was located in a catchment area that had it competing with the likes of Crystal Palace and Brighton & Hove Albion for supporters. If I were going to invest in a club at that level, I would've gone for Luton Town or York City – bigger clubs who had fallen on bad times but had the potential to regain past glories.

The way I understood the venture was the investment was not just a business decision but a sentimental one too, as the mystery investors were apparently lifelong Crawley fans. I think Evo used some poetic licence, however, because when I met one of them – introduced to me as Paul – he had as broad a Birmingham accent as you are ever likely to hear.

Rumours were rife regarding what the new players were earning. It was clear there must have been some financial incentives offered otherwise a lot of these players would not even have contemplated joining us. Sergio Torres, for example, had been playing in the Championship the previous season but had somehow been 'persuaded' to drop to the Conference. The gaffer was a great salesman but not that good.

'PROJECT PROMOTION' (PART I)

I had no problem with who was earning what: you sign the contract you're happy with; if you don't like what's offered then you don't sign it. So, if there were players earning double what I was getting – and I suspected there were – then good luck to them.

If you were going to give a manager a substantial playing budget, Steve was actually not a bad choice. Between him and his brother Gee (our chief scout), they had an extensive knowledge of the lower leagues. I could mention any player at Conference, League Two or League One level and they could talk about what his perceived strengths and weaknesses were.

The gaffer now had a problem, though. The new investment had clearly come after he had dealt with us existing players and those he had signed up early in the close season. I have no doubt he would have released everyone and built a new team from scratch if the funding had come earlier. He denied that by telling us we all had an important part to play, but he was not kidding anyone.

There was no divide in the dressing room, but all us 'old' players knew we had a fight on our hands. After seeing the new recruits in training – as good as some of them were – I was more than up for the fight. In actual fact, I knew that if I could get in the team, it would benefit me hugely as I'd be playing alongside better players.

Considering the intensity the gaffer liked us to play at, I never found his pre-seasons too tough. The only time training almost got hard was when one of the lads put a Viagra into the jugs of drink I had for lunch. Unfortunately for them, but not for me, it had no effect. The last thing I needed was something popping up and slowing me down – although even if it had, I'm not sure anyone would have noticed!

My attempt to prove my worth had a very inauspicious start during the first friendly of the season against Millwall. I was sub, came on at half-time and played like a bag of shit. It was really hot and I struggled to move my feet, giving the ball away sloppily on numerous occasions. To make matters worse, the lads who started the game looked really good.

Our next outing was against a strong Crystal Palace side and my performance improved considerably – not up to my best, but I played eighty-five minutes in a promising 1–0 win.

We were then split up into two groups – one played at Dorchester Town on Friday night while the other, which I was in, played at my old club Weymouth on the Saturday. The first group won 6–0 so we were on a hiding to nothing. We won 2–0 but Steve had written the script before the game had even started.

At half-time he told us we were all 'big time' and that if we didn't improve we could 'fuck off in three weeks' time'. Then, at the end of the game he told me that I couldn't play in a 4–4–2 and that I was trying to get on the ball too much. I'm not sure that's possible, but he added that, as a result of it, other players weren't moving while I was showing for the ball. I was perplexed as I couldn't work out how that was my fault.

It was good to be back in the groove, though – I hadn't been called a useless cunt since the end of April!

A young Arsenal XI were our next opponents and I started in central midfield. They were technically excellent and we were playing at full tilt just to compete. My hamstring started tightening before half-time so that was me done, but I was really happy with my performance and hoped I'd given the boss something to think about.

It turned out he wasn't thinking about me much: we played a young Chelsea team next and the gaffer named the line-up he clearly had in mind for the first game of the season – with me on the bench. The Chelsea team was nowhere near as strong as the one we played the previous pre-season, though, and we won comfortably. I even got a token 25-minute run-out.

Our preparation continued with a win against a strong QPR side, where Matt Tubbs really started to show his class with two well-taken goals. Steve also gave the new lads an example of his ability to massively overreact afterwards.

Right back Glenn Wilson was holding court in the dressing room, as he regularly did, while bouncing a ball. One of the coaching staff asked him for the ball back, but he said, purely in jest, that they would have to come and get it. Evo waddled in at that stage and went spare, telling Glenn to go to his office immediately.

It all resulted in Glenn being banned from the club and training indefinitely – a stupid move, in my eyes. The gaffer didn't realise Glenn, being the longest-serving player, was a huge asset to him in the dressing room. He was the one explaining to the new players what to listen to and what to ignore – as he'd done for me when I first joined the club.

The gaffer clearly had an agenda – he wanted any excuse to get rid of the players he no longer felt he needed while laying his usual marker to the new arrivals.

I was only being selected for the reserve pre-season games and it seemed clear I would not be in the first team at the start of the season. I anticipated it, but I was also willing to bide my time as I didn't think the balance of the team, especially in midfield, was quite right.

Mine was not a philosophy shared by the management, though, as, on a Sunday two weeks before the start of the season, I got a text from the gaffer saying some semi-professional clubs were interested in taking me and I could go if I was interested.

One was Newport County, then managed by my former Weymouth teammate Dean Holdsworth. If it'd been closer to home, I would've walked there straight away. I wasn't keen on moving but I still had my house in Worcester so I didn't rule anything out completely.

I spoke to Dean the next day and liked what he said, but the financial offer was underwhelming. The maximum wage on offer was £550 per week (£100 less than what I was on at the time) and there was no relocation package. I said I couldn't entertain that offer unless I got a pay-off from Crawley, so I needed to speak to Evo.

One other interesting point came out of that chat: Steve had initially told me Dean had asked about my availability, but, in reality, the gaffer had offered me up.

Now Crawley had come into some money, we were off to the Five Lakes hotel in Essex for a five-day training camp. Upon our arrival, the gaffer and I had a chat about my situation. I said that without my contract getting paid up at Crawley, I couldn't contemplate Newport's offer. He didn't take the bait and said I could stay. I had no problem with that either as the move to Newport didn't particularly appeal – mainly because of the travelling involved.

The training camp finished with our last pre-season game against Bromley, in which we played poorly and lost 1–0. I was restricted to a five-minute cameo and was starting to get annoyed.

The gaffer always justified not playing me by saying I was not mobile enough to play in a 4–4–2. That was rubbish. I was going down to the gym regularly to get myself fitter and fitter, motivated by a desire to prove him wrong.

The season started with a home game against Grimsby. I sneaked onto the bench but was not used during the 1–0 defeat. We played really well but lost after a rush of blood from our new goalkeeper Michel Kuipers. He came careering out of his box midway through the first half, handled the ball and was given a straight red card. To compound matters, Grimsby scored from the resulting free kick. Even with ten men we dominated and we should've earned at least a draw. Watching that game convinced me further that I could work myself into the team, though.

The new signings kept coming and we added both Scott Neilson from Bradford City and Jai Reason on a short-term contract from Cambridge United. Both were midfielders but both were also from the Essex area, so that helped with the cost of petrol. Swings and roundabouts…

They were enough to push me out of the sixteen, though, so I watched the game at Cambridge United from the stands. We started off like a house on fire, with Tubbsy getting a couple of early goals to put us two up – both he and Sergio Torres were really showing their class. However, Cambridge quickly hit back to level it at 2–2 and that was how it stayed.

It was a really good game of football, a great advert for the Conference Premier, and, although we hadn't won either of our first two games, we clearly had the potential to be a really good side. Sergio had especially impressed me. He was clearly a very good footballer but, just as importantly, he was a great guy with no ego whatsoever.

Unfortunately for me, though, it didn't look like I had much of a future at Crawley. The day after our visit to Cambridge I got a call from Paul Raynor explaining I was no longer in their plans and I could have £5,000 to leave. I had a little chuckle to myself and then told him there was no way I was going to leave for such a derisory offer. The remaining term of my contract was worth £27,500 alone. I told Rayns I would leave for £15,000 and that was a non-negotiable figure.

I was pissed off because I had re-signed just three and a half months earlier in good faith. The season had only just started so most clubs had their squads in place already, meaning it was by no means a foregone conclusion I would find a new contract. So I decided there was no way I was going to come out of this situation losing money. In actual fact, bearing in mind the money the club was spending on players, I believed I deserved a premium to leave. In the previous season, while not being amazing, I had been a key player in helping Crawley Town finish in their highest ever League position. Now I was being treated like an idiot.

To top it off, I knew I was better than some of the central midfielders the gaffer already had, yet he was going to pay me to leave. I'd never been so determined to prove someone wrong in my life. If I wasn't going to get that opportunity, I was at least going to be well compensated to move on.

The next day at training, the gaffer pulled me into his office and asked me for my thoughts regarding the pay-off. I reiterated my position and, to be fair, Steve said he would not hold it against me and would treat me with the respect I deserved. He stuck to that for all of two days!

When managers are trying to ease unwanted players out of the club, they begin by trying to make life difficult. For me, that began on a Sunday when a few of us were called in to train – all we did was run. On the Monday, I was again sent up to the gym with another lad to train with the physio, even though we were both fully fit. It seemed pretty petty as Evo could've easily incorporated two more players into his session. If he thought his tactics were going to work on me, though, he had another think coming.

I had no problem doing whatever he asked – in actual fact, I made sure he knew that not only was I going to do whatever he asked, but I was going to do it better than anyone else and enjoy it. After all, worst-case scenario, I was getting paid to keep myself fit.

Steve was trying all sorts of techniques to try to get at me. Sometimes, when training was over, he would tell me I had to train again, even though I'd received no prior notice. I would say I couldn't as I was travelling with other players who were taking me home. It was great to see the gaffer fume and grudgingly accept my reasoning.

Another of his tricks was to bring me in at 9 a.m. on the day of an evening kick-off, make me train and then get me to hang around for the game – which is what happened for our match against Bath City. On that occasion, I was pulled straight into the office and asked if I had changed my mind about leaving. I think Evo and Paul thought they'd worn me down, but they weren't even close to my tipping point.

I felt they took me for some kind of imbecile: they'd told me I wasn't getting any money while boasting about how much money they had at their disposal. I just said my position hadn't changed and left the room.

The gaffer must've been straight on the phone to the owners as I was summoned back into his office and offered a very precise £11,666.66. I felt like I was playing my very own game of *Deal or No Deal*. I thanked him for the offer but reiterated my position: £15,000 or I stayed. I walked straight out of the office chuckling to myself – I was confident that within the next day or two I would get my figure and be off.

I had to suffer some short-term pain, though, as the rest of the unwanted players and I endured a tough double training session. But I didn't mind as all I kept thinking about was the big fat cheque I'd soon be receiving.

My confidence was sorely misplaced, it seemed, as time ticked on and that extra £3,333 didn't appear. I was still in exile. Then the gaffer had a change of heart – something he was prone to do – and decided he wanted me to temporarily go out on loan for a month. I wasn't sure whether he was telling the truth or trying a new tactic but, either way, I wasn't fussed. I was willing to go out on loan all season if he wasn't going to pay me off.

During all that time the first team was actually coming along nicely and winning pretty regularly, but there was still, in my opinion, space for an attacking midfielder.

The end of the August transfer window was dangerously close, however, and any pay-off had to be agreed by then. If I agreed something after it closed, that would mean I'd be unable to join another club in the Conference Premier or higher until January. I'm still not sure how this practice is legal – surely it's a restraint of trade? – but it was, and remains, a major issue for many lower-league players.

But then everything seemed to change. We had a reserve game on the last day of August, away at Peterborough United, which I played in and we won 2–0. I played OK but football is all about perception and, for whatever reason, the gaffer's one of me had dramatically changed. Suddenly, in his eyes, I was a good player again. In that one game, I'd gone from someone who could do nothing right to a player who could do no wrong.

The first-team squad was now up to twenty-six players, including six strikers, and I was back training with them after two weeks in solitary confinement. I was also more confident than ever about forcing my way into the team.

The following day I was pulled into the manager's office before training, told that my recent attitude had really impressed everyone and advised to keep it up. To be honest, I hadn't been doing it for them but I appreciated the recognition. Maybe they'd been doing the whole thing to test certain players and see who fell by the wayside?

One of those who did fall away was my gym buddy Darragh Ryan. He'd received the same treatment as me and left the same day I was re-integrated into the fold. I don't think he was on great money but, by all accounts, he settled for £5,000, which I thought meant he'd sold himself short.

I managed to get on the bench for the next League game against Fleetwood and put in a steady display for the reserves against local team Three Bridges – the sort of performance now perceived as 'excellent' by the powers that be.

I retained my place in the first-team squad away to Histon and, although I was an unused sub again, it was the first time in ages I'd sat in on a team talk and felt like I was in with a chance of playing. We won the game comfortably but we still weren't pulling up any trees when in possession of the ball. I knew my time would come and it would be soon.

During that time, Evo pulled me into his office again as it turned out the FA had queried my contract. What with the gaffer's previous misdemeanours, I think the authorities took a keen interest in Crawley's dealings. (For the uninitiated: when Steve Evans was manager of Boston United, he was found guilty of tax evasion and was very lucky to evade a custodial sentence. In the end, he was given a twelve-month custodial sentence, suspended for two years, and banned from all football activity for twenty months.) My contract said we had agreed another relocation package of £4,000, but the authorities had come back to the club and told them such a payment could only be made in an initial contract to cover moving costs, not subsequent ones. This was something I'd known but I hadn't said anything when we were negotiating.

So Steve said I would have to sign a new contract with the relocation money divided up into my weekly wage. I was wary as I didn't trust him at the best of times, let alone after everything we had gone through over the last month, but I checked it out thoroughly, reading every little bit of small print, and all seemed fine. My new wage was the unusual sum of £788 per week.

Richard Brodie, known as 'Brodes', had been at the club for a couple of weeks now and had taken all but a day and a half to settle in – shy and retiring he was not. He is a great lad who had that brilliant, self-deprecating Geordie humour.

One of the gaffer's favourite training ground games was to offer £50 to anyone who could hit the crossbar from the halfway line, much like the challenge popularised by TV show *Soccer AM*. He always used to have loads of £50 notes, which he called 'pinkies', on him at all times. I swear he must have insisted he got paid in cash!

I never got anywhere near winning anything personally as I could not kick a ball that far. Anyone who has seen me play knows I only pass it about 10 yards and normally on the floor. I used to enjoy these kind of games though as they really helped create camaraderie within our group.

On one occasion the gaffer was feeling particularly generous and raised the stakes. For some reason or another Brodes owed him £250, so the gaffer said he would offer him 4/1 to hit the crossbar from about 30 yards.

If he did it Steve would pay out £1,000. Being the eternal optimist that Brodes was he took the bet and only went and did it!

Evo was laughing through gritted teeth while all of us were running around celebrating. One of the gaffer's mottos was: 'If you owe money you have to show your credibility by paying up promptly.' I enthusiastically reminded him of that while the celebrations continued.

To be fair, as soon as we returned back to the ground to get changed, the gaffer presented Richard with a cheque for £1,000. There was nothing better than seeing a Scotsman part with his money!

Training had become notably more enjoyable since I'd returned to the fold. We were doing a lot more football-based activity – maybe because we had better players and were going to play more of an expansive game. Whatever the reasoning, it was definitely a change for the better.

I finally made it onto the pitch that season on 18 September in a home game versus Gateshead. The match was finally poised at 1–1 when I was introduced with twenty minutes to go. Tubbsy, as he did many times that season, saved our blushes by scoring a last-minute winner. I was delighted with the win – and also the fact I'd played a part in it. I'd provided a spark with my introduction and was now starting to put pressure on the other midfielders in our squad.

Support for me from my teammates was also beginning to grow. A few of the new attackers were recognising what I could bring to the team and were pushing for me to get a starting place.

The fixture computer had been kind to us early on, but we were due some real tests. These started with AFC Wimbledon, whom Crawley had developed quite a rivalry with over the previous couple of years. The game seemed to come a week too early for me as everything we did in training leading up to the game pointed to my being on the bench.

Over the years, the top Conference League has had television deals with a host of sports channels – some well known and others more obscure. That year it involved one of the more obscure broadcasters – namely Premier Sports – and they were to cover our game against AFC Wimbledon, which meant it was moved to a Thursday night.

For any player who didn't realise the game was being televised, that was soon rectified when the gaffer lit up the dressing room the day before the match with a fresh set of highlights. That was always a signal a big game was upon us.

After toying with a 4–3–3 formation in training, the gaffer decided to stick with 4–4–2, which, after evidence from training, was probably the right decision. I was on the bench and Wimbledon started off quickly but, after the opening twenty minutes, we were clearly the better team and took the lead.

We looked comfortable and were cruising until they nicked an equaliser with fifteen minutes to go. Then we inexplicably allowed Wimbledon to go on and win it.

Craig McAllister (Macca) and I came on at the end, but had little time to make any impact. The gaffer was fuming but, in the long term, this result was a blessing as it played a major factor in our subsequent success. Steve realised that night that the most expensive players did not necessarily make the best team. He also finally realised the central midfield partnership of Stevie Masterton and Pablo Mills was not working, as they both lacked the mobility for the position.

I was convinced I would be playing in the next game at Rushden & Diamonds on the Sunday. Well, I was until teammate Eddie Hutchinson texted to say Crawley had just signed Dannie Bulman (Bully), a former player before my time, on loan from Oxford United. That was a kick in the teeth!

We trained the day before the game and, even though we had added Bully to the squad, the gaffer confirmed I would be playing alongside him in central midfield. I appreciated the heads-up as I've always thought giving someone prior warning if they haven't played for a while to be good management.

I had a day to get myself mentally prepared for a game I was sure would be my first to prove the gaffer wrong. I felt no pressure. I was not one of his big signings and I was not earning pots of money. I was just someone he had written off as not good enough. No doubt I was just earmarked to keep a place warm for someone else to come in during January but, the way I saw it, it was all upwards from that point. If it all went tits-up I would be in no worse a situation than I had been for the previous two months.

We won the game 1–0 and I lasted eighty-seven minutes, playing well while not being spectacular.

Bully and I struck up a good understanding straight away. I had played against him many times but, while I respected him, I had never really been overly struck by his talent. I subsequently found out you don't appreciate how good someone like Bully is until you play with them. He went about his job quietly and effectively and played with no ego. If that meant he just gave the nearest player 5-yard passes all game then so be it. What I also really liked about Bully was that he was always available if I couldn't play the ball forward.

The gaffer seemed pretty content after the Rushden game. Before we got on the coach he said the press had commented positively on my performance. He'd apparently told them I'd been suffering with a groin injury. I said nothing but I did wonder why he hadn't just told the truth and admitted he'd made a mistake.

What a difference a game makes. I was suddenly brimming with confidence and couldn't wait to play against Tamworth – a team I always did well against.

The gaffer named an unchanged team and I played like a man possessed – determined to continue shoving the manager's words about me not being good enough down his throat. He wasn't happy at half-time when we came in at 1–1. He told us we were playing 'fucking five-a-side football' and weren't 'getting the ball in the box quick enough' – it was a strange comment as we were dominating both possession and the game.

I explained I thought that, by retaining possession, we were tiring Tamworth out and would be able to capitalise on that in the second half (which we did). But my sentiments were certainly not shared by the management – as they had no hesitation in telling me.

We eventually won 3–1 and I got my first goal of the season.

Next up we faced a resilient Kidderminster Harriers. How I didn't score in the first half of that one is beyond me. I peppered their goal with shots at will and only a combination of bad luck, good defending and excellent goalkeeping kept me off the scoresheet. I felt indefatigable and could not remember the last time I had played with such energy levels. We eventually broke them down with a great strike from Scott Neilson and a tap-in from Macca.

We were starting to play some good football rather than the direct rubbish we'd been serving up the previous season. Having two good footballing centre halves in Kyle McFadzean and Pablo made a big difference as they formed the base from which every attack began.

I played excellently again but I was finding it easy to do so within a good team that was now starting to gel. I had never been so motivated to continuously prove someone wrong. Some may say it was great man management – well, I can think of at least one person who would share that belief!

Luton Town, as always, were billed as one of the favourites for the title so it was an early season showdown when we visited Kenilworth Road at the start of October. There was a big, mostly hostile, crowd of just under 7,000 in attendance.

I loved playing at places like Luton, with its classic, old-school stadium. The crowd is right next to the pitch and you can smell the pungent aroma of beer, burgers and fag breath – the way football should be. Fans in the futuristic, all-seater stadiums seem so detached from the action nowadays. The home fans there were clearly up for it and gave us a lively reception while we warmed up. They were creating the sort of atmosphere any self-respecting footballer would have loved to be a part of.

Brodes had history with the Luton fans after being part of a York City team that had knocked Luton out of the play-offs the previous season – although it was his mum who was getting the brunt of their anger. I'm not sure what she'd done to offend them but it was something to do with Mrs Brodie being 'a bore', if I remember correctly – or words to that effect!

Anyway, the Luton players were clearly as up for the match as much as their supporters, because, during the opening twenty minutes, they absolutely put us to the sword. Only a combination of their bad finishing and our good fortune kept the score level. As the half wore on, we began to get a foothold in the game and threaten them back, but, if it had been a boxing match, Luton would definitely have been ahead on points.

We came out for the second half with a renewed focus and the game began swinging from end to end until Andy Drury – their best player on the night – put Luton ahead with a well-taken penalty. That didn't seem to knock us out of our stride, though, as we continued to press forward in search of an equaliser.

Our bravery paid off in the eightieth minute when Brodes, the most hated man in Bedfordshire, got the last touch on a goal-bound header to make it 1–1.

I think both clubs would have settled for a point each, but Bully seized on a wayward pass late on and expertly put Macca through to score and nick us a whole three points. Macca, like myself, was also highly motivated to prove the gaffer wrong, as he felt he wasn't getting the opportunities his performances deserved.

We left the pitch to a chorus of abuse and boos – most of which was aimed at our loveable Geordie. There was no chance I would walk back to the changing rooms by his side!

There was a real feeling of elation in the dressing room after winning such a battle. In reality, a draw would have been a fair result. Mine and my fellow midfield colleague's performances could have been described as 'workman-like', but it was our hard graft that helped us to victory.

The result also sent out a message to the rest of the League and proved, in case anybody was in any doubt, that Crawley had become the real deal.

Games were starting to come thick and fast, and a trip to Holker Street to play Barrow was next up. After not kicking a ball for the first six weeks of the season, I was now in line to start my fifth game in fourteen days – I wasn't complaining!

As always seemed to be the case when travelling that far north, the weather conditions were not conducive to good football: a howling wind blew from one end of the pitch to the other and, as a result, the match was the proverbial game of two halves. We dominated the first half with the wind behind us and took the lead; Barrow dominated the second and equalised.

In the end we were happy enough to grab a point from a tricky fixture. I'm pretty sure the gaffer felt that way too, but it was not a sentiment he was going to openly share with us. He came roaring into the dressing room and moaned about how the second-half performance was not good enough – which was true, but we didn't deserve such anger, especially considering our recent form.

I tried to remind him of that with a conversation that went as follows:

Me: Fucking hell, gaffer – we've taken thirteen points from the last fifteen, that is pretty good.

SE: Who are you? The fucking stat man? Did you think that second half was good enough?

Me: No, I agree it wasn't, but let's keep a bit of perspective.

SE: Keep a bit of fucking perspective! We cannot afford to drop points against teams like that; we need to take these opportunities.

Me: Yeah, but we probably didn't expect to get three points at Luton, so four points from two tough away games is a good return.

SE: No, it is not fucking good. Fucking hell, Rayns – he thinks he is the fucking stat man! (*Storms out of dressing room.*)

I refused to get involved in slanging matches with the gaffer but I would always try to argue my point if he was talking unjustified bollocks. Even though Steve would never admit it at the time, I think he did later reflect on what I said and even took some of it on board.

He soon forgave me for our disagreement too because he came up to the back of the bus and, saying nothing, gave me one of his snack-size Twixes. It was one of those occasions when no words are needed...

Even though I didn't feel like I had anything to apologise for, I was conscious of keeping the gaffer on side, so when we returned to training on the Tuesday I popped in to see him. I explained I hadn't been trying to be a smart arse – I'd just wanted to give some balance to the post-Barrow debate. He seemed fine about it and we chatted some more in the less emotionally charged environment.

After two tricky away games it felt good to be back at our Broadfield Stadium, where we were due to entertain Newport County. They had won the Conference South at a canter the previous year and were turning out to be the surprise package in our division, challenging near the top. I was doubly motivated for that game because I wanted to prove to their manager Dean Holdsworth that he'd been right to try to sign me at the start of the season.

Unfortunately, we lost 3–2, our first defeat since the Wimbledon game. We were poor defensively and, despite going into half-time at 2–2, we couldn't handle the movement of the vibrant Newport side and eventually succumbed to a winner. I was replaced with five minutes to go and told Steve what I thought of his decision as I left the pitch. A sure sign, in my eyes anyway, that I was in the right was the fact I received no reply. The gaffer had gone mad at the break and I felt a few of his bigger signings had gone under. They really should have been replaced ahead of me.

As I'm sure you've guessed by now, there were recriminations after the game. The main recipients of the criticism were our defenders, as we'd given away some terrible goals. Macca came in fuming and said, 'How come I never get the opportunity to score the type of shit goals we gave away today?'

He was right, but I also felt that, bearing in mind the amount of stick we received from the gaffer, the last thing we needed to be doing was turning on each other.

'OK, Mac,' I chipped in. 'But remember nobody digs you out when you miss a chance. People aren't making mistakes on purpose.'

'Yeah, but it's not fucking good enough,' he quite rightly replied.

'He's fucking right, Smudger – we cannot afford to give away such shit goals,' added the gaffer. 'It's not fucking good enough. How are your stats looking now, fucking stat man?'

Not too bad actually, I thought – we'd taken thirteen points from a possible eighteen – but I didn't want to needlessly antagonise him further. 'Of course we're not happy with it, but we're all in this together,' I simply replied. 'There's no point in the forwards having a go at the defenders and vice versa.'

Evo was not having it and insisted that it was just how great teams did things behind closed doors. I begged to differ.

That was the sort of discussion that regularly happened after games, but there was no falling out – definitely not between myself and Macca anyway. He was someone I got on really well with in the team and, by Monday, there was no reference to the incident again.

Steve still wanted to have the last word, however, and pulled me into his office for another chat. I felt quite comfortable in the surroundings of his office – understandably so, bearing in mind how much time I'd spent in there over the preceding months! – although he went on to tell me that I was not the spokesman for the team and that if he wanted my opinion he would ask for it. Fair enough. I made a conscious decision then to be more reserved with my comments. I was playing well and didn't want to talk myself out of the team.

Rumours started going around the club the following week that Crawley were trying to sign Robert Pires who, the previous season, had been playing in La Liga for Villarreal. The way our season was going, anything was possible. Steve may have had his faults but you had to admire his front. After all, if I was going to lose my place to anyone, it might as well be a French World Cup winner!

The FA Cup draw had given us a chance to exact quick revenge on Newport. We had drawn them away – as tough a draw as you could hope to get for a fourth qualifying round tie, bearing in mind they had not lost at home for eighteen months.

Before the game, the gaffer reminded us of their rather exuberant celebrations after beating us the previous week, which added even more fuel to our fire. An already tricky tie was made harder after Tubbsy made a rare mistake and missed a penalty. From then on, the game could have gone either way but we put in a thoroughly professional performance and won off a second-half goal from Macca.

During the game I got an accidental knee in the ribs from Kyle McFadzean as we both challenged for a header. It was a little sore but I thought nothing of it. However, during my usual Monday afternoon session down the gym, I managed to aggravate it while on the treadmill. I was in agony.

I went into training the next day but had to pull out of a practice match. The gaffer was fuming. It turned out I had damaged the cartilage that sits between the ribs.

I arrived for training on Thursday but the gaffer pulled me straight into his office and told me he wasn't sure whether he could have me in his team. I told him he had to do what he had to do. He had loads of players lined up to replace me apparently, so I wondered why, if that really was the case, he didn't just go ahead and do it.

That was a good meeting, though, because it showed me how much he wanted me in the team.

Mark Stein, the former Chelsea striker, was our physiotherapist at the time, and he tried to explain to the gaffer that, as it was only Thursday, I needed another day of rest to give me a real chance of playing on Saturday. Steiny was unfortunately not the most eloquent of people, however, and we faced a losing battle. The gaffer insisted I train and then proceeded to go through an amusing sketch with Rayns whereby he kept asking his assistant: 'What day do players have to train to be available for selection on a Saturday?'

Rayns kept saying Friday until about the fifth loaded question, when he eventually realised the gaffer wanted him to say Thursday. They were just like Laurel and Hardy!

One player who definitely wasn't joining the Crawley Town revolution was Pires, who had made the tough decision to go and play back in the other Premier Division with Aston Villa. It was a shame as, although it would have probably led to me losing my place, it would also have been great to train with such a top player.

Although there wasn't much I could do about my injury, I was gutted it had cost me my place. The gaffer must have sensed this because he told me not to worry about it and insinuated I would get my place back. That was a good piece of management on his behalf as it put my mind at rest.

As I didn't report the injury immediately I was liable to receive a club fine. We settled on me buying him a bottle of his favourite tipple – pink champagne – I was happy with that as it could have been a lot worse.

In the end, I was only unavailable for one game and the lads clearly missed me because they only won 4–1 at Mansfield!

Our next game was against Guiseley in the first round of the FA Cup and I was on the bench. My ribs were not completely pain-free and it made perfect sense to maintain the unchanged line-up that had managed a 4–1 away win.

We cruised to a 5–0 victory so, having missed two games in which we scored nine and conceded one, it looked like it could be a while until I won my place back.

That proved to be true. After not playing for ten days I was selected to join the reserves against Leyton Orient – Steve always liked to keep his players busy. However, after twenty minutes, I had to hobble off with a dead leg. I knew it was nothing serious but I also knew I would be struggling to be available for Saturday. That was all I needed: another niggly little injury setting me back.

Sure enough, I was ruled out of the long journey to Darlington. I suppose if I was going to miss a game that one was close to the top of any 'wish list'. Every cloud…

I was back in the fold within a week and had the dubious pleasure of playing in the Sussex Senior Cup away at Horsham. Both the team and I were useless and we were lucky to escape with a 2–0 defeat. Steve was surprisingly calm and reflective after the game – a reaction that unnerved me more than his usual ranting and raving.

I was swiftly brought into the gaffer's lair the day after to have both my effort and desire put into question. I retorted that if they were questionable, then I would be sitting on my sofa with a fat cheque in my pocket having taken his pay-off in August, rather than standing in his office talking to him about my game. I also added that I knew he was going to bring another midfielder in during the January window and that he should do it so we could see who the better player was.

I was starting to think the gaffer was perhaps cuter than I had given him credit for. He knew if he laid out a challenge for me I would take the bait. Maybe there was a method to his madness.

Everything we discussed was not enough to get me in the first team for our next game at home to Altrincham, although my performance in the reserves had not warranted it anyway. The lads cantered to a very comfortable 7–0 win in any case.

Now I really was in trouble.

It was mid-November and I effectively had six weeks to save my full-time career. If I was not playing by January I had very little chance of fighting for a place against any new arrival as they would most definitely rank above me in the pecking order.

I thought I'd already ridden all the lows this season had to offer but there was still more to come.

On my thirty-first birthday I was due to go to a place called Loxswood to play against Loxswood FC. The game had been arranged to celebrate the turning-on of their floodlights. As it was 2010 and not 1960, that reason alone should tell you how high up the footballing pyramid our hosts were. It wasn't even really a reserve game as there were only a couple of senior players involved.

I was very frustrated – I felt I should have been one of the first names on the main team sheet, not reduced to filling numbers in such insignificant games. To top it off, I had to play central midfield alongside a porky auburn moaner by the name of Paul Raynor! He didn't shut up either – the poor old ref must have had to ice both ears at half-time as Rayns questioned every single decision made.

The only positives were that I scored and that the gaffer took pity on me, subbed me at half-time and let me go home. It was a lovely gesture as it meant I managed to salvage the last couple of hours of my birthday...

Next up was a big second-round FA cup game on a bitterly cold Friday night at home against Swindon Town, who, at that time, were in League One. The occasion was again marked by a dazzling new full set of highlights on the head of our esteemed leader. After my appearance on Tuesday, there was absolutely no chance of me playing – but I did sneak onto the bench.

We started quite tentatively and were lucky not to be behind at half-time. It became more obvious that the gaffer wasn't happy so I was introduced early in the second half. The two players identified as 'key men' by the TV pundits got the goals in a 1–1 draw: Charlie Austin put Swindon in front and Matt Tubbs equalised sublimely for us.

Our performance improved in the second half and we were deserving of a draw – although it did look like we had perhaps missed our chance to go through. I didn't perform very well as I was lacking a bit of confidence, but at least I'd played a part in our recovery.

That was a good example of the highs and lows football can encapsulate within such a short space of time. I had gone from playing in what was effectively a third-team game on the Tuesday to playing forty minutes live on ITV on the Friday.

I was really looking forward to the replay but I wanted to get a couple of games under my belt first so I would be on top form. Unfortunately Mother Nature had other ideas because we suddenly endured a prolonged cold snap and the next two games fell by the wayside.

During that period there was a ridiculous amount of snow and the commute from Essex to West Sussex, which had been relatively kind all season, became nigh-on impossible. I got up one morning and there was a good 8 inches of snow, so I rang the gaffer and told him I would struggle to get in. He was as understanding as ever and said that he didn't care and that I had to be at training.

After three and a half hours I was thanked for my persistence with a £200 fine for being late. I think he expected me to bite, but I just laughed it off. I knew from experience not to confront him immediately and to let him calm down a bit. I was confident he would be willing to negotiate at a later date.

Due to the adverse conditions, the next playable game turned out to be our FA Cup replay at the County Ground. The gaffer unexpectedly changed our formation to a 4–3–3 and named me 'in the hole', while also giving me a specific job to do.

Jonathan Douglas was Swindon's main playmaker and I was earmarked as the man to stop him starting off their attacks. Then, when we got the ball, I was expected to spring off him and make forward runs into the opposition box.

The change of formation was a shock. Training, due to the poor weather, had been very limited and the gaffer had given us no indication of such a modification. I was concerned – I'd hardly kicked a ball competitively over the past two months and was suddenly playing a specific role against a side two leagues above.

I knew I was good enough to compete with anyone in the Conference

National, but the demons in my head were trying to infect my positivity. Two seasons before, Hereford – and, arguably, myself – had proved we weren't good enough for that level.

Playing 'in the hole' was a great position when you were on form but, if you weren't feeling at the top of your game, it was a lot easier to play in an orthodox 4–4–2 because you could get through by just rolling up your sleeves and battling it out with your opposite number.

I started the game apprehensively. The conditions were more reminiscent of the Arctic than Wiltshire, but my work rate was high. I always knew when I was in good form because my first touch was perfect and I was very aware of my surroundings. This was not the case until about fifteen minutes in, though. I made a late run from midfield and anticipated a Craig McAllister knock-down that I could then volley as a left-footed shot into the bottom corner of the goal. The pitch had some frozen patches meaning any shots either side of the goalkeeper were going to be hard for him to reach.

I suddenly felt the adrenalin and confidence surge through my body and the shackles came off. We were playing a League One team and we dominated them on their own patch … until Jon-Paul McGovern equalised and Charlie Austin put them in front before the break. But we still felt we were the better team.

Another positive occurred on the stroke of half-time when Jonathan Douglas, my direct opponent, lunged into Glenn Wilson and was given an immediate red card. I was now relieved of all my defensive responsibilities and had the space to utilise my newfound confidence.

We knew we could beat them and continued pressing for an equaliser. I was at the heart of many of our best moves. Swindon eventually succumbed when Glenn Wilson's cross/shot – he said shot, everyone else said cross – deflected off my former Hereford United teammate Michael Rose to level the score.

There was only one team winning this now as we camped in their half for the rest of normal and then extra time. Just as I was beginning to panic about having to take a penalty, Jamie Cook went on a mazy run across the opposition's penalty box before sliding the ball to me. I instinctively flicked it with the outside of my left foot into the bottom right-hand corner, giving the keeper no chance to set himself.

I hadn't had a second to think about what I was doing and was as shocked as anyone when the ball nestled in the goal. There was just under two minutes of extra time left, which we survived comfortably.

The final whistle went and it was a surreal moment; photographers ran on the pitch and wanted pictures of me doing cheesy poses, holding my arms aloft in triumph while looking straight into their cameras. I did not feel comfortable and didn't like being the centre of attention – although I did enjoy seeing that the *Daily Telegraph* named me as the most influential player on the pitch.

Before I knew it I had been coerced into a picture with the gaffer. It was like one of those moments when your ninety-year-old great-aunt gets hold of you at Christmas for a kiss and you can't get away. By the time I got into training on the Thursday, someone had managed to blow a copy of the image up and put it above my peg in the dressing room.

I was buzzing after the game and held the team coach up afterwards for about half an hour as I attended to numerous press interviews. The lads welcomed me onto the coach with a song: 'Two goals and you were going to pay him up! Two goals and you were going to pay him up!'

Even the gaffer couldn't help but chuckle at that one.

What an amazing game football can be. I was finally reaping the rewards for all the hard work I'd put in by myself down the gym, proving the people who had doubted me wrong.

The Swindon game took a lot out of me, plus I was now struggling with a gash on my ankle. We were playing Dartford in the FA Trophy on Saturday and I was determined to build on my two recent goals, but the gaffer had other ideas. He made eight changes to the team and I was in the stand. After ten minutes, we were 2–0 down and I was smugly thinking I had dodged a bullet. We eventually secured a 3–3 draw, but I was left out of the replay as well (which we lost).

The weather took control again and we didn't play until New Year's Day. The transfer window was about to open and the gaffer did his business early, signing Scott Shearer from Wrexham, Josh Simpson from Peterborough and both John Dempster and James Dance from Kettering. He also added David Hunt, on loan from Brentford, for the rest of the season. That was worse for me than I'd been expecting. I'd known he'd bring in one central midfielder, but Josh Simpson and David Hunt were both recognised midfielders.

But, to be fair, the gaffer did manage me brilliantly during that time. He firstly praised me in front of the whole group – saying how hard I had worked and how I was an important part of the squad – and he then privately reiterated that I was going to have a big part to play in the rest of the season. He was as good as his word.

Every one of his signings went on to make a contribution on the pitch – though some more than others. They were also all great characters in the dressing room, each adding something positive to an already really lively group.

Whether by luck or judgement – probably a bit of both – the squad that had been put together over the summer was gelling brilliantly. There was a core group of five or six nutcases – namely Scott Neilson, Brodes, Kyle McFadzean, Tubbsy and Macca – who egged each other on to do more stupid things, while the rest of us 'normal' people enjoyed being entertained by them. This group of lunatics was then added to in the New Year by Scott Shearer and John Dempster, who were more than willing to match and surpass their new teammates' antics.

There were so many hilarious incidents – some not suitable for print – but I will give you a flavour of the sort of stuff they did while keeping the individual culprits nameless.

One of the nutters decided to put yoghurt-coated raisins up his bum before returning them back into the packet and trying to get one of the other lads to eat them. As a result, most of us very quickly learnt not to take any food unless it had come out of a packet you had witnessed being opened. However, one of our more trusting (read: dopey) players was more than happy to take up the offer and didn't believe us when we told him what had happened. Unfortunately he couldn't ignore the evidence when the culprit pulled down his trousers, bent over and revealed the remnants of the yoghurt coating around his arsehole!

The same perpetrator then decided to see how many Minstrels he could get under his foreskin. The number escapes me but I remember it being a lot more than I thought possible!

The victim of the yoghurt-coated raisin incident was also stupid enough to leave his water bottle unattended in the dressing room once. As soon as he left the room, the cap was removed and the tip of the bottle wiped around someone's ring piece. He duly came back, took a massive swig of his drink and was greeted by sniggers from those in the dressing room.

The same mischief-maker yet again decided on another occasion to see how far he could get a broom handle up his arse. Do not ask me how far it went as I could not look, but whoever cleaned the dressing room that night may have wondered why someone had put a peanut butter-like substance on the handle!

New Year's Day saw us up against Eastbourne Borough in a local derby. After our enforced break and the new additions, I was again feeling a little insecure about my position within the team. I kept my place though, as promised, and repaid the gaffer by scoring the opening goal. Tubbsy continued his one-man assault for the 'Golden Boot' with another two goals, including a Andrea Pirlo-esque dinked penalty.

Within forty-eight hours we had another game, away to Forest Green Rovers, and again the gaffer played me very well. I was left out of the team in favour of Josh but Evo qualified the decision by saying I was guaranteed to be playing against Derby County in the third round of the FA Cup.

I didn't have enough time to sulk as I was busy telling all the lads I was the only player definitely playing the following week. In reality, he wasn't offering me much as Josh was cup-tied (plus I still had to play in a reserve game midweek), but it was a good piece of psychology.

My absence from the team made absolutely no difference whatsoever as the lads cruised to a 3–0 win on a pitch covered in a light dusting of snow.

We had a full week to prepare for the FA Cup tie at home to Derby County. Even though they were a Championship club, the gaffer's arrogance was rubbing off on us and we really fancied our chances. After all, they were going through a consolidation period at the time and trying to recover from overspending in the Premier League.

As promised, I was selected to play 'in the hole' as part of a 4–3–3 but, again, I was nervous – the standard of opposition had gone up yet another notch. I still hadn't had a regular run in the team but, as with the Swindon game, I had another important job to do: pick up the experienced Robbie Savage.

Everything seemed to be building towards a cup upset. When Derby came out onto our pitch they were met by torrential rain and a gale-force wind. We had the wind behind us in the first half and we tried to take a stranglehold of the game. As always, we set our stall out to be competitive and not give them a second on the ball. Kris Commons, Derby's best player, was welcomed by a robust Glenn Wilson tackle that resulted in both him and the ball finishing up on the opposite side of the advertising hoardings.

Our strategy looked like it was going to backfire when keeper Michel Kuipers had one of his more impetuous moments and gave away a penalty. Thankfully he instantly redeemed himself by saving it with his legs.

We continued our high-tempo pressing game. There was a great clip shown by Setanta Sports, who were covering the game live, in which four of our players were hunting down one Derby player deep in his own half and forcing him to kick the ball out of play.

Our superiority paid dividends shortly after that incident when Craig McAllister put us ahead. We fully deserved the lead and even received a little bit of good fortune just before half-time when our talisman, Matt Tubbs, was lucky to stay on the pitch. The ball had fallen between him and Robbie Savage, and Tubbsy fully committed himself to the tackle. He ended up taking both the ball and the pantomime villain. At the time it had looked like a very aggressive but ultimately fair tackle; after seeing it again on telly though, it was actually a very naughty one. Robbie, as I'm sure you can imagine, was not best pleased. Almost immediately after that, the ball fell between him and me. I could see he was going for the ball irrespective of whether I was in the way or not so I moved just in time and he smashed it out of the ground.

I started laughing and he went off on one: 'Don't fucking laugh at me. When you've played 300 games then you can fucking laugh.'

Actually, Robbie, I've played about 400. Is that OK with you? No doubt he would have cut me down with something about the number of Ferraris he owned or the millions he had in the bank, so I kept my thoughts to myself.

Derby improved in the second half but we were still going toe-to-toe with them. It looked as though our chance had gone when Derby equalised midway through the second half, but we continued to press for a winner.

Right on full time, Sergio Torres had a great strike flicked over the bar by Paul Green on the line. I'd love to say that, from the resultant corner, Dean Howell performed a well-thought-out set-piece routine, but the truth was he shanked his cross to the edge of the box. Thankfully it fell to Sergio, who managed to strike the ball through a clutch of bodies and into the bottom corner of the goal.

The whole place erupted and Sergio eventually appeared from beneath a sea of bodies after about five minutes. The goal came so late that Derby had no chance to recover. Crawley was through to the fourth round of the FA Cup for the first time in the club's history.

I was happy with my own performance too. After another nervy start, I got into the game and caused the opposition a lot of problems by getting into those little areas between their midfield and defence.

The dressing room was buoyant after the game. Evo, being the hard taskmaster that he was, had us in for training the next day so I stayed in Crawley and we all celebrated with the supporters in the club bar.

During that evening I got talking to one of our mystery owners, Paul. He was very complimentary and praised my performance. He believed the influx of new players had made me raise my game. I begged to differ, and said that nothing had changed except the manager's opinion of me.

Paul was obviously in a buoyant mood as apparently he gave the gaffer a Rolex, allegedly worth £25,000, as a reward for the triumph. This cup run was financially beneficial for everyone, though. Our bonuses for League victories were minimal but we were entitled to 40 per cent of any prize money due from a win in the FA Cup, which was now getting pretty substantial. For reaching round four we received 40 per cent of £67,500, shared between the eighteen-man playing squad.

It was a strange time overall for me as, even though I was playing well when selected, the gaffer had a lot of midfielders available and was rotating the squad. I say rotating, but there were only four or five of us who were regularly rested; everyone else seemed to be untouchable. It was clear Josh and I were competing for one place and I was pretty sure Steve favoured Josh, but my performances meant the gaffer couldn't ignore me. It was an interesting one as, although we were both midfielders, we played the role in totally different ways. Josh was a lot more athletic and threatened the opposition by stretching the play with his forward runs; I played the position by coming towards the ball and knitting the play together.

I was left out of the squad for the next game at home versus Kettering (where we laboured to a 2–1 victory), then I was back in for our away trip to Bath City (which we won 2–0). I was desperate to play every game but, I must admit, maybe the gaffer was doing the right thing by selecting which games I did and did not play in as things were going well.

That trend continued as I was on the bench for the long trip to Grimsby (where we ground out a creditable 0–0 draw), but then, surprisingly, back in for a midweek game at home against Cambridge United, even though we had our next cup game that Saturday, for which Josh was unavailable.

We beat Cambridge comfortably 3–0, although the gaffer did get a little stressed at half-time because it was goalless. We blocked out his normal over-reaction, ignoring it to go on and make our superiority count. Jamie Cook reminded everyone of his quality with a wonderfully composed finish – the main thing holding him back was his almost horizontal outlook on life. I put in another decent performance but was especially happy with my set pieces, which I had put a lot of work into over the year.

We were up, out and on the road early on the Friday as we travelled to Devon to play Torquay United in the fourth round of the FA Cup. Steve had developed a taste for the finer things in life because, with the club's newfound riches, we were now staying in some lovely hotels.

On that occasion, we stayed at Woodbury Park – a hotel once owned by Formula 1 driver Nigel Mansell, boasting a beautiful complex and excellent training facilities. It was a far cry from my first away trip with Crawley the previous season, when we'd stayed at a Travelodge in Gateshead, full of boozy Swansea City fans.

We couldn't wait for the Torquay game as we all knew the vast majority of us would never get a better chance of making it to the final sixteen of the FA Cup. Initially we were – as I'm sure Torquay were too – disappointed with the draw because we wanted to play a Premier League club, but that all changed when we got to Plainmoor.

Even though it was a showdown between a humble League Two club and an even humbler Conference National club, we could soon sense how big a game it actually was. Kick-off was delayed by fifteen minutes to allow the 5,000-strong crowd into the ground, including a contingent of 1,200 from West Sussex – quite an achievement considering we were averaging around 700 for home games just a year before.

The game was as competitive as you might expect, but we quickly got into our stride and took control. We looked like the higher-ranked team and Torquay tried to hit us on the counter-attack. Tubbsy put us into the lead six minutes before half-time.

The second half continued in the same vein and, at around the hour mark, we had a chance to put the game out of sight. I delivered an in-swinging free kick from the left that was inexplicably handled by Torquay's Chris Zebroski. The referee awarded a penalty and Zebroski was sent off upon receiving a second yellow card. Unfortunately Scott Bevan produced an excellent save to deny Tubbsy. However, we now had the added advantage of an extra man and, ten minutes later, we were awarded another penalty after Jamie Cook was felled in the box. After a slight disagreement between Jamie and Macca over who was going to take it, Macca stepped up but the Torquay keeper thwarted us again. We saw the game out though and it created a great buzz. At that time, we were only the second non-League team in the history of the competition to reach the fifth round of the FA Cup. The money was mostly irrelevant, but it didn't go unnoticed by some of the team that we were sharing 40 per cent of £90,000 for that victory.

The only downside to our success was that it wasn't shared by the neutrals. Normally the underdogs were embraced by the nation but, because of our financial backing and the unpopularity of our manager, we were receiving the opposite reaction. Everyone but our own fans seemed to want to see us get a very public hammering.

That was illustrated during ITV's FA Cup highlights show in the evening. The panel, which included Chris Coleman, seemed to take a very dim view of Crawley. They highlighted an argument that Paul Raynor had with Torquay's groundsman before the game. Our strikers had wanted to practise some finishing in goal – a fair request really – but the groundsman had thought otherwise. We'd gone ahead and practised regardless, which the TV pundits said showed a lack of respect.

They then went on to point out our robust tactics, which, incidentally, were no more combative than Torquay's, and also highlighted Jamie and Macca's disagreement over the second penalty.

What were they expecting? We were never going to get another chance to reach the fifth round as a non-League club. Were we meant to just go there and let Torquay roll us over? In their eyes, we didn't deserve any credit, despite the fact we had beaten teams from League Two, League One and the Championship to get where we were.

Theirs was not the view shared by other media outlets, though, as I did a great interview with Danny Kelly for TalkSport radio on the coach home.

The next day I was at home by myself when the fifth-round draw was made. The numbered balls were slowly being whittled down and we had not yet been pulled out. The two teams I'd really wanted, though – West Ham United or Arsenal – had already been drawn, so we just had to wait and see.

In the end, we were one of the last two remaining and then it dawned on me who else was left at that point.

We were going to play Manchester United.

The penultimate ball was lifted up and shown to the nation. We would be playing at Old Trafford!

The phone calls started coming in straight away and they didn't stop. I was getting requests for tickets from family, friends and people I hadn't spoken to in ages.

On the Monday I went to my local BBC studio and did an interview for Radio 1, then, later that evening, I did another for Radio 5 live, not to mention interviews with several local papers. There were still three weeks to go so I wondered how mad everything would be in the week leading up to the game itself.

I felt the pressure mount almost immediately. This was going to be a great occasion and I was absolutely desperate to play. During my career I had seen former teammates play in similar sorts of games and I really thought such a chance had passed me by. I certainly wasn't going to get another opportunity to play at Old Trafford.

One problem we had was there were still three important League games before our glamour tie. As much as the gaffer told us to concentrate on those games, he knew everyone's focus was on making it to the week of the big game injury-free and in good enough form to be selected.

Just before the transfer window closed, another player was added to the squad. Willie Gibson, a whinger – I mean winger – joined us from St Johnstone. He seemed nice enough, but, for someone who'd just signed for a new club, he was a bit of a miserable git – something that didn't really change during his time at the club.

Our game on the first Saturday after the draw had been brought forward to Thursday because it was being screened by Premier Sports. We laboured to a very uninspiring 0–0 draw with Kettering. As a result of the rescheduling, we had a free weekend and were to be treated to a short training trip over in Portugal.

I personally, without wishing to sound ungrateful, would have preferred a few days' rest – I wasn't sure whether the trip was a treat or just something the gaffer could quote in the press to show how 'professional' Crawley were.

Evo, as usual, did not let us down with the accommodation. We stayed on the Algarve at a lovely resort. The complex had also just had a brand new pitch laid, which was better than anything we were used to. It would've been immaculate had it not been re-turfed just a few months before and not quite knitted together properly.

We had a night out on the Saturday and, although the town was quiet, some of our new signings made their mark. Two players drank a fair amount of urine – more than a shot and less than a pint – as part of their initiation, and another new recruit, who was a little worse for wear, had to be carried home to bed before midnight just after being showered in urine, seemingly the theme of the night.

We returned to Gatwick on Tuesday evening and, despite my initial doubts, I'd really enjoyed the trip. The weather was nice, I hadn't missed my daily commute and I'd even been able to forget about the Manchester United game for a while.

The next two games were, strangely enough, both against Wrexham – firstly at home, and then in north Wales the following Tuesday.

I started in the first game but it was a disaster. We were 2–0 down at half-time and I had one of those games that could be an occupational hazard when playing 'in the hole'. I received very little service and found myself constantly trying to battle for balls that seemed to be endlessly up around my neck.

The gaffer was, quite rightly, not happy with us and he said he had to make a change at the break. He admitted it could have been any one of a group of seven or eight players, but that was no real consolation when he revealed I was to be replaced. I wasn't happy but I also accepted that when a manager wants to change his formation, it is often the so-called 'luxury player' who is sacrificed.

I'm going to be really honest here and reveal that things didn't get any better for me: we went on to win 3–2. The fact we turned the game around, in my mind, vindicated the manager's decision to take me off. In reality, we hadn't really played much better in the second half than in the first, but the sheer will to win that had been instilled in us by the management was enough to drag us through. Well, that – and Tubbsy's brilliance in scoring a hat-trick.

There was only a week to go until the biggest game of my life and I had been dragged off at half-time – I was sweating over my place in the starting line-up.

We went up to north Wales a day early to prepare for the return game against Wrexham. I was named on the bench, which further confirmed my doubts. It was hard to decipher the thinking behind the decision, though, because there were players who were cup-tied for Saturday, so they were more likely to play in Wales. We ground out a 0–0 draw in a game watched by the then Manchester United manager Sir Alex Ferguson and his assistant Mike Phelan.

Maybe the gaffer knew they were coming and purposefully put me on the bench so I could be unleashed as our secret weapon on Saturday?

All joking aside, their presence showed the level of detail someone as successful as Sir Alex went to during his career. He could have easily sent one of his coaching staff to Wrexham on that wet February evening, but the fact he went himself gives some insight into why he enjoyed such longevity at a single club during an illustrious career.

Although we hadn't been playing at anywhere near our top form, we had negotiated our three League games since *that* FA Cup draw without defeat. We were ready to concentrate on the biggest game of our lives.

CHAPTER 23

'WHO YOU PLAYING SATURDAY?'

'**M**ANCHESTER UNITED AWAY...'

We had the day after the second Wrexham game off and I woke up feeling stressed. After not playing any part in the previous night's game I was worried I would not be playing at Old Trafford. But I resolved with myself there and then that, whatever happened, I would make sure I enjoyed what promised to be a great experience.

We were due to travel up to Manchester on the Thursday but, before we could leave, we trained at our Broadfield Stadium before having a rare press conference. I climbed the stairs to our lunch area and it was packed wall-to-wall with journalists, ranging from tabloids to broadsheets to individuals from all around the world.

I had the customary chat with *The Sun* about what cars we all drove so they could compare them to our opponents. They particularly loved me because I was, and still am, driving a battered old Ford Focus. The reporter was unsurprisingly not as keen to talk to the lads who drove the BMWs and Audis – after all, that would have broken the lazy stereotype that all lower-league footballers earn just above minimum wage.

I then did a rather more insightful piece with Henry Winter for the *Daily Telegraph* and spoke to football magazine *FourFourTwo*.

Sergio Torres was the darling of the mainstream media, portrayed as an Argentinian Dick Whittington who had come to England to find fame and fortune. The first time he told me his story I had found it fascinating but, after hearing it for the thirtieth time on this cup run, even I was getting pretty blasé about it.

After an hour or so of these people treating us like superstars and pretending our opinion was important, we began our journey to Manchester. One thing that time with the media gave me was a little taster of what it must be like to be a top Premier League player. Those types of players have a press conference like ours every three days before a big game. Don't get me wrong, I really enjoyed myself, but I could see how doing it on a regular basis could become boring and monotonous. I was already looking forward to Monday when I could go back to a life of anonymity.

As soon as we arrived in Manchester we went straight to Old Trafford to have a look around. That was a good idea because it allowed the lads who wanted to act like tourists to get it over with. Once Saturday arrived, we could just concentrate on the job at hand.

To be honest, I had never been one for all that. Whoever I was playing – whether a Sunday League player or Wayne Rooney – I had to, at least on match day, believe I was their equal. If you start believing you're inferior to someone then you have no chance.

We entered the stadium and someone was immediately on hand to show us around. Two things really struck me.

Firstly, the away dressing room was quite basic. I could have been in any changing room in the Football League. It was not terrible but I was expecting more opulence.

Secondly, the pitch did not seem that big. Whenever I had watched games at Old Trafford, or even seen it on the TV, I'd always thought the pitch was huge. Once standing on it, however, it didn't seem to be much different to ours size-wise.

As we wandered around, we asked our steward what sort of crowd they were expecting on the day. I'd imagined a figure of around 50,000, but he replied that it had sold out!

Cue twenty players taking a big gulp of breath…

We checked into a lovely hotel called Mottram Hall. I roomed with Sergio and the magnitude of what was about to happen really begun to sink in as we unpacked.

I would often get apprehensive before games but not nervous. This was a different scenario though. We were still two days away and I was already nervous. I was concerned about whether I would be starting and, if I did, I was then worried about my performance. I hadn't been in great form leading up to the match and I was desperate to play well in front of a capacity crowd and millions of people watching live on ITV.

We trained at the hotel on Friday morning. The gaffer had originally told us we would be training at Man City's training facility, but that was another one of those occasions when he was being a little economical with the truth.

During our session we did a lot of work on the shape of the team and the manager looked at different formations. I was in and out of the first eleven depending on the shape. If we played a 4–4–2 I would be on the bench, but if we played a 4–3–3 I would start.

The rest of that day dragged, followed by an anxious night when I hardly slept a wink. As the game was not due to kick off until early evening, we did a light training session on the Saturday morning before a pre-match meal at 2 p.m. The gaffer, as always, did not name the team until just before we set off for Old Trafford.

However, before that happened, he pulled Sergio outside for a private chat. Sergio returned stony faced but gave nothing away. All the lads were shocked: surely he had not been left out?!

On this occasion, rather than read the team out like normal, the gaffer just flipped a sheet of paper over and revealed the line-up.

My heart rate was going at about 180 beats per minute as I scanned the sheet for my name. I looked for where it should be, just behind the strikers, and there it was: *7) Smith*.

I could relax momentarily: I was in. I just had to make sure I performed!

Turning my attention to the rest of the team I noticed Sergio was in and wondered what his chat with the gaffer had been about. There were two shocks within the selection – a really big one and another that had been on the cards for a while.

The big shock concerned Glenn Wilson. He had played the vast majority of games that season and had still only missed a couple when David Hunt had joined to compete with him for the right back slot. It was Glenn's fourth season playing under Steve and I always joked with him that one year with Evo was worth two under anyone else.

Glenn had been a loyal lieutenant to Evo, regularly translating his rants to players not as familiar with them as himself. He would let people know what bits to take on board and which to let go over their head.

What made it even more galling for Glenn was the management did not even have the decency to tell him face to face in private. Instead he found out, like everyone else, when the team was revealed. Glenn and I were talking the day before about our fears regarding not being selected but I was convinced he had no worries. He had his doubts but I am pretty sure that, deep down, he thought he would be in.

I know managers have to be ruthless sometimes but that was ridiculous. David Hunt was a very good player and also a great guy and he was not going to turn down such an opportunity. He was the first to admit that Glenn deserved to play though.

To compound matters, the gaffer did not even get Glenn on the pitch. It was a measure of what a well brought-up guy Glenn is that he managed to repair his relationship with Steve enough to play for him for another eighteen months. I know many players who would have never played for him again.

The second, more predictable, shock was the fact new signing Willie Gibson got the nod ahead of Jamie Cook on the right wing. Scott Neilson, who regularly held that position, had broken his foot at the end of January and the position had been up for grabs ever since.

Jamie was another that had history with Steve, having played for him at both Boston United and an earlier spell with Crawley. It could have been argued Jamie had not done enough to earn a place – he was a very talented player but lacked the heart and motivation to really make the most of his ability. I loved playing alongside him though as he was intelligent and a ridiculously composed finisher.

I felt he was definitely more deserving of a start than Willie, who was a 'glass half empty' kind of guy. Jamie illustrated how pissed off he was when he came on during the game with the bit between his teeth to make a really positive impact.

Once we got to Old Trafford everything settled down and each player went into their usual routine. Striding out on to that pitch for the warm-up was a great feeling and it could have gone on for two hours – I just loved being out there soaking up the atmosphere.

People still ask me now what it felt like and I still say the same thing: it was a surreal experience, none more so than when we lined up in the tunnel and I looked over to see the likes of Michael Carrick, Javier Hernández and Rafael da Silva.

All I could hear in my head was all the people telling me I should enjoy the occasion. Easy for them to say but I knew I would not enjoy it if I played crap or we got hammered. I did not care who we were playing against, I had my professional pride and did not like losing.

There was a loud roar as we emerged from the tunnel. The atmosphere was great but it did not seem a great deal different to a lot of crowds I had played in front of. I think if you play in front of a capacity crowd of 5,000, 20,000 or 75,000, then yes it was a bit louder, but all you hear is noise. Plus if, like on this occasion, you know you have to be on top of your game to be competitive, then you just try to block everything out.

The game started off quite tense and we were holding our own before my own Ronnie Radford-esque moment came.

Tubbsy battled for possession and cushioned the ball into my direction about 30 yards from goal. It sat up perfectly and there was no way I was going to turn down the opportunity. I hit it well, on the volley but just slightly off-centre, which meant it was always just veering off to the right. I was right behind the shot and could see it was going to deviate just wide of the post – although it was close enough to have United goalkeeper Anders Lindegaard scrambling across his goal.

United then took hold of the game and, although we were not getting battered, we were sacrificing territory while trying to hit them on the counter attack. My job was to pick up Michael Carrick when we lost possession. This was easier said than done as, I am sure you can imagine, he used some cute and sharp movement to make that yard of space for himself.

The United player that really impressed me in that half was Brazilian midfielder Anderson. He was willing to take the ball in any situation and, when he received it in tight areas, he displayed strength and composure on it.

We held out until the twenty-eighth minute when Wes Brown opened the scoring with a header but we saw the rest of the half out without conceding again.

We knew as a group we had more to offer and the gaffer felt the same way. He did not care we were playing Manchester United, he was not happy and let us know. He came for me pretty quickly: 'Are you fucked? Are you? Because I'll fucking take you off if you are.'

I was blowing out of my arse, there was no doubt about that, although I did not feel like I looked any more knackered than anyone else. There was no way I was going to admit that though. 'No, I'm fine.'

'Well, you do not look fine. Pull your fucking finger out,' came the reply.

I felt I had done OK when I had the ball but physically I was at full pelt trying to keep up with their superior athleticism.

We came back out for the second half with the gaffer's words ringing in our ears. As we were waiting for referee Lee Probert I noticed they were making a substitution. The number eight went up. *That's good*, I thought. *Anderson is going off.* Then I saw who was to replace him...

Wayne Rooney!

We started this half with more belief and began to dominate possession, a feat which continued as the game wore on. We moved the ball around well and Kyle and Pablo kept bringing it out of defence majestically, like they were born to play in such arenas. Bully and Sergio also made it really tough for their midfield to play.

A combination of these two things meant I was able to start picking up some dangerous positions in advance of their midfield and feed Tubbsy with a bit more quality. It felt like we could do the unthinkable and actually score a goal.

With just under twenty minutes left we had the first of our two really good chances. A cross came over from the left and David Hunt, who had rushed up from right back, met the ball just outside the 18-yard box with a volley that just flashed past the far post.

Then, with just two minutes remaining, Brodes looped a header on to the top of Lindegaard's crossbar from a corner.

The game finished with us camped in their half trying to force the equaliser but my participation had finished nine minutes earlier when I was replaced at eighty-one minutes. I was pretty satisfied with my performance, however.

Steve was, for once, lost for words after the game. It was clear he was just immensely proud of our performance and was a little choked-up. We had come really close to earning a draw against one of the biggest clubs in the world, and on their own patch to boot.

It was a relief to have come through the game with our self-respect still intact. I sat back in the dressing room and began to soak up the occasion while reflecting on what we had achieved.

All the lads had an abundance of family and friends at the game so we all went our separate ways that night. I had some of my friends I grew up with staying in Manchester so we went out for a few drinks.

Once the hysteria had calmed down we had to focus on the most important task at hand – getting back to reality and securing promotion to the Football League.

CHAPTER 24

'PROJECT PROMOTION' (PART II)

WE WERE IN for training as usual on Monday as we had a home game against Southport the day after.

The gaffer was like a dog with two dicks at training, regaling us with stories about his new best friend Sir Alex. The gaffer had gone in to see him after the game, like most managers did, and had taken a nice bottle of wine (apparently worth £350) with him. He had spent a good couple of hours with the United manager talking about the game and football in general. It must have been a great thrill for him, to be fair, as it would have been for any ambitious manager.

I was not expecting to play after my exploits on Saturday but the gaffer obviously did not want to tinker with the team too much because I kept my place. Before the game the gaffer said, having now spoken to Sir Alex, he was worried about this game being a case of 'after the Lord Mayor's show'. He compared it to when Manchester United had a League game after a big European match.

As a result, he revealed, just for this specific game, we would be on a win bonus of £10,000 to be shared between the whole squad. This worked out to around £500 per player. This revelation definitely made my ears prick up because, believe it or not, we received no bonus whatsoever for the Manchester United game.

Players would normally receive an appearance fee for such a game, bearing in mind the club got a share of the gate money and a substantial fee from the television broadcasters, which I believe was £250,000. We attempted to argue our case before the game but, to be honest, it should have been negotiated into our bonus schedule before the season started. We were still entitled to 40 per cent of the prize money but even the most optimistic of us were not expecting to receive that.

The club had been quite clever about exploiting the big game after the event. We had taken nearly 10,000 supporters to Manchester so, to capitalise on that, anyone showing their ticket stub at the turnstiles on Tuesday was let in at a discounted price – I think £5 a head. This meant we had a really healthy attendance of 3,765 for a pretty unappealing Tuesday night game – we would have struggled to get the 765 a year ago!

We started like a side that had just played against Premier League opposition, passing the ball around confidently, but unable to find a final ball. This was not good enough for the main man, of course, who was going mad calling us all 'Big-time Charlies' – a little hypocritical, as the only person constantly talking about the game and his new best pal was actually him.

Anyway, as a result, we went more direct during the second half and I drifted out of the game. We eventually ground out a 1–0 win though, as Pablo scrambled home a Willie Gibson free kick, which the Southport keeper spilled.

I had not particularly enjoyed myself but I was happy the gaffer was now regularly giving me a starting berth.

The big pre-match incentive the gaffer announced definitely had a positive effect but we never saw any of that money. Whether it was a genuine offer, a tactic he employed to get us going or simply a figment of his imagination, we never found out. It never hit my bank account despite numerous promises throughout the rest of the season.

We had now not lost a League game since that defeat to Newport last

October and we looked to continue the run at home to Barrow. I was left out of the squad entirely but, despite this clear hindrance, the boys went on to edge a thriller by the odd goal in five.

The League had turned into a two-horse race with AFC Wimbledon leading the way and us lurking menacingly on their tail with games in hand. Luton Town were not totally out of the equation but it was looking like they lacked the necessary consistency to mount a sustained challenge.

After my little rest I was back in the team for our next game against Histon. When naming the team Evo said, 'If this were a cup final, this would be the team I'd play', which I took as a nice compliment.

We had way too much experience for a young Histon side, which was being managed by my former Arsenal youth-team colleague David Livermore, and we ran out 5–0 winners. I got on the scoresheet with a lovely left-footed volley, after a trademark Dean Howell surge and cross from the left wing put us two up.

It was my best performance for a while so I was a little disappointed to be replaced in the second half, but I comforted myself with the fact that the gaffer and Rayns must have just wanted to save my legs for our game at Kidderminster Harriers on Tuesday.

That confidence was misplaced, however, as I was named on the bench. At this moment in time I was really struggling to read the gaffer. When I thought I would be playing I was not and vice versa. We reverted to a 4–4–2 but had to settle for a draw.

It was the same story for the next couple of games as I was an unused sub in a great 2–1 away win at Fleetwood, then I got a couple of minutes in a scrappy but eventually comfortable 5–2 win at home to Hayes & Yeading. I found myself feeling a little bit confused and frustrated.

Every year, usually around March or April, there always seems to be a game to define the season. Our next game was just that. We were playing AFC Wimbledon at home. If we won, it would give us a pretty much unassailable lead at the top of the League, with games in hand. If we lost, it would give Wimbledon faint hope of catching us.

I was back in the starting eleven and playing just off Tubbsy. The gaffer subsequently told me I had been specifically earmarked for this game a few weeks earlier – I wished I'd known that sooner as I would not have been so annoyed about not playing.

We started the game at a blistering pace and were two goals up within the first ten minutes. Tubbsy scored first, finishing a well-worked team goal by getting onto the end of a great cross from Josh Simpson, and then Kyle scored a header from a corner. All this surprisingly did not affect Wimbledon and they persevered with their patient passing game.

The whole complexion of the game changed on the stroke of half-time.

Wimbledon pulled one goal back and then they quickly broke forward again. Dannie Bulman was aware of the danger and cynically fouled their attacker on the halfway line. It was definitely a foul and a yellow card, but amazingly the ref showed him a straight red.

Suddenly we were in a spot of bother – going down to ten men played perfectly into their hands. It would give them more space to play their slick passing game. Thankfully we held on to half-time where we could re-group.

We were 2–1 up so it seemed pretty clear that our first strategy would be to protect our lead, but Steve disagreed. After a bit of flapping he decided I was coming off. I could not believe it – I had been really effective and it seemed a more obvious decision for me to drop into Bully's vacant position. We still had Josh in central midfield who had the athleticism to support Tubbsy, who I assumed would be in a lone forward role.

I made my dissatisfaction pretty clear as I took off my shin-pads and boots. I was just about to get totally stripped off when, after a short conference with Rayns, the gaffer said in fact I would be staying on – Brodes would be replaced with James Dance instead.

We reverted to a 4–4–1 with Dancey playing out wide, Josh and I in central midfield and Tubbsy up front by himself.

Wimbledon came out smelling blood and attacked from the outset. We survived an almighty scare in the first few minutes of the half when we managed to scramble away a shot that hit both of our posts.

Less than ten minutes later, the game was over when James Dance smashed in an effort from outside the box that eluded Seb Brown in the Wimbledon goal. It was a great strike and instantly alleviated all the pressure. It was also a great moment for Dancey as he had received few opportunities to show his talents since joining in January. He is a lovely guy and it was always good to see people like him get their rewards.

I played a much deeper role than usual but really enjoyed it, keeping possession and plugging gaps. Josh, Sergio and Dancey did a great job supporting Tubbsy, whose level of performance was so high we hardly noticed we only had a solitary front man. He had a great ability of holding the ball up and keeping it under pressure, irrespective of the quality of the service.

I must have played well because I even managed to complete a rare ninety minutes. Once the final whistle went everyone knew the League title was effectively ours.

Mathematically there was still work to do but, with a nine-point advantage and four games in hand, even Blue Square, the League's sponsors and official bookmakers, were paying out.

There were no post-match celebrations though, just that lovely sense of satisfaction after a job well done. We were now focused on getting those remaining points we needed to confirm the inevitable.

The next step on our quest was away to Eastbourne Borough, a game we won 2–1. Sergio and defender Charlie Wassmer, who had joined from Hayes & Yeading in March, scored the goals.

Charlie had been signed through that little loophole in the transfer window – he joined us on a 'temporary loan' but he had also signed a contract, which meant, as soon as the window re-opened, he would become a permanent signing.

When Charlie first joined I could not see him lasting long. He seemed like a nice guy but was painfully shy – a demeanour not suited to our lively dressing room nor working with an even livelier manager.

Nothing changed my thought process when, on his first day, Charlie came into the dressing room and Simon Rusk compared him to a cross between Eminem and Lee Ryan from the old pop band Blue. The lads thought it was hilarious but he did not even flinch, let alone crack a smile.

I was wrong, however, as, against Eastbourne on his debut, Charlie scored the kind of goal any striker would have been proud of, let alone a centre back! The ball fell between him and the on-rushing keeper and he arrived at the ball first and coolly lifted it over him with just enough power to get it over the line.

He wheeled away and celebrated as cool as you like, as if he did that sort of thing every day. It was an exquisite finish and a great way to introduce himself to the club. He might have scored more if I had been able to get my corner kicks above knee height.

I was happy with my performance despite my set-piece deliveries being terrible, and I got replaced with ten minutes to go.

We followed up that win with a solid 0–0 draw at Gateshead on an atrocious pitch. Normally Steve would be seething about such a result but he knew now was the time to just keep chipping away at the points tally we required, especially picking them up in away games as we had become unstoppable at home.

The next team trying to stall our dream was Mansfield Town and the game turned into, without a doubt, my proudest moment as a Crawley Town player. Pablo was injured and Bully was still suspended, so this meant I was named captain.

Technically that made me vice vice-captain. When said like that it does not sound too impressive. However, when you think at the start of the season I was told, on more than one occasion, I was not good enough and would never play for the club again, I was delighted.

After all that treatment, for me to lead the team out for this game felt like the ultimate vindication. It was like, in doing this, the gaffer was publicly admitting he was wrong. Obviously he did not actually do this but he may as well have.

I had always revelled in the extra responsibility of being captain and I gave a virtuoso performance, one of my best since joining the club. I set up Tubbsy for our second goal in a 2–0 win and was only denied a goal of my own by the woodwork and some good goalkeeping. A couple of minutes before the end, the Tannoy man went to announce the 'Man of the Match' but I knew it would be me.

Bully was back for our next game at home versus Darlington but the gaffer seemed to have settled on his midfield four. We now played a diamond with Bully at the base, Sergio left, Josh right and myself at the tip.

It seemed to work really well: Bully gave us security, Josh and Sergio were energetic and helped support both in defence and attack, while I linked the play going forward. Those three took most of the physical work away from me. I lost count of the amount of times I would look back at them and think: 'Blimey, that looks like hard work!' They would get the ball and feed it into me with the sort of quality service I needed to have an influence on a game.

The Darlington game was no different although we struggled initially. They were a strong, organised team and I think we all felt the exertions from Tuesday night's game. It also seemed I was being man marked – not something I was used too.

We went into the break all square. The gaffer gave one of his more sedate analysis of our performance but let me know, very fairly in this case, that he needed a little bit more from me. He got it as I went on to score the winning goal – the ball broke to me just outside the box and I hit a left foot strike that went in via a post.

When I was replaced with five minutes to go, as I left the pitch, I asked the gaffer if that was enough for him! I was awarded with my second 'Man of the Match' award in a row – although this one was less deserved.

We now only needed six points to be guaranteed a place in the Football League, although in reality it looked pretty certain we would go up even if we did not win another game. We had a tricky game away at York City to negotiate next and squad rotation had now gone out of the window as I was selected for my fifth game in a row.

York seemed determined to knock us off our pedestal. They harried and pressed us all over the pitch before deservedly taking the lead. The hairdryer was back on full power as the gaffer went mad at half-time. These indiscriminate shouting matches were hard to take at the best of times, let alone when we were twenty-four games unbeaten, so I decided to switch off.

Luton Town, the only club that could mathematically catch us, drew that night too so all we needed was to beat Tamworth away to secure the League title. Disappointingly for me the gaffer switched to a 4–4–2 for the match, so I would be on the bench.

We confirmed our place in the Football League for the 2011/12 season with a 3–0 win. It seemed fitting that Tubbsy grabbed two goals as he had been arguably the gaffer's best signing that season. I had played against him the season before and, although he scored a lot of goals and was clearly a good player, I did not realise just how good until I played alongside him.

Matt had a bit of everything – the vast amount of goals scored during his last couple of seasons clearly illustrated his finishing prowess but he offered so much more than that. His work rate was phenomenal and made him our first line of defence. He also displayed clever movement, could bring people into play and was intelligent enough, when the occasion required it, to give the ball to others in a better position.

The only thing I felt may have held Tubbsy back from playing in the top two divisions was a lack of blistering pace, although he was more than quick enough for our level.

I managed a five minute cameo at the end of the Tamworth game, but it felt good to be on the pitch as we finally secured our reward for a season's work. I have always found, when you actually achieve what you set out to do, the buzz is never quite as good as you thought it would be. This was one of those times, mainly due to the fact we had effectively sealed our promotion a month earlier.

This did not stop the lads celebrating in style, however. As I mentioned previously we had a small group of lunatics in the squad, and goalkeeper Scott Shearer was very near the top of the list. The night before the game he decided we were going to have a naked coach on the way home if we clinched promotion. Most of us laughed the idea off but Scott was adamant.

We had stocked the coach up with alcohol and, before we got out of the Tamworth car park, Scott, along with four or five of his cohorts, were nude and acting like it was an everyday occurrence. Thankfully the seats were leather so any unwanted fluids could easily be wiped away. It is fair to say a few people on the M40 got a shock on the London-bound carriageway that evening!

The atmosphere on the coach was amazing; the music was blaring and the drink was flowing. I could have stayed on there all night. John Dempster was on the microphone at the front of the coach, in his own words, 'spitting lyrics'. For a middle class white boy from Northamptonshire he was impressively adept at rapping.

As soon as we got back to Crawley we went out to continue the celebrations. I say that very definitely although I have little recollection of the evening itself.

After basking in our triumph for a couple of days, we were back preparing for a now meaningless game at home against Luton Town. However, the word 'meaningless' here only applied to any ramification it would have on the League table; the gaffer was intent on us breaking the longest unbeaten record in the Conference National and posting the most points collected. There was no way he was going to let us take our foot of the pedal.

I was, as promised on Saturday, back in the team and we drew 1–1. We took the lead but Luton gained the ascendancy and equalised before half-time. After two days' celebrating, the sort of preparation we would never have dreamt of normally, you would have thought Evo may have cut us some slack.

He had none of it though, entering the dressing room all guns blazing and I was first in line for his wrath: 'You cannot fucking play for me!'

Are you taking the fucking piss? I thought. After everything I had gone through this season, he was treating me like that?!

He repeated himself just in case I did not understand: 'You cannot fucking play for me, you take too fucking long on the ball.'

I was just doing what I always did. If I had no pass available I held the ball until someone was available. I had never resorted to lumping the ball long and I had no intention of starting now. Yes, there would be times when I got caught in possession but it was not always my fault.

It was not often Steve's scattergun comments got to me but they did that night. I lasted until around sixty-five minutes before I was subbed, but I was frankly happy to get off the pitch. The situation just proved to me that, no matter what I did, he was never going to give me the respect I deserved.

We were presented with the League trophy and were meant to be celebrating but I was now in no mood for this. As we did a lap of honour Evo whispered in my ear: 'You were shit tonight, but we would not have won the League without you.'

Nice words but they rang hollow after what he had said at half-time. On an evening that should have been an opportunity to reflect on a great achievement, I just went home and sulked.

It was now a case of seeing the season out. We remained unbeaten for the rest of the season by beating Southport, Rushden & Diamonds, Newport County and drawing with York City.

In the last week of the season the gaffer started discreetly offering new contracts to players. I say discreetly but, as usual, everyone was talking about it in the dressing room. It seemed quite ominous for me as I had no contact whatsoever.

I was eventually called for a meeting in which he said they would like to offer me a new deal but if it was perceived as 'too rich' then they would leave it. I asked for £900 per week and a £5,000 signing-on fee, which I felt was pretty reasonable. I pitched the signing-on fee as a retrospective promotion bonus because I had not received anything extra for playing regularly in a team that had earned it.

The gaffer played it very cool and made it clear that, although he would like to keep me, he was not overly fussed. He showed me a sheet of paper that listed who he was retaining and who he was letting go. I was on the released list but he explained he'd had a change of heart. It could have been true or an elaborate bluff – he was capable of either.

Steve dismissed my terms and made a counter-offer of £800 a week – a full £12 a week increase on my current obscurely numbered wage.

He then added there would be an 'across the board' appearance fee of £150 for every game any player started, while simply being named on the bench would earn you £75.

It was a clever offer – not amazing enough for me to bite his hand off but good enough to be considered. We were both aware of the economic situation at a large majority of football clubs, many were cutting their budgets back. I was viewed as a liability on the balance sheet as I was now thirty-two years old and had no resale value.

I felt I deserved a little bit more though because there were players at the club that had contributed less than me but were earning more money. I asked for a £5,000 bonus to be put into the contract payable only if Crawley gained promotion from League Two, which he agreed to.

I told Steve I would have to think about it but he gave me the normal rubbish about how he needed to know my decision within forty-eight hours.

I took advice from a few managers and players and they pointed out that if I was regularly playing, or at least involved in the match day squad, there was every chance I would be earning an average of £900/£1,000 a week.

Where else was I likely to earn that sort of money and not have to move home yet again? I had not put my name out to any clubs but had received a phone call from Wayne Hatswell, who was on the coaching staff at Newport County. He enquired whether I would be interested in talking to them about a contract but it was not a move that interested me while I had a firm offer from Crawley.

I decided the sensible thing to do was to take Crawley's offer of another year. I knew the club would spend heavily during the summer to strengthen the squad but I was confident, if given a fair opportunity, I could compete for a place in the team.

In hindsight, it was one year too many, but more of that later.

Although we did not receive a monetary bonus for promotion the club did live up to the gaffer's regular boasts and we were to be taken on a special holiday. The destination had changed over the season from New York to Abu Dhabi to Dubai but we eventually settled for three nights in Las Vegas and four in Los Angeles.

It was a great trip that allowed us to unwind after a hard season and solidify the bonds we had created. The £10,000 bonus promised after the Manchester United game for beating Southport still had not transpired, though we were told it would be given as spending money.

Steve did treat us to an Italian meal in Santa Monica though, which was dominated by Willie Gibson and the gaffer bickering like an old married couple over what type of wine Willie was allowed to drink. Even on holiday, Evo was not ready to give up control!

He then told a very underwhelmed group of grown men that we were going to Universal Studios the next day, again financed by the big man. I am sure you can appreciate, after being out every night, going to a theme park was not at the top of the list of priorities for most of the lads.

What made it even funnier was that it transpired that, in actual fact, he had not spent any money on the theme park and they were actually free tickets from Virgin after a mix up with our flights from Vegas to LA.

You had to admire his front!

These funny episodes just added to what was a great trip and, along with a visit to Wembley for the FA Cup final, where we picked up our award for 'Giant Killers of the Year' upon our return, was a fitting way to finish a brilliant season.

After a really tough start to the campaign I made thirty-six appearances, including twenty-eight starts, and contributed six goals. Considering I had not started a game until the end of September I felt proud of the way I had fought my way back into contention, captained the team on a few occasions and earned a new contract.

I did not think it had been my best season ever, but it was not far off, and it had given me great pleasure to prove a few people wrong. I knew I would not have been up for such a fight six or seven years ago. I was looking forward to playing in the Football League again immensely.

· · ·

25 AUGUST 2013

We are about to embark on a new school year. The relief that I no longer have to go back and teach a multitude of subjects is still palpable.

It is going to be a really busy year as I will have four job roles, although

I'm not sure if talking about, playing and coaching football counts as work? It never has for me.

One of my new jobs is for a company called SCL where I will be delivering a City & Guilds qualification in sport on a part-time basis. The difference between the working practices of the school and SCL is like night and day. I've already had four training days before I've even started and SCL have given me all the information for the classes I'm teaching. This was the sort of support and preparation I'd expected from the school.

On reflection, although the past year was tougher than I could ever have imagined, I learnt a lot and it clarified what I really want to do. I want to coach football full time and preferably at a professional club. If I can spend as much of my working life as possible on a football pitch then I will be a happy man.

CHAPTER 25

ONE YEAR TOO MANY

SEASON: 2011/12
CLUB: CRAWLEY TOWN
DIVISION: LEAGUE TWO
MANAGER: STEVE EVANS (EVO)

BEFORE THE 2011/12 season had even started I knew it was going to be a challenging one, but I had total confidence in my own ability. After all, if I didn't believe in myself how was I going to convince anyone else?

The club had strengthened its squad over the summer considerably adding the likes of John Akinde, Tyrone Barnett, Scott Davies, Wes Thomas and Hope Akpan. David Hunt's loan was turned into a permanent transfer too. There was also a change to the dynamic of the management team as Craig Brewster, the Scottish-born former striker of clubs such as Dundee United and Dunfermline Athletic, joined the coaching staff.

I liked Craig from the off. He clearly looked after himself and seemed keen to learn and better himself. This philosophy was not entirely in line with his colleagues but I thought he was a good appointment.

I felt the management set out their intentions for me from the very first day back for pre-season training. I walked into the dressing room and saw my squad number had been changed from number seven to twelve.

Ordinarily I could not have cared less about what number I wore, but what did annoy me was my old number had been given to Willie Gibson, who had done very little since joining the club other than moan.

It was obvious what they were trying to do – it was an attempt to wind me up and put me in that psychological place I was in twelve months before. That was not what I needed – I wanted the management to show they valued and respected me after I had shown them how determined I was to be part of this team.

The club was moving forwards, proved by us returning to Portugal for a training camp. We stayed at the same place we prepared at for the Manchester United game.

It was great and I felt like a proper footballer. It was a brilliant exercise and allowed us all to spend time together without having to rush off to pick up the kids, go down the bookies or beat the traffic. That is all without mentioning the great weather and training facilities. There was no dog shit to dodge here!

We trained hard all week before we played a friendly against a Portuguese Premier League team called SC Olhanense. I played in the first half and we went 1–0 up thanks to my goal. That moment was the highlight of a poor display from me. I always struggled to be at my best in high temperatures and, on this day, it was 30°C and I felt very lethargic. We eventually lost the game 2–1.

Steve was not happy and set down a marker to the new players. As I mentioned earlier I was pretty sure these outbursts were pre-planned and the only really spontaneous thing about them was the recipient of his anger. Scott Davies was in the firing line on this occasion.

I was sitting about 60 yards away when I saw some angry finger-jabbing, Phil Brown at Manchester City-style, going on in the middle of the pitch.

This was in full view of the hundred or so spectators and it continued until Scott threw his hands in the air, got up and walked off.

It subsequently transpired the reason for the gaffer's anger was that, as our two centre halves split, Scott had the audacity to try to get the ball on the edge of his box. Anyone who had played for the manager knew this was a heinous crime, one punished with a public dressing down that normally sounded like: 'He can't fucking play for me! No, it's over. Rayns, it's fucking over.'

If you are playing that last sentence in your head, it needs to be in a thick Scottish accent with the hand going across the neck signifying a throat cutting gesture and phlegm showering anyone in the vicinity.

You could put an argument forward saying the gaffer was within his rights to tell people if they were in the wrong, but I believe screaming at someone in the middle of the pitch was not the way to do it. We played a specific way but this was never laid out in any detail to new players. This was how you were expected to learn – if you got a bollocking, you clearly did something wrong. If you did not then you had probably done the right thing.

For the next few days Scott got the full treatment. On our last day in Portugal he was stripped of all his training gear (not naked – he was allowed to wear his own stuff! – that would have been too far even for Evo) and made to train in the basement gym by himself. Steve said he would never play in the first team.

The more experienced of us did not bat an eyelid but for Scott, who had been used to the relative sanity of Reading FC, it was a shock to the system. As was often the case Scott had to go through a period of redemption before being reintegrated into the group as though nothing had happened.

After a relatively good pre-season the year before, I reverted to what had been 'the norm' and struggled through the friendlies. It really frustrated me as I worked so hard through the off-season. I felt fit but my touch and confidence were low. It was like I was wading through treacle when playing.

I was worried how far my stock was falling in front of a man not known for his patience.

I put in nondescript performances against a young Chelsea team, Bognor Regis Town, Crystal Palace (where one of my own fans was kind enough to call me 'a cart horse') and Peterborough United. Worryingly, they did not seem to be improving.

Due to a freak set of results that saw Birmingham City win the League Cup and therefore qualify for Europe while also being relegated from the Premier League, the FA implemented a preliminary round for the League Cup to be contested by the two lowest-ranked teams in the competition. That meant our competitive season started early, against our nemesis AFC Wimbledon.

I always performed well against Wimbledon but that was not going to be the case this time. The gaffer called me into his office the day before the game and asked how we were going to get me back to my highest level. It was a totally valid question and I was actually pleased he said it because we now had it out in the open.

The gaffer said he could not play me and, on this occasion, I totally agreed with him. In the end my absence was irrelevant as we won our first ever League Cup tie 3–2 in a really entertaining game, although Hope Akpan received a red card during it.

Due to that unique situation we had another friendly, against a strong QPR team, before our first League game of the season but the less said about my performance the better.

The fixture computer had thrown up an away encounter at Port Vale for Crawley's inaugural game in the Football League. I was pretty sure there was little to no chance of me playing.

So imagine my surprise when, on the customary pre-game walk (which all managers must get taught to do at managerial school), the gaffer said he was thinking about playing me. He asked for my thoughts and I replied that I would at least give him a disciplined performance.

He told me if things were not going to plan he would not hesitate in replacing me after twenty minutes. Just the reassurance I needed!

It was clearly a toss-up between myself and Scott Neilson. Form-wise there was no contest; Scott had easily been more effective in the friendlies but the gaffer knew I was tactically astute and would be more disciplined when we did not have the ball. After this conversation I knew I would be playing and that was confirmed an hour and a half before kick-off.

We drew 2–2 despite going 1–0 and 2–1 up. Bearing in mind I felt more out of touch than I had during any part of my career, my performance was acceptable. I was only subbed on seventy-eight minutes because John Dempster got sent off and we needed to bring on a centre back.

As was always the case within the Football League, apart from this year, our second official game of the season was a League Cup game. We had been drawn away against Crystal Palace but the game was cancelled due to the rioting that engulfed London that week.

Our first home League game was against Macclesfield Town and it became evident during our build-up that I was not going to be in the team. We were doing some formation work, which, to the uninitiated, was basically attack versus defence. The team playing on Saturday was defending against the rest. As I was playing as a roving left back for the attacking team that told me all I needed to know.

I was not even named in the squad. I knew I was fortunate to play against Port Vale but I felt my competent performance was deserving of at least a place on the bench. Admittedly part of the reason I started the last game was because Hope had to serve his suspension, but that was not my fault.

We won 2–0 against a Macclesfield team that got exactly what they deserved – they had set up as if they were playing Manchester United and hardly ventured out of their half.

I snuck back into the squad for our next game and made a fifteen-minute cameo during a 3–0 win against Southend United. It was a tight game until Dean Howell scored with a fortuitous cross and Tubbsy grabbed his first two Football League goals for the club. We all knew the step up to League football would be no problem for him.

Games were coming thick and fast and next up was the long trip to Plainmoor to play Torquay United. The fact I was not playing had caught a few people's attention because Craig McAllister, who had left us to join Newport County, contacted me to say their manager was interested in taking me.

When I had played there last season I thought Newport was a really nice club, but I just did not fancy the commute, plus there was no way I was going to re-locate.

Garry Hill, my former boss at Weymouth and then manager at Woking of the Conference South, also rang me but I felt I should be playing at a higher level than that.

We arrived at Plainmoor and the gaffer pulled me to one side to reveal I was not playing. I told him I did not expect to but he assured me that I was close to selection. It sounded like the sort of bollocks managers tell young players, not experienced professionals. He tried to cushion the blow, however, by adding I would play in the re-arranged cup fixture against Crystal Palace.

That seemed like a strange comment to make; I was not good enough to play against Torquay but would be used against a much higher-ranked club? I had played for Steve long enough now to know when he was telling the truth and when he was trying to placate someone – this was definitely the latter. What confused me was he did not need to say it as I was not expecting to play.

The lads went on to win the game comfortably 3–1. We played our best football to date, retained possession confidently and the result was sealed by a sublime goal from Scott Davies.

The highlight of the day for me was, even though we were in Devon, the

Cornish pasties made available in the Torquay boardroom. I eased the pain of not being involved by eating my body weight in those – their hospitality was nearly as impressive as our performance.

Our focus immediately switched to the Crystal Palace game, the one I was apparently due to be playing in. I did not expect to get the nod but I was still really apprehensive and nervous. I did not feel ready to play against players of such quality.

On the way to Selhurst Park I got a phone call from Garry Hill, who told me a group text had been sent (which he forwarded to me) outlining my potential availability. It was something I was not aware of, but it did not surprise me. I suspected it but it would have been nice to have had a chat about the situation rather than be told by another manager.

The one thing this did confirm was that I would not be playing that evening. I am ashamed to say I was relieved. For one of the first times in my career I did not want to play because my confidence was at an all-time low.

I was an unused sub but I enjoyed my half-time warm up. Normally I would do some running, dynamic stretching and passing. But this time we had the pleasure of watching the Crystal Palace dance troupe, imaginatively called the Crystals. I must admit they momentarily broke my focus as I concentrated on how tight their choreography and dance moves were.

After having plenty of chances in the first half we eventually lost 2–0 to a Palace side inspired by winger Wilfried Zaha, who scored both goals. We had been well in the game but got taught a typical lesson by a higher ranked club – if you do not take your chances when in the ascendancy, you get punished.

That was not good enough for the gaffer though and he cancelled our day off.

The following morning we had a crisis meeting as a few issues had clearly got up Evo's nose, like people not putting their kit in the laundry baskets after training. He also added Gayle, the club secretary, had to remove some chewing gum that had been spat or dropped onto the carpet of the coach on an away trip. We all agreed that was disgusting.

Gayle came to the training ground two days later and Scott Davies asked her about the incident. She gave him a blank look and said she did not know what he was talking about.

Vintage Evo – it was just a figment of his imagination to back up his gripe about the training kit. Unfortunately he did not have the foresight to warn Gayle about his cunning plan.

A trip to Cheltenham was next on the agenda and I did wonderfully well to retain my place in the stand. I would have preferred to be left at home, at least then I could go to the gym and do some fitness work.

The game as a contest was over by half-time as Cheltenham sped into a 3–0 lead and comfortably saw the game out 3–1. After playing so brilliantly against Torquay, we were the exact opposite in this game, although credit must go to Cheltenham. They played excellently and had a midfielder, Marlon Pack, who put in as good a performance by any player I saw that season.

Steve was livid, made three changes at half-time and had not calmed down by the end of the game. We were called in for training at 8.30 a.m. on Sunday.

At our new training ground, which we had moved into at the start of the season, we had a games area plus satellite television in the changing rooms. The TVs were switched off and the games room closed as a punishment. I was not really sure what that was meant to achieve; whatever it was it seemed pretty petty.

The gaffer and I had another chat about my situation and he asked what I thought about going on loan to Woking. I said I just wanted to play games and did not want to waste the season in the reserves. He made no commitment but gave the impression he would let me go.

We had a Johnstone's Paint Trophy game away to Southend United on the Tuesday night. It was really a glorified reserve game but, after Monday's training session, there seemed no chance of me playing – or so I thought.

That morning the gaffer rang me to say I was not going on loan, I was playing that night. This was one of the gaffer's traits – he was hard to read and my selection had come from nowhere.

He stuck to his word and I played in a 1–0 defeat but the result was irrelevant because I finally found some form. After a steady first half everything clicked into place, I felt my confidence return. I knew I was playing well as I rarely wasted possession and was composed on the ball.

Suddenly I could not wait for the visit of Bristol Rovers – an amazing turnaround after not wanting to play just two weeks earlier.

I kept my place and, although they were one of the biggest teams in the League and tipped for promotion, we tore them apart. I continued my performance from midweek, caused them lots of problems and opened my goal-scoring account with a header as we won 4–1.

After a few dodgy results it seemed like we were adapting to League Two until we were brought back to earth away at Morecambe. I retained my place for the third game in a row but that was the end of the good news.

The gaffer, when he announced his line-up for this one, said he was happy with this midfield because he knew what sort of performance he would get. I do not think a 6–0 defeat was what he was referring to.

We had a few injuries and a makeshift defence but that was no excuse for such a resounding defeat. We started the game positively but Morecambe had done their homework and continuously picked us off on the counter-attack. They were 2–0 up by the break.

We got a pasting at half-time but nothing was addressed tactically – we were just told what poor players we were and what was going wrong. My performance was by no means the worst; in actual fact I thought I was our most effective midfielder.

This did not stop me getting tugged ten minutes into the second half. As I left the pitch I told the gaffer what I thought of his decision. He had taken the easy option and he knew it.

In hindsight, coming off was not the worst thing that could have happened to me as we capitulated to the eventual 6–0 scoreline. In his post-match interviews the gaffer was prone to over-exaggeration but when he said it could have been twelve he was spot on. We absolutely folded and they looked like they were going to score every time they went forward.

Whenever we lost an away game there was an unwritten rule: there had to be a period of mourning on the coach journey home. Before we had even left Morecambe, someone on the coach laughed, which Steve did not like. He warned us the next person who laughed would be removed from the coach and have to make their own way home.

How the whole team did not get thrown off after the next incident was a minor miracle!

We had fish and chips provided on the journey back; not exactly a cutting edge refuelling technique but I was not complaining. The food must have been ordered before the result filtered through. There was a portion for everyone onboard.

Craig Brewster asked the gaffer if he wanted some but he declined – the result had obviously put him off his food.

The lads, as you might expect after a game, were like vultures and hoovered everything up. The smell of fresh Lancashire fish and chips obviously got the better of the boss because he suddenly changed his mind. Craig was sent to the back of the coach to get the portion but, unfortunately for him, he had to go back empty handed and explain to an angry, ravenous Scotsman there was no food left.

Steve was apoplectic. I was sat near the front and could see his head getting redder by the second.

Paul Raynor was immediately sent to the back of the coach to bring the perpetrators to justice. After a severe post-game dressing down and our day off cancelled there was a siege mentality between the players. Nobody was talking, even under the severest of questioning.

This situation ended up as Evo's second big loss of the day as no evidence was found.

The 'Morecambe Two' were never brought to justice. I have my suspicions who the guilty parties were, however, and I am pretty sure both their names start with Scott!

We were in for training at 9 a.m. on Sunday and had the customary crisis meeting. You would imagine, after the previous day's performance, we would maybe review the match DVD or talk about some of our tactical deficiencies, but we talked about 'fish-and-chip-gate' instead. Steve was determined to get to the bottom of the situation and, at times like these, he inadvertently gave us some funny moments – and this occasion was no different.

Without a hint of irony he firstly asked: 'Where has all the honesty gone?'

How I suppressed my laughter I will never know. This was a man who lied about his lies, yet expected honesty from everyone else. After receiving nothing but deafening silence it was Rayn's turn to take centre stage.

As eloquently as ever he announced: 'If you want us to be cunts, we can be cunts!'

And normally you are so nice and approachable…

Thanks for that, Paul, I thought, as I pondered how much he got paid for such insightful comments.

Swindon Town and their newly appointed manager Paolo Di Canio were next up for us at our Broadfield Stadium. I was dropped and, to make matters worse, the gaffer came up to me after naming the team and said I was right about not deserving to come off at Morecambe. But I was being left out as I looked tired.

That really frustrated me. Other players could seemingly have three or four average performances and the management would say they had done 'alright'. It seemed I was not allowed to play like that – I had to be 'excellent' or I was left out, this time under the guise of being 'tired'.

We lost 3–0. We looked nervous and reverted to playing a very risk-free style of direct football. Swindon were not three goals better than us but, as we pressed for an equaliser at 1–0 down, they hit us twice on the break to give the scoreline a more flattering look.

Another defeat, another day off cancelled…

We were stuck in a rut but, luckily for him, Steve was well supported by the owners who allowed him to go and buy his way out of trouble. He signed two really influential players – Andy Drury on loan from Ipswich and defender Claude Davis, who had previously been with Crystal Palace.

Andy was someone I had played against many times and I thought he was an excellent player, but his arrival signalled that my time at Crawley was coming to an end.

A couple of managers rang to say they had been told I would be going on loan. Again, I was disappointed to find this out through third parties but it merely confirmed what I already knew – I was never going to get the respect I deserved.

I was left out of the squad for a Saturday home game against Bradford City, which we won, before having the dubious honour of travelling to Cheltenham Town for a reserve game the next Tuesday.

I spent eighty minutes of that game trying to ignore Evo, who was going mad at any slight mistake or error of judgement by any player. With ten minutes to go I was hauled off as the gaffer called me a 'tippy tappy player' (which, incidentally, I took as a compliment). Judging by the look on his face however, he did not mean it as one. The driving rain and gale force wind compounded what was a bad day.

Football has got to be one of the fastest-moving and most dynamic industries in the world.

I turned up to training on Thursday morning and was called into the gaffer's office as soon as I arrived. I was told Kettering Town, then of the Conference Premier, wanted to take me on loan.

I instantly said yes and that was it, deal done. I did not speak to their manager Mark Stimson, I did not liaise with any friends or family and I had no real ambition to join Kettering permanently. I knew this move would give me the opportunity to put myself in the shop window and that was enough for me.

As soon as I agreed Steve and I were best pals again and he waxed lyrical about how I was still part of his plans. He was lying, I knew he was lying and he knew that I knew he was lying, but we still went through the rigmarole of pretending he was telling the truth. I am not sure what makes him do this, I just do not think he can help himself.

I was off the next day to meet my new teammates. As was normally the case, especially at my age, there were a couple of players I knew or was aware of, which helped. As soon as I got there I met Mark Stimson, who took me into his office and went through on a tactics board what he expected of me. This sounds pretty simple but it was not something any of my managers had done before.

My first impression of Mark was great but the rest of the club was a shambles. Kettering played and trained at the newly defunct Rushden & Diamonds ground, which was a lovely venue but now looking very shabby. There were still pictures of Rushden & Diamonds players on the walls and we used their old training kit.

After coming from a club like Crawley, which was moving forward and investing in its facilities, that was a bit of a shock. The club was also struggling on the pitch and it was reflected by the atmosphere within the dressing room. At Crawley, after nearly eighteen months of success, there was a real buzz about the place and always something going on. The opposite was true of Kettering: the mood in the dressing room was sombre and dominated by several cliques.

I made my debut the next day away to Bath City, which we won 1–0. I enjoyed myself and put in a strong performance. It was nice to feel like an integral part of a team again. We were not anywhere near the same level as Crawley quality-wise but we attempted to implement a patient passing game, which I always approve of.

We entertained Hayes & Yeading FC next and the optimism generated from our previous win quickly dissipated as we got well and truly taken to the cleaners. We lost 5–3, which insinuates the game was close, but we were never really in it (being 3–0 and 4–1 down at different times).

I witnessed another career first late in that game. We were awarded a penalty, which, after an unprofessional disagreement between Moses Ashikodi and JP Marna, resulted in Moses missing it. We scored from the subsequent corner and, as we were still two goals down, the majority of us were in a rush to get the ball back to the centre spot.

However, JP and Moses were still 'discussing' who should have taken the penalty and, before the game could resume, the pair launched into a full-on fight in the middle of the pitch. The referee had no option but to send them both off. I remembered the incidents between Kieron Dyer and Lee Bowyer, and Graeme Le Saux and David Batty, but had never personally been involved in a game where such an incident had occurred.

We had played like a pub team and now looked like one, playing out the last few minutes with nine players. It was embarrassing to be a part of and what the manager made of it I do not know.

However, Mark did expertly diffuse the situation after the game. Tensions were still running high in the dressing room and our two protagonists wanted to continue their disagreement. The gaffer removed one of them from the room and, instead of carrying out an inquest into the altercation, he began talking about the game. There was plenty to discuss after such a crap performance and this ten-minute debrief took the heat out of the situation.

I dread to think how things would have ended up if he came in ranting and raving.

The manager was very complimentary regarding how I had performed in the first couple of games and I was enjoying myself, but my initial fears about the place being a shambles were being confirmed. For the previous three days we had no hot water to shower with and the lack of enthusiasm from people who were fortunate enough to be professional sportsmen was embarrassing. Although, in mitigation, it probably did not help that after the previous game the chairman put eleven players on the transfer list.

Morale further declined as we lost our next game 1–0 against Kidderminster Harriers. It was a match that could have, in all honesty, gone either way, but we just did not have the stomach for such battles.

Although the place was a bit of a joke, excluding the football management, I was enjoying a bit of a renaissance. Unfortunately disaster struck during a full-scale practice match when I suffered a calf injury. At the time it seemed pretty innocuous, but it eventually curtailed my loan.

It was now the middle of October, the injury was worse than I first feared and I went back to Crawley to get treatment.

Nothing much had changed: the team was doing well but Steve was still prone to the odd rant. The rise of social media was causing problems for a lot of football clubs as it was giving players an open forum to air the sort of opinions their employer did not want to be associated with. Crawley was no exception.

Hope Akpan, the talented young midfielder who the club signed from Everton and eventually sold to Reading, was alleged to have posted a homophobic comment on Twitter. Evo immediately called a meeting and took his usual dictatorial approach – all social networking was now banned until you signed a disclaimer agreeing to your contract being terminated at the club's discretion for any misuse.

This was clearly not in the players' best interests so, in my role as PFA representative, I explained that to the manager. Unsurprisingly he did not take kindly to this and threw a barrage of abuse at me. The rest of his staff – Rayns, Craig and Steiny – just sat there embarrassed until he ran out of steam and sloped off to his office. I looked at all three of them and said with a straight face: 'That went well then...'

I should have known better and not bothered even mentioning it. David Hunt, a prolific tweeter, was willing to sign the disclaimer and called Gayle to arrange it the next day.

'What disclaimer?!' she replied.

Classic Evo!

I recovered from my injury by early November and was back on the training pitch but things had changed. Unlike previously, I no longer had a burning desire to prove the gaffer wrong. I was, quite frankly, sick of continuously having to prove myself to him. Whenever I had an 'average game' it felt like I was back to square one.

I played a couple of reserve games while regaining fitness, including a dire defeat to a young Forest Green side that played round us like we were not even there. The closest I got to anyone was the handshakes at the end.

The boss continuously brought in new players, good ones to be fair, so I could not see any real possibility of nailing down a regular place in this team. I always felt exasperated when I could not see my life moving forwards and this was one of those times. I just wanted to move on, whether that be to a new football club or perhaps into a new career.

By mid-November my lack of motivation was obvious to everyone and, the Friday before we were due to welcome Oxford United, Evo pulled me aside and asked if I would be interested in a pay-off. I said yes – I was owed £34,000 and was going to ask for half, or I'd take £15,000 at a push.

Unfortunately this pay-off never came to fruition. But by the end of the next week I had left the club anyway, albeit temporarily.

Garry Hill, my former manager at Weymouth, was still trying to persuade me to join him at Woking. It was nice to hear a manager really wanting my services but, to be honest, I would have signed for anyone at that time.

I knew I was better than Conference South level but I just wanted to play, so said if he could agree a deal with Evo, which was by no means a foregone conclusion bearing in mind their history, then I would sign a one-month loan.

Steve and Garry had a mutual dislike for each other after the tax evasion scandal in the 2001/02 season. Boston United and Garry Hill's Dagenham & Redbridge had been going toe to toe at the top of the Conference. Boston eventually prevailed on goal difference. However, Garry and a lot of people within football felt this was an injustice, as although Boston was subsequently punished with a £100,000 fine and a four-point penalty, the points deduction was not applicable until the 2002/03 season, which allowed Boston United to take their place in the Football League.

Within an hour, I was told Woking had agreed to pay 50 per cent of my basic wage (£400 a week) and so I was on the move again.

It was a weird feeling – I should have been happy at the prospect of playing games but I felt miserable. I think it was a realisation that, if things went as expected, I would probably be finished as a professional footballer by the New Year.

My month at Woking passed by unspectacularly. It was evident, once I began playing matches, that I was nowhere near match fit. I should have been standing out but I was not. We won games but they were quite often turgid affairs and we were just grinding out results.

Even scoring the winner on Boxing Day against Farnborough in front of over 3,000 people could not lift my mood. It was my only decent contribution throughout my last scheduled appearance.

Garry wanted to extend my loan, which I was willing to do – but only because it was better than the alternative. To be honest, I had not really enjoyed the games, mainly due to the quality of my own performances, plus it was a nightmare journey. I had to navigate the M25 from Essex on Tuesday and Thursday nights for training sessions, which did not begin until 8.30 p.m. I was normally falling asleep on the sofa by then.

The decision was taken out of my hands anyway and I was back at Crawley by 27 December.

I found myself in the office with the gaffer upon my return and he said that Crawley – by which he was referring to himelf – was not interested in a longer-term loan while Woking only paid 50 per cent of my wages. He proposed giving me two months of my net wage to leave, which amounted to £5,000. I looked at him like he was mad, telling him there was no chance.

I wanted out but I was not stupid. If I stayed until the summer I would get paid through May, June and July, so there was no value in me accepting such an offer.

While I was at Woking I received a call from Nas Bashir, then manager of Hayes & Yeading in the Conference Premier, about a loan move. It transpired they could not contribute money-wise much more than Woking but I assumed the financial side of that deal was really only a problem because of the animosity between Evo and Garry.

That thought was misplaced as Steve stuck to his guns and reiterated I would not be going anywhere unless the loan club paid the vast majority of my wages. To be fair, he understood I was not going to leave Crawley for a pittance and did not seem to hold it against me.

I was even involved in the squad for my first game back at the club against Barnet. This was by default however as we only had sixteen players available. I even got on the pitch for a token minute and got a warm reception from our supporters, which I appreciated. The game itself was a dour affair but we narrowly won 1–0.

I could not decide if I was happy that I had not fully participated in such a game or depressed that I was not deemed good enough to start. Everyone around the club seemed pleased I was back in the squad but I felt being a sub for a League Two team aged thirty-three was not anything to celebrate. The squad remained the same for our next game against Oxford United, so I retained a place on the bench.

It was now early January and my situation seemingly altered by the day. First I would be off to Hayes & Yeading, then I was not, then I was. However, on the eve of the third round FA Cup game at home to Bristol City, the gaffer pulled me into his office to say I may well start the next day.

It was a strange situation – I knew I would not be playing and he knew I would not be playing, but it left me with a 2 per cent chance I actually might, so I prepared accordingly. I could not fathom out the thinking behind this situation because I had not started a game for Crawley since September.

As expected I ended up on the bench. The boys put on a vintage Crawley Town performance, unsettling Bristol City from the off, and we thoroughly deserved our victory courtesy of Tubbsy showing once again that he could comfortably step up to the next level.

As I settled back into the club I could feel my performances in training improve. The loan move to Hayes was still a non-starter but, mid-January, Rayns called to say Newport County wanted me on loan. Ordinarily I would have jumped at the chance but I had a lot of things going on and did not fancy travelling up the M4 every two days. There was also no way I was going to relocate to Newport permanently, so I turned it down hoping it would force the Hayes situation.

I expected this action to cause problems as the gaffer did not normally take kindly to players not doing what he asked them but, again, he was good as gold and respected my decision. He had also stopped taking me on away trips when I was not going to play, something else I appreciated.

If I travelled to such games I would end up preparing, especially eating, as if I was playing and end up putting on about half a stone after sitting in the stand. At least when I stayed at home I could spend a couple of days working in the gym improving my fitness.

Just as we were moving into February and I was losing hope, I got a text from Paul Carden, then assistant manager of Luton Town, enquiring about my availability. I tried to say I was free without sounding too keen.

Luton were a club playing at least two levels below themselves. I had always enjoyed playing in the spiky, aggressive atmosphere of Kenilworth Road and would have loved to have performed there every other week. But Paul explained that they had to get a couple of players out before they could bring me in. He obviously thought I was earning more than I actually was.

Unfortunately, as was often the case, that was as far as it went and I heard no more.

For the second year in a row we had made it to the fourth round of the FA Cup, where we had drawn Hull City away. As influential as my role had been in the competition last year it was irrelevant this time. I had not even stepped on the pitch during this run, but had pinched a few win bonuses by sitting on the bench.

I played in a reserve game against Brighton & Hove Albion before the Hull game. I always enjoyed playing against their development squad as they played the sort of style I loved. It was a beautiful, controlled, patient game with a fluidity and movement rarely seen in English football.

I became frustrated when I was replaced with fifteen minutes to go and I threw my captain's armband toward the vicinity of my nearest teammate as I trudged off he pitch. In a rare moment of awareness Evo noticed my disappointment and told me that, if we played with a player in the hole against Hull, then it would be me.

I will never know how he or I managed to keep straight faces as he went through that complete bollocks. To just illustrate what a load of shit this was, he signed Sanchez Watt on loan from Arsenal the next day. This move obviously had not just come about over the previous twelve hours, so why he blatantly lied to the face of someone who could not be further out of the first-team picture I will never know.

The lads put in another fantastic performance away to Hull City and deservedly won 1–0, with Tubbsy scoring the goal. That turned out to be his last meaningful action as a Crawley Town player because he was sold to AFC Bournemouth not long after for reportedly over £600,000.

The next day we were off to Portugal, for the third time in a year, for another mid-season training camp. As we were about to leave for the short trip to Gatwick we were joined on the coach by Billy Clarke, who had signed from Blackpool as a replacement for Tubbsy.

Billy turned out to be an excellent signing and, overall, the quality of players Crawley were bringing in continued to be impressive. The more I saw of Billy play, the more I realised he was a lot better version of myself. He could do everything I could do and a whole lot more.

The transfer window was about to close while we were away. On its final day I received a call from Dean Holdsworth, then manager of Aldershot, asking if I would like to join them on loan for the rest of the season.

I could not say yes quick enough. I never imagined I would get a chance to join up with a fellow League Two club after the season I'd had. Initially he had offered to pay 75 per cent of my wages, but the gaffer had said no. Dean came back and said Aldershot would cover the whole £800 a week if we could get the deal done.

I went straight to the golf course on our resort to find the gaffer and tell him how keen I was for this to go through. Strangely he did not want me to leave, but I was adamant this opportunity would not pass me by. Thankfully the management did see my side of the argument and sanctioned the deal.

For the first time in a while I was both genuinely excited and a little nervous, which is never a bad thing, about the chance to possibly earn myself a new contract, either at Aldershot or elsewhere. I had forgone all my appearance bonuses and was only getting a small percentage of the travelling expenses I was entitled to, so there was nothing from my end that could hinder the temporary transfer.

What you hope for and what you get can often be two totally different things however. I cannot believe, in hindsight, how something I felt so positive about became such a disaster…

I returned from lovely weather in Portugal to arctic temperatures in England. These conditions automatically meant my first game at Aldershot was in doubt.

CHAPTER 26

LAST CHANCE

SEASON: 2011/12
CLUB: ALDERSHOT TOWN
DIVISION: LEAGUE TWO
MANAGER: DEAN HOLDSWORTH

I **TURNED UP** for my first session on a Friday before a home game against Bristol Rovers and my initial impressions were positive. The club had a larger staff than I was used to at Crawley, which included an assistant manager, first-team coach and fitness coach.

I assumed, at the time, Dean was confident the game would be cancelled as we did a near two-hour session – unheard of for a Friday. It included some 'team-shape' work, which is when what is usually the starting team goes through potential match-play scenarios, plus the manager tells individual players what he wants them to do when in or out of possession.

The match day line-up can regularly change during these types of sessions through a combination of keeping everyone on their toes and the management still deciding who is going to play. However, on this occasion, I stayed in what was to be the first team the whole time. I performed well, which was always nice when trying to earn respect from new teammates.

Unfortunately the game was called off because of a frozen pitch. Dean texted me the same afternoon to ask if I had enjoyed my first day. I said I had, and that little piece of man management made me want to play for him even more.

I felt the most motivated I had for quite a while, being determined to thank Dean for the faith he had put in me while rediscovering a desire to prove Steve Evans wrong.

The adverse weather conditions continued for another week, which meant we had very few opportunities to train outside. I was really impressed with our indoor sessions though as Russ Clash, the fitness coach, was very good and clearly put a lot of thought into his sessions while making sure we worked hard.

Ten days into my loan period the snow started to subside, which allowed us to get back on the training pitch. My Aldershot debut seemed fated to be against Hereford United.

To add extra spice to that game Gary Peters, my old adversary, was now working for the Bulls and he was someone I still wanted to stick two metaphorical fingers up at.

Our preparation for the game was not dissimilar to my first day; another long session the day before and I was involved in what seemed like the starting eleven at all times. I was deployed in central midfield before getting moved out to the left, a position we know I was never particularly comfortable playing. As long as I was in the team, however, I would be happy.

My performance level was good and I had seen enough now to know that I was one of the stronger players in the group. The session finished with the manager being unhappy regarding some players' performances but I was confident that I was not one of those he was referring to.

Whether a manager names his team the day before a game or not, as a player you can make three decisions on your participation: you can decide you are definitely in, definitely out or unsure. I used to call it correctly more often than not throughout my career, the exception being the Conference-winning season with Crawley.

When I decided I was not playing, I would not even give the match a second thought. However, on this occasion, I was 100 per cent sure I would be starting and prepared accordingly.

I arrived at the game just after 6 p.m. and watched as certain players were called into the manager's office, safe in my knowledge that I would be playing. A little later Dean came into the dressing room, did a pre-match speech and then revealed his team on a flipchart. I looked for my name but it was not in central midfield.

Shit, I thought. *I'm going to have to play left midfield.*

But my name was not there either. Surely I was right midfield then?

Nope.

I was on the subs bench.

I was amazed I was not playing and was fuming. I had performed excellently in training plus, although I had not been promised to play every week when I joined, I could not see much point in signing a player of my age on loan and not playing them. I held up my end of the bargain, which was to do the business on the training pitch, and I wanted the opportunity to do it in a proper game.

What annoyed me more than anything was I had clearly seen the manager talk to other players and explain decisions, but he said nothing to me.

We won 1–0 in a pretty poor game between two very average teams. Being in the totally selfish mindset that I was, a win did me no favours as it was unlikely the manager would change a winning team. He was going to get a knock on his office door first thing on Thursday morning that was for sure.

My only consolation of that evening came after speaking to my old friend, and then manager of Hereford, Jamie Pitman. After initially being taken in by Gary Peters's charms, Jamie's opinion of him was now very similar to mine!

After a day off, I went straight to the manager's office.

Unfortunately he was off through illness so I was left speaking to his assistant manager Matt Bishop. I told him I had been training really well and I was pissed off I had not played, both points he agreed and sympathised with. But he gave me no real reason for the situation other than the management decided they did not want to make too many changes.

This did not really stack up though because, a couple of days after I signed, Aldershot also brought in Darren Murphy on loan from Stevenage, who also played in my position. Getting my grievances off my chest helped though and lifted my mood slightly.

Due to the bad weather this was also the first time I had seen the club's training ground. Throughout the cold snap we had trained on an AstroTurf pitch, which was part of the local army barracks.

I was really impressed with their facilities, it was a big area and a good surface. It was a lot better than what I had been used to at both Crawley and Hereford.

Our next game was away to Macclesfield Town, which meant an overnight stay and the dreaded initiation song. As is the norm at a lot of clubs these days, a new player has to sing in front of the squad after dinner on their first away trip. On this occasion the club had seven new signings so first-team coach Matt Gray decided we would have an *X Factor*-style competition. I sang the 1980s classic 'Never Gonna Give You Up' by Rick Astley.

I would like to take this opportunity to publicly apologise to Rick. For some of the younger players it was the first time they had heard the song, and most probably the last after I murdered it twice having been voted in the bottom two by the audience.

My first mistake was the song choice. I went for a pop tune but had no dance moves to accompany it. As a result I just stood on the stage looking like an awkward teenager at a house party.

I then decided to give it a right go and, after initially forgetting the lyrics, I belted it out. What with the lads not knowing my sense of humour I was met by a combination of bewildered looks and stifled laughter. It was a painful situation for everyone involved.

Josh Payne absolutely brought the house down with his rendition of *Valerie* and Guy Madjo thankfully pipped me to last place – although considering he sang in his second language I took no satisfaction in that feat whatsoever!

Even though Darren Murphy got injured during that afternoon's training session I still could not get myself into the team and was named as a substitute again. We ground out another 1–0 win but this time I managed to get on the left side of midfield for the last twenty minutes.

Entering the field of play made me feel more a part of the team and I felt I made a positive contribution, being nice and composed when in possession of the ball.

Southend United came to our place next. I was on the bench and, for the first time since I had been at the club, the lads put on a really dominant performance from start to finish to win 2–0. The whole team played excellently but Josh Payne in particular was on a different level to anyone else on the pitch. To me he looked like someone capable of playing at a much higher level.

I made a ten-minute cameo.

Aldershot had won three out of three since I joined and, with Barnet next on the agenda, I expected to be sat on the bench again. However, the day before the game, Josh Payne did not train. I assumed if he was out I would be a like-for-like replacement.

Yet again I was wrong. To my amazement, I was still on the bench as Troy Brown, predominantly a centre half, was named in Josh's place. By my reckoning this made me fifth choice central midfielder at best. Josh and Darren Murphy had started there upon my arrival, now they were both injured and had been replaced by Aaron Morris and Troy.

I had nothing against these guys but I could not understand why any manager would want to bring in a loan player to be fifth choice?

To add insult to injury the gaffer said to warm up on fifty-five minutes and I did not even get on. On the plus side, for the rest of the team anyway, we cantered to a 4–1 win.

This was a strange feeling – I enjoyed being at Aldershot, I liked the lads and the training environment suited me, plus I was performing well day-to-day but I was constantly left frustrated by not being able to display that on a match day.

I relayed all my concerns to Dean but all he would say was he 'loved me to bits and that I would get game time' – all well and good, but it did not exactly answer my question of why I was not being selected. I liked the gaffer as a person but his management style was not working for me.

The good run continued as we defeated Morecambe at home to make it fifteen points out of fifteen. It was another solid, if unspectacular, performance but defensively we looked strong.

I was still no closer to getting a starting berth and it began looking even less likely when we signed my former Crawley colleague Michael Doughty. He had been on loan from QPR and was now doing the same at Aldershot. He was a talented boy and someone who I believed would go on to have a good career, but he was another midfielder to contend against.

Although I was frustrated and annoyed with this situation I knew I had to do everything I could, both while training with the team and working by myself, to ensure that I was ready to perform if I got the chance.

The approach at Aldershot was totally different to the one I was used to at Crawley. Steve Evans, in case you had not already worked out, took a very dictatorial stance. He looked to be in charge of everything and his philosophy was 'if you give a player an inch, he will take a mile'.

While that rang true with certain individuals, I found this approach insulted my intelligence as I got older. Once, for example, Steve decided while we stayed at a hotel on a Friday night that we were not allowed to have breakfast the next morning. I had breakfast every Saturday and wanted to continue my normal routine.

Aldershot was totally different – it was a lot more laid back. When we travelled to Torquay on a Monday before a Tuesday night game, we were allowed to go to a local pub and watch a televised game. We did not drink, of course, but it was refreshing to have a management team that treated players like adults.

But even the novelty of that soon wore off as I sat on the bench for yet another ninety minutes while we lost our first game since I had joined. We were behind for the whole of the second half but I still did not get close to being involved. I freely admit I was never one of the most dynamic substitutes in the world, but if I was not going to get on in this type of scenario then when would I? To make matters worse Dean was now bringing the recovering players straight back into the fold.

I sat on the coach during the long journey back from Devon stewing about how I would word my, now weekly, moan in the gaffer's office when I received a text. It simply read: 'You deserve a chance and will be playing Saturday.'

About fucking time!

We had a team meeting at the next training session and the gaffer moaned about a series of things, including players' body fat. He explained that anyone over 12 per cent would not play, which had not been the case as there were players over that threshold.

I was recorded at 7.9 per cent, which the manager seemed to be very impressed with, but it only further exasperated me. Surely being that lean aged thirty-three illustrated my professionalism? You do not get that kind of result by spending your afternoons sitting on the sofa eating custard creams and chocolate bourbons.

I was not about to tell Dean that though because I was already preparing myself for our game at Northampton Town, the one I had been told I was definitely playing in.

Matt Bishop took the Friday session as the boss was not in. At the end he took some players off to do some set-piece routines, while Matt Gray took a few others to work on throw-ins. Three players, including me, where just sent off to do some passing.

My head was about to explode. If I was playing why was I not involved in the set pieces? It was either rank bad management, where it had not been discussed who was playing, or I was being left out again. Either way, it was rubbish preparation.

Thankfully for my sanity Dean stuck to his word and I was in the team. Not only that, but I was to take all the set pieces, which made the last session seem even more shambolic. I was playing right midfield but I was not going to let that affect me.

I started the game well and Ben Herd, who was playing right back, and I were linking up productively – by far and away our biggest attacking threat. Unfortunately we went 2–0 down before the break after not dealing with two long throws. Dean was not happy at half-time and was particularly critical of individual mistakes. He even kicked the flipchart but his aggression did not have much of an effect.

Even though Northampton were comfortably the better side I was happy with the way I was playing. Early in the second half we gave away a penalty and we went 3–0 down. By fifty-eight minutes Michael Doughty was being primed to come on.

I knew what was coming next – my number came up and I trudged off the pitch. I was severely pissed off and the gaffer was about to find that out. He tried to shake my hand as I walked past, so I held onto it and said: 'What the fuck are you taking me off for?'

'We had to change it,' he replied.

'Well, take someone off who fucking deserves it,' was my particularly abrupt response.

Matt Gray, as I went to sit in the dugout, put his hand out for a high five and I slapped it so hard that mine stung for about ten minutes. I was so angry. All the manager had spoke about during half-time was about people making individual errors yet, when he made his changes, he punished me for their mistakes. I would be the first to hold my hands up if I had a bad game but I also knew when I had played well and this was one of those occasions. Even after the game a couple of my teammates, unprompted, asked why I had been taken off.

I cannot remember being so wound up after a game. I kept replaying it over in my head all weekend. Was I deluding myself perhaps? Maybe I had not played as well as I had thought.

I was still brooding about it on Monday. I contemplated apologising to Dean for my reaction – not for what I said, as I stood by that, but my body language and aggressive nature was not very professional. However, in my opinion, he was in the wrong so I quickly dismissed that idea.

We had a team meeting and were shown the goals again. They were crap from our perspective. The manager had every right to really dig a few people out but was almost apologetic as he talked about the errors. These lads were obviously not used to any criticism as, despite even a fairly tame appraisal of individual players' performances, it all led to some very defensive reactions from certain people.

Sometimes you have to take your medicine and that was one of those times. I know for a fact players would not have reacted like that if Steve Evans had been leading that debrief.

Nothing was said about my reaction despite me half hoping it would be so I could discuss the reasoning behind it.

Unfortunately our next game was away at Crawley so I was not allowed to play. Before the game I saw Gee, Steve Evans' brother and Crawley's chief scout. I was still bristling about the Northampton debacle and asked him if he had the scouting report for the game. He did and I was not deluding myself. It confirmed what I thought and said I had played well. The only criticism it had was that I overplayed at times – which, in my book, was a compliment.

Aldershot ground out a creditable 2–2 draw, which gave the management an easy excuse to leave me out of the team again. The next three matches saw us win 1–0 against Bradford City, Southend United and Bristol Rovers, and I played a combined total of one minute. The normal stuff was happening, centre halves were coming on in midfield ahead of me along with players who had been injured for months.

As the club was doing well we were treated to a two night break in Bournemouth. I was not particularly up for it but it turned out to be a good trip. The highlight was when Guy Madjo turned up at the village hotel in Farnborough, where we regularly trained at its gym, instead of the one in Bournemouth – only a footballer would do that.

However, nothing fundamental was changing. I was counting down the days to the end of the season and most probably my career. By the start of April, even though I had no ambition to stay at Aldershot, I still wanted to know why I was not getting more opportunities.

I went looking for Dean after one Tuesday training session but, as was often the case, he proved quite elusive. I was left with Matt Bishop to whinge at again. He sympathised without giving me any real answers. It was funny to watch his reaction when I said I knew our relationship was going to be coming to an end soon. He said nothing but I do not think he is much of a poker player.

I finally managed to trap the manager in his office that Thursday and told him how I felt. He said he was trying to build a team that was not going to play attractive football. I had no problem with that inherently but, if it was always the plan, what was the point in me being there? He went on to say I was too much of a footballer and, in the same breath, I was to play against Port Vale on Good Friday.

It was really weak management because I was sure I had just talked myself into the team. I wondered how many times other players had done the same thing. Being the person Dean is, he was too concerned with upsetting people rather than doing what was right for his team. I think he would have commanded a lot more respect from his players if he was just straight with them, rather than trying to please everyone.

The Port Vale game panned out exactly as I expected. I started off in an attacking central midfield role, which we stuck with for about twenty minutes before the gaffer reverted to a 4–4–2, shunting me out to the left.

I managed to last an extra three minutes overall this time and was replaced on sixty-one minutes. I had not been as effective as at Northampton but was still one of our more potent attackers. I have no doubt the substitution was planned before the game because it definitely was not decided on performance.

There were no histrionics or words exchanged as I left the pitch this time but I was pretty sure Dean was aware of what I thought about his decision. We lost the game 2–1 and, while I could complain all I liked, ultimately we had lost both games I started.

We were back in training on Easter Sunday before travelling down to Plymouth for a game on the Monday. To my surprise I actually retained my place in the team and, even more surprisingly, I was deployed in my preferred central midfield position.

We lost 1–0 and I played crap.

I found it hard to get on the ball and, when I did, my quality was rubbish. To confuse me further I stayed on the pitch longer (seventy-five minutes) than I had in either of my other two starts. The manager would have been well within his rights to drag me off earlier and I would have had no complaints.

Whether it had meant to or not, that move dispirited me. I had played well twice without reward or recognition and now could not see how that was going to change. It was a strange feeling. I was playing on loan for a club where I had no future rather than playing for my parent club where I also had no future.

News broke during that same day about Steve Evans leaving Crawley Town to join Rotherham United. I had no particularly strong feelings about it at the time because I did not think it would really affect my future.

I was wrong, however.

On the second of two days off, Dean called me and I assumed he wanted to speak about my underwhelming performance at Plymouth.

'Alright, gaffer. How are you?' I asked.

'Not happy,' came the reply.

Oh shit, what have I done now?

'Crawley want to recall you from your loan,' he continued. 'It is a blow.'

It is a blow…?! Was it really, Dean? I mean, *really*?!

Aldershot had played thirteen games while I was there and I had played in three, all defeats. I did not think the people of Aldershot were going to be crying into their beer when hearing this news.

Dean wanted me to tell Craig Brewster, Crawley temporary manager, that I wanted to stay at Aldershot. The problem with that was I did not want to. Do not get me wrong, I was not doing cartwheels about being called back but I did not want to sit on the bench at Aldershot for the last month of the season either.

CHAPTER 27

COUNTING DOWN THE DAYS

IT WAS A weird sensation – I had only been away from Crawley for just over two months but it felt like I was joining a new team. The management had totally changed with Craig Brewster in temporary charge and Steve Coppell brought in as Director of Football.

Even though I did not agree with everything Steve Evans and Paul Raynor did, at least I knew what to expect from them. This felt like a step into the unknown. One thing I was looking forward to, though, was seeing how Steve Coppell worked.

I felt a little nervous, which was strange as I had nothing to prove. Realistically whatever I did was not going to have any effect on my future.

The whole vibe at the club had changed. Steve and Craig were not doing anything spectacular but what they were doing was treating players like adults. It led to a lot more relaxed feeling around the place.

Every day when we were training and the lads were laughing I kept expecting to see Evo come roaring round the corner and start screaming obscenities at someone for having the audacity to misplace a pass – it felt like I had been institutionalised.

Within a day of being back at the club I had a chat with Craig and Steve and they offered me the newly vacated Head of Youth role for next season.

Simon Rusk, my former teammate, had moved on to Brighton & Hove Albion to run their youth team.

It was a great opportunity and pretty well paid but I still felt I had the ability to play at a high level and did not want to stop playing. Also, to do the job properly, I would need to move to Crawley and I was not sure I wanted to relocate.

I canvassed a few trusted people's opinion and the general consensus was I should take the role. Perhaps I was not as good a player as I thought!

I obviously did not take it and it turned out they were all right and I was most definitely wrong. It is a decision I regret to this day and I just hope I get another chance in a similar role because I think I could do a good job.

As the month wore on, whether we achieved promotion or not was clearly going to go down to the wire. There were two reasons why I was desperate for this to happen. Firstly, I had a £5,000 promotion bonus in my contract. Admittedly I had not done much to earn that this season but I saw it is a retrospective bonus for my efforts in the Conference winning season.

Secondly, I was desperate for the season to not be extended for another month via the play-offs. I just wanted to be put out of my misery.

The lads put us all through the mill but we eventually secured the third automatic promotion place after winning at Accrington Stanley on the last day of the season.

The season ended like the previous one: a party on the coach as the club moved up another level to League One. The progression was quite spectacular really and I was proud to say that I had played a role in it. However, on this particular occasion I did not feel a part of the success.

The season was brought to an end by individual meetings between the players and management to discuss how the season had gone and to discuss the future.

Mine seemed like a waste of time but we went through with it anyway.

'How do you think the season went?' asked Craig.

'For me personally?'

'Yes.'

'A fucking disaster,' I retorted.

Craig laughed, which I guessed was his way of agreeing with me, before he went on to thank me for what I had done for the club but that there would be nothing for me going forward. I had been aware of this outcome since about September so had no problem with it at all.

Even though I ended up leaving Crawley through the back door, my spell at the club had surpassed my expectations. I initially joined as I had nothing else and was just happy to guarantee myself another year in football. In the end I had two out of three really enjoyable years there.

It was a roller coaster few years which, I think, anyone who has played under Steve Evans will tell you is normally the case, but I certainly came out of it a stronger person.

Steve constantly tested me both as a person and a footballer and, even though I did not like some of his techniques, more often than not he motivated me in some way. In that third year, as I went to play under different managers, I realised why he behaved the way he did at times. I still did not agree with a lot of it but I could see the method behind some of the madness.

Once you stripped away all the hot air and bullshit there was often a lot of thought put behind his rants. I have tried to give you an insight into how he works, and yes there were funny incidents where we would all cringe at some of things he said and did, but you do not get the success he has achieved in his managerial career without knowing what you are doing. It is not for me to say what is right or wrong – after all, there is more than one way to skin a cat.

One thing I did notice both during my time working with Steve and since is how ruthless he is. When at Crawley and now Rotherham he never rests on his laurels. As soon as he achieves success he is immediately planning for the next challenge. He shows very little loyalty to players. He does not wait to give them an opportunity at the next level. If he thinks he needs to improve the team or squad he goes and does it without any sentiment. The more I progress in my career in coaching the more I understand why he does that.

During my three years at Crawley I made over eighty appearances and scored fifteen goals. My last season as a professional yielded seven appearances for Crawley, three for Kettering, five for Woking and eight for Aldershot, chipping in with two goals.

CHAPTER 28

WHAT MIGHT HAVE BEEN

I **THINK IT** was Gordon Strachan who said: 'Football is a game of lows punctuated by a few highs.' (Although I may be paraphrasing him slightly.)

I am not sure I take such a pessimistic view but for every win against Leeds United, Derby County or heroic games against Manchester United, there was an abundance of defeats on cold Tuesday nights against the likes of Dagenham & Redbridge, Accrington Stanley and Morecambe.

However, I had some memorable games and seasons throughout my career: the game at Old Trafford it goes without saying, although probably an even prouder moment for me personally was captaining Hereford United to our FA Cup win at Elland Road. Scoring two goals to help knock Swindon Town out of the same competition also gave me a great thrill, along with playing a big part in the win against Derby County that same season.

I will always look back with a sense of 'what might have been' after a brilliant first two-thirds of the 2003/04 season, when I had already scored fourteen goals from central midfield before dislocating my shoulder for a second time. I was out of contract at the end of the season and am still convinced I would have either helped Hereford United get promoted or secured myself a move to a much bigger club than Shrewsbury Town.

I thoroughly enjoyed proving Steve Evans wrong and being an integral part of an excellent Crawley Town squad that broke all sorts of records to romp to the Conference Premier title during the 2010/11 season.

My biggest achievement, however, was without doubt winning promotion to League One with Hereford during the 2007/08 season. We were tipped to be closer to the relegation zone than the top but, after a good start and managing to maintain our form, we more than competed against the likes of Darlington, Peterborough United and MK Dons. Despite a shaky start, I was a virtual ever-present in the side and developed a great midfield partnership with Toumani Diagouraga, who was a pleasure to play with.

On the downside, the 2008/09 season was a disaster as we were humiliatingly relegated from League One with a whimper and an embarrassing points tally.

My last season as a professional 2011/12 was also disappointing as I never got the chance I felt I had deservedly earned during the previous two seasons.

My spells at Southend and Shrewsbury were unmitigated disasters but helped mould my character as much as my more successful spells. The spell at Shrewsbury was especially underwhelming for a variety of reasons, but I knew I should not have gone there before I even put pen to paper. I suppose I got what I deserved for chasing money.

I realise my failure to make any impression at either Arsenal or Reading was down to the fact I was not good enough for the former and I acted too immaturely while with the latter.

I only have two real regrets: moving from Yeovil just before Gary Johnson took over; and leaving Hereford United the first time around. I strongly believe that if I had remained where I was at either point then I would have gone on to develop a lot quicker, under two highly experienced football men, into both the player and person I was capable of being.

On reflection, though, four promotions and only one relegation was a decent return on all the hard work I put in during my career, especially when I really knuckled down in the second half of it.

I hope this book has given you an overall insight into life of jobbing foot-ballers. For seventeen years I was lucky enough to get paid a decent wage to do something I would have done for free. During my career I used to saunter into training about 10 a.m. and would wonder what went wrong if I wasn't home by 1 p.m. However, the trade-off to that was I moved house nine times and never really settled in any area – although I could have gladly stayed in Weymouth or Worcester for the rest of my life.

Over nearly two decades I came across all sorts of characters and learnt something from all of them, even if it was sometimes how *not* to do things. I would often look enviously at the likes of my old pal Terry Skiverton, who managed to stay at one club (Yeovil) and make a real impression on its his-tory. There was nothing I would have liked more than to make 300 or 400 appearances at the same place, but I was always too obsessed with moving on to pastures new. The problem being, once I got there, I often realised the grass was not always greener.

The closest I came to making an indelible mark was with Hereford United. When I joined them for the second time I was ready to give them the next five or six years of my career. Unfortunately, by the end of my contract, they did not share that ambition and my nomadic lifestyle continued.

By some twist of fate I seemed to find myself drawn back to the West Country and I particularly loved my times in Yeovil, Hereford, Weymouth and Crawley.

Ultimately I did not quite have the career I had hoped for. Let's be hon-est – when I signed for Arsenal as an eleven-year-old I did not dream of playing for Yeovil, Hereford or Crawley. However, when I look back at some of the players I played both with and against over the years, who had double the ability I had but did not have half the career, I can look back with pride at the fact I managed to earn a living in the cut-throat world of professional sport.

I will always have that 'what if' feeling at the back of my mind – if the penny had dropped earlier for me, I am convinced I would have played at a higher standard for longer.

During my whole professional career I made 475 first-team appearances and scored eighty-two goals.

INDEX

INDEX